The Businesses That Built San Antonio

Living Legacies
San Antonio, Texas

The Businesses That Built San Antonio

By
Marianne Odom & Gaylon Finklea Young

Published by Living Legacies, San Antonio, Texas

Co-sponsored by Living Legacies and the Greater San Antonio Chamber of Commerce

Conceived, Written and Edited by Marianne Odom and Gaylon Finklea Young

Special Photography by Harry Young

Printed in the United States of America by American Printers, San Antonio, Texas

First Edition
ISBN 0-934371-00-8
Library of Congress Catalog Card Number 85-050832

FOREWORDS

How appropriate that an excellent and historically significant book like *The Businesses That Built San Antonio* has been readied for distribution in 1986, exactly 150 years after the founding of the State of Texas. For like the state itself, San Antonio's growth as a city over the past century and a half has been clearly and directly linked to the development of its business community. As its businesses have prospered and progressed, so, too, has San Antonio.

As co-sponsor of this volume, the Greater San Antonio Chamber of Commerce has done more than just observe and chronicle the tremendous strides made in commerce and industry in the Alamo City. We are proud to have been both a leader of and a representative for the business community in San Antonio since our own beginnings in 1894.

Those of you who are as fond of San Antonio as we will certainly enjoy and savor every page of this book. In its chapters are the firsthand accounts of not only the businesses that helped make the city such a success story in the 20th century, but of the men and women who gave birth to those successes and nurtured them throughout the years. At the same time, these men and women served as the civic, cultural, governmental and community leaders as well; their business lives were only part of the important role each played in the creation and building of this All-America City that we now enjoy.

Construction of office towers, a healthy sign of a booming economy, is a common sight in San Antonio.

Market House, San Antonio, Tex.

It has been said that the past is prologue. If true, then our city's rich heritage — and that of its business community — can only mean that San Antonio is destined to provide a rewarding and bright future for all of its citizens.

Enjoy your reading. The Greater San Antonio Chamber of Commerce is as proud of this book, our gift to the Sesquicentennial celebration, as we are of our city.

SAMUEL P. BELL
Chairman of the Board
Greater San Antonio Chamber of Commerce

WILLIAM V. McBRIDE
President
Greater San Antonio Chamber of Commerce

From the prime of the Market House in the first part of this century to the businessmen and women of the 1980s, San Antonio has offered economic opportunity.

The largest snowfall in a century blankets San Antonio's most famous shrine, the Alamo.

The popular River Walk welcomes tourists and makes San Antonio one of the country's four unique cities.

President William H. Taft in 1909 laid the cornerstone of the chapel at Fort Sam Houston, one of five local military installations.

The celebration of Texas' Sesquicentennial offers San Antonio the opportunity to examine and celebrate the history and heritage of Texas, Bexar County and San Antonio. For more than 260 years, San Antonio has occupied a position of key importance in Texas. San Antonio's growth and stability are due to three main sectors of our economy and their history: (1) the military presence, (2) the tourist industry, and (3) the medical community.

The onset of World War II attracted thousands of military and civil service personnel to the city. Once the war ended, the military installations remained and have become an integral part of our economy and have made substantial contributions to the quality of life we enjoy today. The military installations have contributed in areas such as the training of personnel, medical care and biotechnology.

With respect to the tourist industry, HemisFair '68 was the catalyst for the city's new image as a major tourist attraction. San Antonio is now a leading choice for major conventions due to the ambiance, historical sites and excellent facilities along our beautiful River Walk.

In recent years, the medical community has developed and grown through the auspices of The University of Texas Health Science Center and the South Texas Medical Center. Public and private sector organizations such as the Southwest Research Consortium, the Institute of Biotechnology and the Texas Research and Technology Foundation have strengthened San Antonio as an emerging leader in the health care and biotechnology arena. This leadership has already gained national and international acclaim.

The book you are about to read will provide much insight into the development of the business community in San Antonio and the obstacles that have been overcome. It will reflect the commitment of many individuals to the growth and prosperity of their city. It will show the continued participation and coordination in public/private partnerships by many dedicated individuals. All these elements have made this city what it is today and will pave the way for its future strength and growth. The future holds many wonderful things for our city, among them growth, prosperity and a strong economy.

San Antonio is moving in many directions toward many goals, but this could not be possible without its people. San Antonians are the factor that has made this city prosper and will continue to help San Antonio toward a bright, optimistic future.

Henry Cisneros

HENRY G. CISNEROS
Mayor
City of San Antonio

Technician works with an automatic blood cell sorter used in hemotology and oncology at the Audie L. Murphy Memorial Veterans Administration Hospital, part of San Antonio's extensive medical complex.

J. Frank Dobie once observed that every Texan has two homes — his own and San Antonio.

Thus, in this year when Texas celebrates the 150th anniversary of its independence, all Texans will be looking to this city where so much of the history of the last century and a half has been made.

The Sesquicentennial is a special birthday. In celebrations from the Panhandle to the Rio Grande and from El Paso to Texarkana, Texans will be looking at the past to gain inspiration for the future. In Texas, the past is only prologue. It has been that way since 1514 when its recorded history began.

Thus, it is appropriate that San Antonio, seat of the oldest municipal government in Texas, observe the Sesquicentennial while looking to the next 150 years. It has chosen to do so by recounting some of the past success stories of its businesses. Not only did these businesses build San Antonio, but their stories stand as guideposts for those who will come after.

San Antonio's history spans almost twice that of Texas independence. It was on June 13, 1691, that a troop of Spanish soldiers and padres found an Indian village. It was at the headwaters of a beautiful river and it was called Yanaguana. Because it was St. Anthony's Day, they renamed it San Antonio de Padua. Later a mission was established, followed soon by the first business. Now almost 300 years later, San Antonio is the 10th largest American city.

The Sesquicentennial will be celebrated by hundreds of communities in myriad ways. Some will emphasize the colorful history of Texas, others the varied ethnic groups and some will focus on its cultural amenities. All of these are part of San Antonio's heritage, too. However, in this volume, this city points with pride to the contributions business has made to it.

Once again, San Antonio has demonstrated that it is a unique city.

As far back as the missions' aqueduct system built in 1725, San Antonio has appreciated youth as the key to its future.

Lively dancing is an integral part of Mexican fiestas which San Antonio celebrates at the drop of a hat.

JACK R. MAGUIRE
Executive Director
The University of Texas Institute of
Texan Cultures at San Antonio

Member
Texas 1986
Sesquicentennial Commission

CONTENTS

A glistening nighttime skyline shows why San Antonio is a city of promise.

PROLOGUE

The lifeblood of a city is measured by the vitality of its corporate community.

Business leaders not only nurture a prospering economy, they help determine a city's direction, provide responsible leadership and foster a vibrant cultural climate.

To flourish, a city must maintain a broad base of deeply rooted businesses, inspire entrepreneurial firms and attract national companies.

Such is the enviable environment in San Antonio.

The state's oldest major city enjoys a dynamic business community, which includes the military, medicine, tourism, real estate and development, agriculture, manufacturing, research, banking, education, insurance, communications, oil and gas, retail, service and high technology.

Thus the history of San Antonio's businesses is the history of San Antonio's growth.

As the Alamo City commemorates the 1986 Texas Sesquicentennial, it is appropriate that the business community chronicle its contributions to San Antonio's history.

The Businesses That Built San Antonio is a compilation of success stories behind firms that built — and continue to build — this sparkling city. Combined with a pictorial overview of San Antonio's past and present charms, this volume is fondly intended as a most fitting and lasting tribute to the Sesquicentennial.

The text is based on oral history — a classic and increasingly popular research method involving personal accounts. More than 80 hours of taped interviews were conducted with spokespersons from 58 leading San Antonio firms resulting in more than 700 pages of single-spaced transcripts.

In these interviews, prominent business leaders shared their perspectives on their companies' past, present and future. The interviews then were transcribed, edited and intertwined with pertinent supplemental material.

Executives share a laugh on a sidewalk in downtown San Antonio, which remains the financial hub of the city.

Space shuttles stop over at Kelly Air Force Base, illustrating San Antonio's contribution to the future.

Chili vendors showed enterprise in 19th century San Antonio.

A bicycle rider in 1893 exemplified the gaiety of the annual Fiesta celebration.

Oftentimes, corporate histories could not — and should not — be separated from the personalities who developed the companies and direct them today. To capture that humanity behind the corporate image, anecdotes, conversation and company legends are interwoven with essential chronological development.

The book's design reflects a feel for the past as well as the future. Chapters are arranged chronologically by the year companies were founded in San Antonio or opened in San Antonio. From literally thousands of possibilities, historical and current photographs were selected to etch in time the images of San Antonio businesses then and now. For the convenience of the reader, thumbnail histories are provided in a "History at a Glance" with each chapter.

The stories of many of San Antonio's leading businesses captured herein are interesting, inspirational and representative of the spirit that makes San Antonio the All-America City.

Many more stories are yet to be told. However, this initial effort at describing San Antonio's business community adds significantly to public knowledge and will endure long past the Sesquicentennial year.

It is hoped *The Businesses That Built San Antonio* provides an entertaining and enlightening look at our past and future. It is also the unabashed intention of the authors to mirror San Antonio as the lively, charming, progressive, expanding metropolis we love.

Marianne Odom
MARIANNE ODOM

Gaylon Finklea Young
GAYLON FINKLEA YOUNG

The Tower of the Americas and the annual Fiesta carnival symbolize the city's love of festivities.

An early market day on Military Plaza was the scene of energetic buying and selling.

SAN ANTONIO: THEN AND NOW

As Texas celebrates its Sesquicentennial, its oldest major city, San Antonio, occupies an enviable economic position. The pleasant climate and Sun Belt location, the expansive land and the capable work force, all make it a desirable spot for economic investment and a propitious site for development.

How different from the first half of the city's history, when wide open spaces held the threat of hostile bands and isolated the settlement far from civilization. In its beginning, San Antonio was an unlikely place for anyone to settle much less prosper.

From its founding in 1718 to independence and statehood, San Antonio de Bexar showed little indication it one day would be a thriving metropolis. Its strategic location drew Spaniards to establish an outpost between Mexico and the British and French Americas. The military role equaled the religious as soldiers protected mission priests and the Indians they hoped to Christianize. European colonists were expected to follow. But except for one major party of Canary Islanders, the Spanish found it difficult to attract settlers to San Antonio.

Opportunity beckoned immigrants to San Antonio.

Spectacular displays of wildflowers continue to enchant South Texans.

The beautiful countryside remained unspoiled and unsettled while the mission to the Indians failed; the fierce Comanches, Kiowas and Apaches wanted nothing from the foreigners but scalps and plunder, and the more docile tribes died from smallpox and other European diseases. By the end of the 18th century, the missions were closed and the only economic force was the Army. One quarter of the 3,000 inhabitants were soldiers. Otherwise, San Antonio's only enterprises were subsistence farming and cattle trade for hides.

Mexico's independence from Spain caused little change in the economy of frontier towns such as San Antonio. The settlement was still attacked at random by Indian raiding parties who rode through the center of Military Plaza to steal horses. But Mexican authorities were willing to listen to American entre-

Palm Sunday processionals are a tradition at Mission San Jose, which was established in 1720.

preneurs who offered to bring colonists from the States, homesteaders willing to leave the backwoods of Tennessee or the Eastern Seaboard for the promise of cheap or free land. These dirt farmers with their few tools, horses and mules did not bring much immediate economic growth to Texas. But they provided a foundation for subsequent businesses, a growing market that would need staples and later luxuries.

The independent Anglo pioneers never liked Mexican rule, and revolution was perhaps inevitable. San Antonio was the scene of much fabled and heroic action during the war for Texian independence. But after the victory, the city lay stagnant, paralyzed with fear of raids by the Mexican Army or the Indians, and the population decreased until after statehood in 1846 and the end of the Mexican War in 1848.

Texas' economic future opened dramatically with its annexation as settlers arrived in greater numbers. The major export was cotton, and some planters on the Gulf Coast were making fortunes working slaves on the newly cleared land. In San Antonio, however, farmers saw far more modest gains because of less fertile land worked with little extra help. But by and large, the area prospered during the cotton boom.

An oxen-drawn wagon stopped in front of the Alamo in 1900.

Industrious cotton farmers made a living off the land.

The progressive businessmen of the day were merchants who supplied settlers and soldiers, smiths, warehousemen, and traders who freighted goods in 7,000-pound loads by ox wagon or mule train. Their trade came from Indianola on the coast, Louisiana or all the way from Mexico City. The enterprising freighters also brought with them Mexican silver money hidden in the wooden axles of their wagons. For many years, this was the only money with any value in San Antonio. Otherwise, the townsmen traded with promissory notes or agricultural products.

The 1850s brought a wave of German immigration to South Central Texas, more than 30,000 before the Civil War. Those who stayed on their small farms, working the land intensively as in the old country, made a living. But it was the group who came to the towns to ply their trades and skills — the mechanics and merchants, tradesmen and even some intellectuals from the rebellious generation of 1848 — who provided towns like San Antonio with a solid middle class of industrious, sober citizens.

Blacksmiths were among tradesmen who developed a solid middle class in the mid- to late 1800s.

Perhaps not always sober. One of the first businesses in San Antonio was a brewery built by William Menger behind his boarding house in 1855. Another Menger, Simon, had started the first industry of note in 1850, a rendering plant on Laredo Street to make soap.

General store dealers, hide traders, smiths and more freight companies as well as attorneys opened offices and shops around Military and Main plazas. Even luxury now could be had in San Antonio's shops, from window glass to crystal, oil lamps to musical instruments — the first piano was imported in 1860. But other than food grown here or rudimentary products made at home, durable goods were imported.

The Louis Bizy Saloon located in 1917 on Produce Row, now El Mercado, was among hundreds of popular watering holes.

The Lone Star Brewery, the largest brewery in Texas during the early 1900s, now houses the San Antonio Museum of Art.

The Gold Rush brought some business to San Antonio when the city became a staging area for the overland route to California. In 1849 the city saw its first newspaper printed here, the Western Texian. The population in 1850 was 8,000.

The roots of a thriving banking business began in the San Antonio of the 1850s. Early banking was a sideline of some of the more respected merchants. Their customers asked to keep their savings in store safes, which often were nothing more than deep holes under the floorboards into which strongboxes were lowered on ropes. Merchants also began taking their customers' goods on consignment, holding the cotton, wool or hides until the market price went up and loaning the customer money in the meantime. Although not a major business, this early form of banking was profitable and a convenience for customers. Simple merchant banking was more acceptable to settlers who had bad memories of bank failures back East. San Antonio would not see a nationally chartered bank until after the Civil War.

San Antonio lost many of its sons in the Civil War, but the city was never attacked. Sentiments here ran high before and during the war, both for and against secession.

One enterprising newspaper here, the Alamo Express, was burned in 1860 for its pro-Union editorials, and a number of citizens fled to Mexico rather than fight against the Union. But there was no question which side Texas as a whole would support: The Union garrison stationed in San Antonio in 1860 surrendered to Confederate forces before fighting broke out back East.

The Persyn family was among Belgian farmers who brought their native farming methods to South Texas, contributing stability to the local economy.

The first bank in San Antonio was reputed to have been housed in this adobe building on Main near Houston Street.

An 1889 view of Alamo Plaza showed the economic and cultural achievements San Antonio made after the Civil War including a three-story Opera House at right.

Early 20th century sculpture downtown pays tribute to Indian tribes who lived along the San Antonio River.

San Antonio was cut off from its eastern and European markets during the war, but trade was nonetheless brisk. The Union blockade of the Gulf of Mexico made this the major route for Mexican trade with the Confederacy. Local hides and cotton were in demand. Dozens of new freight companies sprang up to handle the traffic including one bossed by Judge Roy Bean, later known as the "only law west of the Pecos."

At war's end, the survivors limped back to pick up their lives. But San Antonio was never part of the Old South and did not carry long-lasting resentment. The city was left intact, but impoverished. There was no money for civic improvement, no business to be done. Real estate was worthless, its value destroyed by taxes. The Indians got bolder in their attacks on the frontier folk and the town was full of gunfighters, gamblers and other flotsam of the war. The town was filthy and diseased; cholera epidemics killed hundreds.

Slowly San Antonio recovered. Two newspapers were started in 1865 to inform and unite the citizens.

San Antonio's strategic military location was not forgotten by the Union. The military post was soon strengthened and supplying the soldier continued to be big business. Trade and traffic returned. Hotels, wholesale stores, gunsmiths and locksmiths, grocery stores, dry goods stores, saddleries and blacksmith shops opened for business.

Wool from Merino sheep and Angora goats brought to the Hill Country was a new export product. Wool replaced cotton, which was struck with disease and boll weevil infestations. The Hill Country became the wool and mohair capital of the 19th century. Wool trading created fortunes for the dealers in San Antonio and the Hill Country who had connections in the East and Europe.

The Texas Hill Country was so well-suited for sheep ranching that wool made fortunes for 19th century San Antonio businessmen.

Cattle ranching has remained a staple of the South Texas economy for more than 150 years.

But nothing compared with the postwar fortunes of the cattle barons now that the railroad extended to Kansas City. Cattle had run wild over South Texas since the days of the Spanish vaqueros. But now that a cow worth $3 in Texas was bringing $30 in hard cash in the railroad stockyards, enterprising Texans rounded up and branded all they could. Ranchers recruited the footloose Civil War veterans to herd the cattle north. Although the era of the great trail drives lasted only some 20 years, the romantic image of the cowboy became fixed in the world's folklore.

Money poured into San Antonio for provisions to equip the trail riders, and cowboys and ranchers put their profits into banks, businesses, saloons and bawdy houses, all of which flourished in the 1870s. For the first time, San Antonio's downtown real estate became valuable and speculators made more than the tradesmen who crowded the choice plaza locations. San Antonio was the largest city in Texas and would remain so until 1930. The 1870 population of 12,256 almost tripled in 20 years to 1890's count of 37,673.

The soldier was a welcome feature of San Antonio society. The Indian wars were a deadly serious business on the frontier until the last war parties were vanquished in 1880. San Antonio got a scare when the Army moved its Texas headquarters to Austin in 1873. So San Antonio's city fathers quickly deeded a large tract of land northeast of downtown to the U.S. government for a military post. The Army returned to its headquarters here in 1876 and built Post San Antonio, renamed Fort Sam Houston 14 years later.

San Antonio lived up to its Old West image with cowboys such as this trio posed on Veramendi Street in the late 1800s.

Also in 1876 in San Antonio, an invention which was to change the free-ranging cattleman's life was demonstrated for the first time in the West — barbed wire. Before a crowd of skeptical ranchers and cowboys, a fence across Alamo Plaza stopped a herd of bewildered cattle and started a trend that meant the end of the frontier — fencing of the land.

The romanticism of the cowboy lives on in San Antonio through the annual Stock Show and Rodeo. Today the event also includes carnival thrills as promised by this mural.

Another landmark, the long-awaited railroad, was greeted with a torchlight parade by the entire populous in 1877 when the first train of the Galveston, Harrisburg and San Antonio line pulled into town.

Real estate transactions took on more importance in San Antonio's economic picture. The city's first planned development was designed as an elite neighborhood. The strong local German element was obvious in the name chosen for this development: King William, after the ruler of Prussia.

The first electric streetcar in San Antonio was captured in this 1890 photo.

A survey of businesses in 1880 showed four breweries and four ice factories, three bookbinderies, factories and tanneries, one wool scouring plant and an iron works. The city had a mule-drawn streetcar line built in 1878 but replaced by electric cars in 1890, and the streets were illuminated with gaslights. Modernization and industry boomed across the country during the last quarter of the century and San Antonio experienced it, too. A cement plant opened in 1880, and the next year residents read a new newspaper. Telephone lines were strung to the first 200 patrons in 1882, the same year the San Antonio Electric Company was founded. And in 1883, the Kampmann Building was erected with four floors served by an elevator.

Cattle was still king in San Antonio. Twenty-seven livestock commission companies ran cattle through six stockyards. For the cowboys and soldiers looking for relaxation in 1890, there were 300 bars and saloons.

Telephone poles were a new addition to West Commerce Street at the turn of the century.

The city, however, could not progress beyond the basic industries that served local needs. San Antonio lacked water and natural resources necessary to manufacture products for national distribution; it was outside the major railroad routes and market areas. The local industry was devoted to processing raw agricultural materials. Even some ranchers suffered after President Cleveland in 1895 reduced a high tariff against importation of wool, which forced many sheep

The homestead of Edward Steves is an elegant example of the King William neighborhood inhabited by German settlers in the late 1800s.

ranchers out of business.

Retail businesses continued to diversify, a sign of a healthy economic base. The turn of the century saw new dry-cleaning shops, sporting goods stores, funeral directors, photographers, jewelers and the invention of the new nickelodeon to compete with vaudeville.

But then as today, government was the largest employer. The federal payroll grew, and the city got national attention in 1898 when Theodore Roosevelt organized and trained the 1st U.S. Volunteer Cavalry, better known as the Rough Riders, at Fort Sam Houston. The bluebloods of Boston mingled with cowhands from Cotulla and their after-hours revelries at the Menger Hotel bar are legend.

Teddy Roosevelt posed with two of his Rough Riders in front of Mission Concepcion in 1898.

The stories the Spanish-American War veterans took home about San Antonio added to the city's color and reputation. During the first decade of the new century, the city also became a tourist spot and health spa. Brochures proclaimed it "the healthiest city in America" as patients sought rest cures and tuberculosis treatments. The number of hotels accommodating sightseers rose from 22 in 1907 to 58 five years later.

The city grew in another way with the start of the 1910 Mexican Revolution. This was a hotbed of plotting by revolutionaries and counterrevolutionaries-in-exile and thus at the center of arms dealing. The U.S. Army was put on alert with the marauding activities of guerrillas on the frontier.

Mexican immigrants kept alive Spanish culture in San Antonio as these spectators dressed in Mexican costumes watched a bloodless bullfight on South Laredo Street in 1938.

El Mercado continues the tradition of markets with imported and handmade goods.

But the real impact on the city was made by refugees from the interior of Mexico. Many were from the poorest desert villages and could offer only menial labor. But there were tradesmen, too, and members of the middle class and former aristocracy, all finding a way to make a living north of the border.

The U.S. Army's involvement in the Mexican Revolution was a minor exercise compared to the training necessary to put an expeditionary force across the Atlantic. More than 70,000 soldiers were stationed in San Antonio during World War I, and Kelly and Brooks

The 22nd Infantry prepared to pitch tents at Fort Sam Houston in 1911.

fields were opened to train pilots in the fledgling air corps. The economic impact of those troops slackened with the end of the war, and the city had another economic setback with Prohibition's closing of bars and breweries.

A natural disaster with far-reaching consequences occurred in 1921: A great flood caused millions of dollars in damage to downtown and killed a score of people. The devastation was the impetus for development of a downtown flood control system which became the River Walk, an enduring and scenic resource. It also made the city look to expansion of its boundaries, and new sections were annexed to widen the tax base to pay for flood controls. The major development, Olmos Dam, was completed in 1925.

New products and businesses introduced in the Roaring '20s changed the way San Antonians lived, worked and played. Automobiles and radios became common,

A local woman displayed the latest in radios in San Antonio in 1924, a communications innovation that kept the city at pace with the rest of the world.

and the city gained many auto dealers and three major radio stations. Two full-service advertising agencies helped promote those businesses and many others. The retail trend was toward sales of nationally advertised goods, the growth of supermarkets and self-service stores, and the entry of national chain stores.

The Depression came at the end of a building boom that graced the city with some of its most beautiful classic architecture. Built during the 1920s were the Medical Arts Building (now the Emily Morgan Hotel), Nix Professional Building, Tower Life Building, old Frost National Bank Building adjacent to San Fernando Cathedral, Municipal Auditorium, Alamo Bank Build-

At Christmas the San Antonio River Walk twinkles with lights and echoes the voices of carolers floating on barges. Inset, River Walk improvements are ongoing as shown in this renovated section near the old Texas Theater.

ing, Milam Building and the Plaza Hotel (now the Granada). With few exceptions, no more construction of this grand scale occurred for a generation.

San Antonio was not immune to the Great Depression and had its share of bank closings and business failures. But bad times did not hit the economy here until early in the 1930s and the impact was weaker here than in the East. Poor farming revenues hurt, but the federal payroll, although decreased, provided a buffer. The population, which in 1930 numbered 231,542, grew only 1 percent per year for the next decade.

World War II ended those stagnant times and the air bases here filled their role as training centers for U.S. air power. The way had been paved for the huge training command effort in 1928 when the city acquired and donated a large section of land in the northeast part of the county to the Army. Randolph Field was established there and earned the title of "West Point of the Air."

One salubrious effect of the mobilization for World War II was more social than economic — the Army forced the city to close down its

Replicas of 1933 streetcars, part of Via Metropolitan Transit system, offer commuters a charming ride into the past.

infamous red-light district in 1941.

At war's end the city had about 400,000 inhabitants. The principal enterprises then were finance, distribution and mercantile trade. The fast-growing construction industry was called on to house the city's newcomers. There was a national trend of migration from the country to the cities, and that, along with servicemen and veterans, retirees and continuing migration from Mexico, created a housing demand on all sides of San Antonio. Shopping centers and highways followed the suburban growth, and giant regional shopping centers were the innovation of the late 1950s and early '60s. The large retail stores downtown built branches in the malls as did national chains and discount stores. Major office buildings and apartment complexes sprang up far from the central city.

An age-old practice with a 1960's look made unexpected economic strides here: the health care industry.

Java blue peacock is one of the more colorful residents of the San Antonio Zoo which draws more than 1 million visitors each year.

Patriotism is revered in the All-America City as demonstrated in a flag-lowering ceremony at Fort Sam Houston.

San Antonio had long been the hub of health care for South Texas and northern Mexico, and now new hospitals and a medical school were built in what has become the South Texas Medical Center. The city became nationally respected for its research and treatment facilities, a reputation that enhances its outlook for progress into the biotechnical fields in the 21st century.

The city's trend of deserting downtown for the suburbs copied most other American urban areas. But San Antonio hosted an event in the late '60s that sym-

From the original Battle of Flowers Parade, Fiesta now features three city-wide parades. Below, a float decorated with peach blossoms rode in the 1913 Battle of Flowers Parade. Right, the brightly illuminated Fiesta Night Parade is considered America's greatest night parade.

San Antonio means home to military personnel stationed at four air bases and an Army post as well as thousands who retire here. Below, the Paseo del Alamo connects the city's most popular tourist attractions, the Alamo and the River Walk.

bolically and materially turned that trend around. HemisFair '68, a celebration of San Antonio's 250th anniversary, helped revitalize downtown business and trade and introduced millions of visitors to the city's beauty and charm. The vigilance of the San Antonio Conservation Society and business and government groups to keep downtown a pleasant place to live and work has provided a testament to the city's unique quality of life. Meanwhile, that movement also spawned a tourist and convention business that now is the second most important enterprise.

The Greater San Antonio Metropolitan Area, now 1 million in population, looks to a future of continued national importance, an attractive image of a city in the sun, an example of well-planned growth, a city where endeavors as diverse as agri-business and electronics prosper together. ◧

BUSINESS CHRONOLOGY

1852	St. Mary's University	1942	Trinity University
1859	Menger Hotel and Motor Inn	1946	Guy Chipman Company, Realtors
1859	Pioneer Flour Mills	1947	Luby's Cafeterias, Inc.
1866	Steves & Sons	1949	Ellison Industries, Inc.
1868	Frost National Bank	1949	KMOL-TV 4
1873	Joske's of Texas	1958	McCombs Enterprises
1880	Alamo Cement Company	1958	Peat, Marwick, Mitchell & Co.
1880	Southern Merchandise & Storage Co.	1960	Lyda, Inc.
1881	Southwestern Bell Telephone Co.	1960	Trammell Crow Company
1883	Friedrich Air Conditioning & Refrigeration Co.	1962	Harte-Hanks Communications, Inc.
		1964	Tesoro Petroleum Corporation
1883	Lucchese Boot Company	1966	Ralph C. Bender & Associates, Inc.
1889	Union Stock Yards San Antonio	1966	La Mansion Hotels
1894	Greater San Antonio Chamber of Commerce	1967	Rand Development Corporation
1903	National Bank of Commerce of San Antonio	1968	Dillard's
1905	The Roegelein Company	1968	Brake Check
1917	Frost Bros.	1969	Crain Distributing Company, Inc.
1920	Azrock Industries Inc.	1971	Orah Wall
1920	Santikos Theatres	1974	Embrey Investments, Inc.
1920	J.C. Penney Company, Inc.	1977	G.I.C. Insurance Company
1920	National Bank of Fort Sam Houston	1979	Nash Phillips/Copus
1922	First Federal Savings and Loan Association of San Antonio	1979	Garden Ridge Pottery & World Imports
		1979	San Antonio Marriott Riverwalk
1922	USAA	1980	Fisher Brothers Lumber Company
1922	Ernst & Whinney	1981	Hyatt Regency San Antonio
1927	Travis Savings and Loan Association	1982	Tetco, Inc.
1930	Nix Medical Center	1983	Diamond Shamrock Refining and Marketing Company
1931	American Security Life Insurance Company		
1934	Redland Worth Corporation	1983	Advanced Tobacco Products, Inc.
1935	H.B. Zachry Company	1984	InterContinental Bankshares
1941	Broadway National Bank		Corporation

San Antonio harmoniously blends the old and new. A reflection of modern architecture is typical of the thriving North and Northwest sides. Inset, the Landmark Building downtown, now the Emily Morgan Hotel, is preserved as a fine example of Gothic architecture.

ST. MARY'S UNIVERSITY

The university had quite a back yard at the turn of the century.

The history of St. Mary's University is one of the oldest stories of educational excellence in Texas.

Founded in 1852 by four French educators, the university's long-term academic reputation is influenced by religious values and a sense of community. The 135-acre campus in the city's northwest neighborhood serves an average of 3,300 students each semester. More than 25,000 San Antonians flock to the campus each year for the popular Fiesta Oyster Bake.

The university is owned and administered by the Society of Mary with headquarters in Rome and 14 provinces around the world. St. Mary's is part of its St. Louis province.

The Rev. James A. Young, S.M., president emeritus and St. Mary's graduate, noted the school's heritage and today's challenges and goals:

"The educational adventure here began as the only Catholic school for boys in San Antonio. We opened near San Fernando Cathedral with 12 students. Enrollment increased to 100 before the end of the year.

"In 1852 the first bishop of Texas had looked around the diocese and was convinced of a great need for education. San Antonio was a frontier town, and he thought the city would not progress without education facilities.

"He returned to France where our society had been founded in 1817. He finally got three Marianists to come from Alsace-Lorraine. Another came from Dayton, Ohio. They were expected to teach in English, Spanish, French and German. In fact, the school was first called The French School.

"Originally, the bishop was going to give us the Alamo for the school. It was a mission which the Franciscans had started. However, it was in such shambles nobody wanted it. Nobody then thought of the Alamo as a symbol of Texas liberty.

"Shortly afterward, property was secured where La Mansion del Rio now stands. The hotel retains the facade of the original school building. Later as the need for education grew, St. Mary's became a junior college and finally grew into a senior college. The doors opened on the current campus in 1894.

"The land developer who built Woodlawn Lake thought the city would move toward the West Side and would need a school. He practically gave us the land.

"The Woodlawn campus was high on a hill — literally in the sticks. Nothing was there but mesquite. Students got off buses at Cincinnati and Bandera roads and had to walk uphill to the school. The kids used to call it 'the longest mile in Texas.'"

Among the famous contributors to St. Mary's progress was an early football coach — Lt. Dwight D. Eisenhower. He coached the 1916 team while he was stationed at Fort Sam Houston and dating Mamie.

St. Mary's became completely coeducational in 1963. Today the enrollment demands expansion of the campus, including the construction of a $5 million student center and an

History at a Glance 1852

Founded: *Aug. 25, 1852, first classes began*
Founders: *Brothers John Baptist Laignoux, Nicholas Koenig, Xavier Mauclerc and Andrew Edel*
Original name: *St. Mary's Institute*
Original location: *Southwest corner of Military Plaza*
Original employees: *5*
Size of original school: *Converted shop above livery stable*
Milestones: **1877** *four-story building built as tallest downtown structure;* **1882** *name changed to St. Mary's College;* **1891** *Woodlawn Hills tract purchased;* **1894** *the new St. Louis College opened its doors for grades 5 through 14 on the Woodlawn Hills campus;* **1895** *received junior college status from State of Texas;* **1904** *regular college degrees given;* **1925** *admitted to Association of Texas Colleges and ranked a senior college;* **1927** *name changed to St. Mary's University;* **1934** *Law School established;* **1936** *Graduate School established;* **1963** *went completely coed;* **1960s** *multimillion-dollar physical expansion;* **1982** *Albert Alkek School of Business and Administration Building dedicated;* **1984** *Sarita Kenedy East Law Library dedicated*
Lineage of leadership: *Brothers Andrew Edel, Charles Francis and John Wolf; the Reverends Louis A. Tragesser, A. Frische, James A. Canning, Robert W. Mayl, Alfred H. Rabe, Walter F. Golatka, Louis J. Blume, Walter J. Buehler, Charles W. Neumann, James A. Young, David J. Paul; all of the Society of Mary*
Headquarters: *One Camino Santa Maria*
Owners: *Society of Mary*
Employees: *424*
Assets: *135-acre campus, $49 million in buildings, $9.9 million endowment*

This chapter was based on an interview with the Rev. James A. Young, S.M.

athletics complex to be built around Alumni Gym.

"Alumni Gym stood relatively unfinished for years," Young remembered. "An aerial team called the Flying Cadonas practiced there in the off season because they could use the beams and girders."

"Originally, the bishop was going to give us the Alamo for the school."

Today St. Mary's University is composed of five schools: the School of Humanities and Social Sciences; the School of Science, Engineering and Technology; the School of Business and Administration; the Graduate School; and the School of Law.

The School of Law limits its enrollment to approximately 600 students. In 1982 the university received a $7.5 million grant to build the new Sarita Kenedy East Law Library and remodel the former law library building.

Young explained, "Our school is called a 'lawyer's law school' because the San Antonio Bar Association began it in 1927. In 1934 the school became part of St. Mary's University and local attorneys began teaching classes at the downtown campus."

The popular Oyster Bake started as a get-together for faculty, students and parents.

The stately facade of the administration building graces the university's Woodlawn campus.

"While the brothers were teaching in the high school downtown, they planned an oyster bake as a social function. It was such a happy occasion, they decided to have it every year. It gradually grew," Young explained. "Some years ago, the St. Mary's University Alumni Association decided the event should be tied

in with Fiesta. Approximately 1,500 alumni and friends from across the city and state volunteer, and the money goes for scholarships."

St. Mary's reputation for academic excellence comes from the Society of Mary's dedication to teaching.

"St. Mary's is a special school because we have a strong sense of community. Our founder liked to use 'family' to describe the religious congregations he established. We try to inculcate that into our faculty, staff and students so the university atmosphere is one of acceptance, of bringing people together.

"Another characteristic is a real sense of community responsibility whether it's in business, law, teaching or medicine. There's also the religious atmosphere on the campus because the society members live here and our chapels are convenient and open to all." L

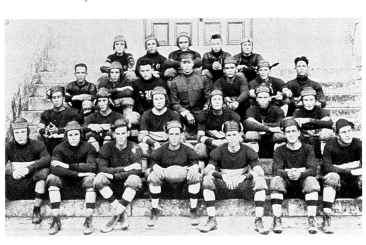

This 1916 football team was coached by Lt. Dwight Eisenhower.

MENGER HOTEL AND MOTOR INN

Next door to the Alamo and a San Antonio landmark in its own right, the Menger Hotel and Motor Inn is one of the oldest and most important hotels in the United States standing in its original form.

When it was built in 1859, the Menger brought refinement to the rough and ready Texas frontier by providing first class accommodations to cattlemen, statesmen, celebrities, socialites and other travelers.

More than 125 years later, the 350-room hotel blends old and new. The original wing contains authentically restored 19th century accommodations furnished with priceless antiques. The motor inn, added before HemisFair in 1968, features oversized guest rooms with private balconies overlooking a tropical pool and patio area.

Art Abbott, general manager for 15 years, traced the hotel's rich heritage and detailed plans for expansion:

"An enterprising German brewer, William A. Menger, started the hotel as a brewery. His was the first brewery in Texas.

"In the second basement of the hotel, the tunnels are still there where he stored his hops, malts and kegs of beer. He could see trail peo- ple and cattlemen coming through here who needed a place to sleep. So he decided if they were here to drink, he might as well have rooms for them to sleep in.

"Menger's 50-room hotel was the first first-rated hotel in San Antonio, which meant basically that you could have ice water in your room. He would ship ice here in kegs from New Orleans. Later there was a bath in some rooms, and the story is, of course, that the people from the trains would run to get here first to try to get a room with a bath. There also was an area where water was brought in to provide baths for dusty cowboys and trail riders."

One of the most interesting suites in the original building is the King Suite where Capt. Richard King of the King Ranch lived and died.

"The furniture he left is Victorian with a classic canopy bed, shaving stand and his desk. We often rent the King Suite to honeymoon couples," Abbott said.

"Legends abound about Capt. King. If he'd get mad, he'd holler down in the rotunda. If he waited too long for ice water, he'd throw the porcelain pitcher down and break it, saying, 'I don't need the darn pitcher if you can't give me ice water.' So they started giving him metal pitchers."

Equally intriguing is the Roy Rogers Suite.

"Roy Rogers and Dale Evans stayed here for many years when they performed at the San Antonio Stock Show and Rodeo. The room is furnished with a settee, coffee table and lamps, all covered in rawhide," Abbott said.

The most famous legend of the Menger is that of Teddy Roosevelt recruiting well-oiled Rough Riders in the hotel bar, now called the

The Menger Hotel, shown in this turn of the century photo, retains its elegant, historic facade.

History at a Glance 1859

Founded: *Feb. 2, 1859, at 204 Alamo Plaza*
Founder: *William A. Menger*
Original name: *Hotel Menger*
Original assets: *$15,712*
Original employees: *27*
Milestones: 1949 *added air-conditioned guest rooms and Texas-size lobby;* **1953** *added swimming pool;* **1959** *celebrated 100th an-niversary with Centennial Ball;* **1967-'68** *added Motor Inn with 110 guest rooms;* **1977** *completed restoration work on original building*
  Lineage of ownership: *William A. Menger, Hermann Kampmann, Gal-Tex Hotel Corporation*
  Headquarters: *Galveston*
  Employees: *185*

This chapter was based on an interview with Art Abbott.

Teddy Roosevelt Bar. The bar is an exact replica of the bar in the House of Lords in London.

With San Antonio on the Chisholm Trail, the bar also was the gathering spot of trail bosses and ranchers.

"Cattle deals involving hundreds of thousands of dollars were cinched over three fingers of rye in the Menger Bar."

The hotel's reputation for cuisine came from serving buffalo hump, wild turkeys and deer loins.

"In the Renaissance Room, which is still used for banquets, Gen. Ulysses S. Grant was served turtle soup made from turtles taken from the San Antonio River," Abbott said.

The Menger has hosted the wealthy, famous and powerful for more than a century.

Roosevelt came back to the Menger in 1905, this time as president of the United States. Other presidents who stayed at the Menger were Taft, McKinley, Eisenhower and Nixon. First Lady Rosalynn Carter spoke to a crowded Colonial Room during Campaign '76.

Theater and film stars who have been Menger guests include Sarah Bernhardt, Bob Hope, Joan

Guest rooms were decorated in Victorian furniture, much of which is still in use today.

Crawford, John Wayne, James Stewart, Jose Ferrer, Robert Mitchum, Steve McQueen and Maude Adams.

Writers Sidney Lanier, Oscar Wilde and O. Henry have been Menger guests. O. Henry referred to the hotel in his short stories.

The hotel long has been at the hub of Fiesta, especially for the Order of the Alamo, which traditionally wraps up its activities with a black-tie Queen's Coronation at the Menger. Dignitaries watch the parades from the hotel's windows and balconies. To ensure their availability, prized rooms on the front are booked from year to year.

"Someone must die to make one of those rooms available during Fiesta. They are passed down through families. We always reserve the most luxurious suite for the parents of the queen," Abbott explained.

Modernizing while preserving its heritage, the Menger added 110 rooms before HemisFair in 1968. The hotel ran 99 percent occupancy during the event.

In 1977 the center section of the hotel was upgraded with new furniture, draperies, bedspreads and carpet. New furniture was added to supplement the antiques in the original building.

On the drawing board for the Menger are plans to connect the historic hotel with the Tiendas del Rio Mall slated for downtown San Antonio. The hotel's plans include a

new ballroom which will seat 650 people, luxurious suites and a bank of rooms. Construction probably will start in 1986 and be completed by 1989. The addition will be behind the hotel overlooking the river to be diverted through the new mall. Bonham Street from Crockett to Commerce streets will be closed to make a pedestrian walkway.

***

"Menger's 50-room hotel was the first first-rated hotel in San Antonio, which meant basically that you could have ice water in your room."

***

The Teddy Roosevelt bar will be moved back intact to its original location facing Alamo Plaza at the corner of Blum Street.

As to what the founder would say if he could see the hotel today, Abbott surmised, "I think he'd be kind of proud of the Menger the way the original rooms are still there. I think he'd be very proud to know that it's still operating as a first class hotel." ⬛

PIONEER FLOUR MILLS

Carl Hilmar Guenther

It began with one man's dream more than 125 years ago. Today Pioneer Flour Mills remains the oldest privately owned flour mill in the United States and one of the country's leading manufacturers of baking mixes.

All it took was commitment and hard work.

Scott Petty, Jr., chairman of the board, traced the company's rise to prominence from its meager beginnings in 1851.

"Abraham Lincoln was still practicing law in Illinois. The population of the 37 united states was 24 million. And Carl Hilmar Guenther stood in the rain and watched the wreckage of his gristmill flood by in the swollen river below. The mill would have been completed in a matter of days.

"When Guenther left Germany three years earlier, it was more than wanderlust. It was an escape from the constraining Old World system of apprenticeship and guilds. He would prove himself, he wrote, 'in a country that offered freedom for all.' On the banks of Live Oak Creek near Fredericksburg, he knew only one option. He started again.

"Finally, after months of labor, the mill opened. Business was good. It stayed that way until 1859 when drought so depleted the crops that Guenther found himself with little grain to grind and little water to turn the wheel. Guenther knew he would have to take one more chance. He closed his little mill and relocated his business to just outside of San Antonio on the more powerful San Antonio River.

"Time passed and business flourished in the growing community. Guenther decided he could continue to produce the highest quality products by adopting the best methods and machinery as soon as they were developed. It was an important decision. It meant his mill would survive.

"Guenther could not have foreseen the changes in technology that would take place when he began his mill, but he certainly would have been proud. The simple water wheels gave way to more efficient turbines, steam power, coal, natural gas and, finally, commercial electricity. The millstones were replaced by the more powerful steel roller. The mill itself was expanded several times, and computerized quality control became an important part of the daily routine.

"**A**part from mill technology, society itself was also changing rapidly. The population increased and became more mobile. Women took on an increasingly important role as they entered the work force — leaving them with little time in the kitchen. This significant change prompted Pioneer Flour Mills to develop an entirely new product line — ready-mix preparations.

"First, a small test facility was established. Then a pilot plant. Its first product was a modern update of an old recipe that Guenther himself would have recognized — biscuit mix. These first production runs were eagerly accepted by a ready public. Convenience in baking had entered the kitchen.

"Today Pioneer Flour Mills boasts a variety of ready-mix preparations.

History at a Glance   1859

Founded: *1851 in Fredericksburg*
Moved to San Antonio: *1859*
Founder: *Carl Hilmar Guenther*
Officers: *Scott Petty, Jr., chairman of the board; Richard DeGregorio, president, chief executive officer; Bill Cothren, executive vice president, chief operating officer; Mary Hitt, vice president, finance; Bill Ault, vice president, sales and marketing*
Headquarters: *129 Guenther St.*
Retail products: *Original Baking Mix, Buttermilk Baking Mix, Buttermilk Pancake and Waffle Mix, White Corn Bread Mix, Yellow Corn Bread Mix, French Doughnut Mix, White Wings Flour Tortilla Mix, White Wings Corn Tortilla Mix, White Wings Flour, Pioneer Flour, Angel Food Flour, Pioneer White Corn Meal, Pioneer Yellow Corn Meal, Pioneer Old Fashioned Country Gravy Mix*
Food service products: *Biscuit Mix, Buttermilk Pancake Mix, Pancake Mix, Old Fashioned Biscuit Gravy Mix, Peppered Old Fashioned Biscuit Gravy Mix, Yellow Corn Bread Mix, White Cake Mix, Yellow Cake Mix, Chocolate Cake Mix, White Icing Mix, Chocolate Icing Mix, French Doughnut Mix, Blueberry Muffin Mix, Corn Muffin Mix, Bran Muffin Mix, Apple-Cinnamon Muffin Mix, Basic Muffin Mix, Belgian Waffle Mix, Cone Mix, Flour Tortilla Mix, Corn Tortilla Mix*
Motto: *Quality*

This chapter was based on an interview with Scott Petty, Jr.

All were developed and tested with the most modern methods available but manufactured with the same goal in mind that Carl Guenther had more than 125 years ago — to manufacture the highest quality product possible that best meets the needs of the consumer.

Pioneer Flour Mills today is located on Guenther Street in the historic King William area of San Antonio.

"He would prove himself, he wrote, 'in a country that offered freedom for all.'"

Mule-drawn wagons, below, delivered flour from Pioneer Flour Mills in the early days.

"The development of new products begins with a thorough analysis of information from the marketplace. Then once consumer wants and needs have been determined, the work in the laboratories begins.

"A staff of trained professionals uses the most modern equipment in developing both products and easy-to-use recipes to meet the demands of the marketplace. Many factors are considered in this developmental process including consumer age, ethnic mix, household size and geography.

"In the final analysis, however, the success of a product depends on one factor — its overall quality. Only after this has been found to meet the highest standards is the testing complete and the product ready for production and delivery.

"Although flour is still one of its staple products, Pioneer Flour Mills also has a full line of other high quality retail products. And each is a proven 'Southern Success.' White Wings Flour Tortilla Mix, for example, has been recognized as a market leader outselling competition four to one.

"New products are continually being researched and developed as are new recipes for existing products. By doing this, Pioneer effectively keeps up with consumer trends and needs in the marketplace.

"Once developed and test-marketed, Pioneer products are marketed through a network of trained, experienced sales representatives throughout the South.

"Pioneer Flour Mills is also committed to providing a full line of products to the food service industry. As with its retail line, food service products undergo continuous research and development to assure a product of the highest quality. Since Pioneer food service products are distributed nationwide, many products are custom designed to meet the specific needs of a region, market or even a customer.

"The mill, which once ground only wheat and corn, now produces a variety of products for both the retail and food service trades. The market for its products, which began in Fredericksburg and San Antonio, now covers the United States. Despite significant growth and change, two things have remained constant: The mill is still owned by the Guenther family and, more importantly, their dedication to quality is still there — and always will be.

"One man's dream is now a successful reality."

STEVES & SONS

One of the world's largest manufacturers of doors, Steves & Sons, is the oldest company under the same continuous family ownership and management in the building materials industry in the United States.

The 119-year-old firm headquartered in San Antonio manufactures 12,000 residential and light commercial doors daily in plants in San Antonio; Richmond, Virginia; and Lebanon, Tennessee.

The company today services an international market area which spans the globe.

Six generations of the Steves family have provided leadership for the firm. Marshall T. Steves, president,

assembled these facts on the history of the company:

The original Steves company was founded in 1866 by Edward Steves, a German immigrant who came to the United States in 1849 at age 20. The family landed at Indianola and traveled by ox cart to New Braunfels to join other struggling German settlers. Then the family moved near Center Point north of Comfort in the Texas Hill Country.

On Christmas Day in 1857, Edward Steves married Johanna Kloepper, another German immigrant who had come to New Braunfels with her mother the same year Steves arrived.

"That was probably the greatest achievement of his life," Marshall Steves said of the marriage. "As in most cases, the women are the movers in families, and she prompted him to go into business in San Antonio."

She was not only an inspiration to her husband, but was known as the "Mother of the Lumber Industry in Texas."

History at a Glance 1866

Founded: *1866 at Blum and Bonham streets*
Founder: *Edward Steves*
Original name: *Steves Lumber Company*
Milestones: **1866** *moved lumberyard to Alamo Plaza;* **1870s** *branch offices established along railroad advancing toward San Antonio;* **1877** *established Sunset Yard on East Commerce Street (closed* **1984***); **1904** *opened first millwork factory at Sunset Yard;* **1913** *established Steves Sash & Door Company at Monterrey and Medina streets;* **1916** *established branch at Corpus Christi (sold* **1967***);* **1917** *manufactured 5,000 "Alamo" propellers for U.S. Army;* **1918** *received Distinguished Service Award for service during World War I;* **1919** *established branch at San Juan (closed* **1922***); established branch at Houston (closed* **1947***);* **1924** *established branch at Wichita Falls (closed* **1932***);* **1925** *established branch at Fort Worth (closed* **1935***);* **1939** *established Superior Woodwork Company;* **1944** *received Maritime "M" with 5 stars for meritorious service during World War II;* **1947** *established San Angelo branch (sold* **1954***);* **1951** *established Victoria branch (closed* **1957***);* **1955** *moved Steves Sash & Door Company headquarters to Humble Avenue;* **1959** *established Superior Aluminum Manufacturing Company (sold* **1961***);* **1960** *established and closed Steves Sash & Door Dallas;* **1962** *established Crest Wood Mouldings (closed* **1967***);* **1963** *established Steves Sash & Door Austin and Steves Sash & Door Harlingen (closed* **1964***);* **1969** *established Wood Door Plant in Easton, Md. (closed* **1971***);* **1971** *established Wood Door Plant in Hannibal, Mo. (closed* **1974***), and established Wood Door Plant in Lebanon, Tenn.;* **1983** *established Wood Door Plant in Richmond, Va.;* **1985** *established Crest Metal Doors, Inc., changed company name to Steves & Sons, and moved headquarters to Heimann Building*
Lineage of leadership: *Edward Steves (1829-1890); Albert Steves, Sr. (1860-1936); Albert Steves, Jr. (1884-1945); Albert Steves III (1908-1969); David P. Steves (1912-1957); Marshall T. Steves*
Owners: *Family of Marshall T. Steves*
Officers: *Marshall T. Steves, president; Monroe H. Voigt, senior vice president; Edward G. Steves, vice president; Sam Bell Steves II, vice president; Gene M. Patton, vice president; Wendell C. Stoneham, treasurer-controller; Marshall T. Steves, Jr., secretary*
Employees: *220*
Motto: *Quality & service*

This chapter was based on an interview with Marshall T. Steves.

> ## "She was not only an inspiration to her husband, but was known as the 'Mother of the Lumber Industry in Texas.'"

Edward and Johanna Steves built a home by Cypress Creek near Comfort where they had three sons, Edward Steves, Jr.; Albert Steves, Sr.; and Ernest Steves.

When the family moved to San Antonio in 1866, it was a small village of Mexican-style adobe buildings. Steves, who had apprenticed as a carpenter in New Braunfels, opened a lumberyard.

He purchased a lot and what he described as a "pretty poor house" at Blum and Bonham streets behind the Menger Hotel. Some six months later, he moved the lumberyard to Alamo Plaza at Losoya Street to join in a short-lived partnership with E. von Hartz.

By May of 1867, he had purchased another location across the plaza on the site of the present day Joske's department store. One year later, he wrote in his memoirs, "I was rather successful in my commercial enterprises."

Steves scoured Central Texas on horseback seeking quality lumber which he paid for with $20 gold pieces hidden under his saddlebags. In 1868 a sawmill on the Medina River became a source of wood, as did another two years later six miles above Belmont on the Guadalupe River.

Directing Steves & Sons are Marshall T. Steves, seated, and his sons, from left, Sam B. Steves II, Edward G. Steves and Marshall T. Steves, Jr.

The lumber yard on East Commerce Street was part of the early-day enterprise.

In 1881 the railroad was an asset to the lumber company near the Sunset Railroad depot.

By 1871 Steves advertised "sash and doors" in addition to Louisiana cypress and longleaf Florida pine. Lumber was shipped by schooner to Indianola and hauled by ox cart 150 miles to San Antonio. In 1872 the wagon haul was shortened when trains began running between Galveston and Austin, a transportation route which also provided lumber from a new mill in East Texas.

As the railroad approached San Antonio, Steves established branch offices along the completed tracks in Luling, Kingsburg, Seguin and Marion. Prior to 1877, Steves moved his lumberyard to East Commerce Street where it occupied four acres which were adjacent to the tracks of the Sunset Railroad when it arrived in the city.

When Edward Steves retired in 1882, his sons, Albert Steves, Sr., and Ernest Steves, assumed leadership roles in the business. For the next three years, they became involved in the great Texas "lumber-

Edward Steves

Albert Steves, Sr.

Albert Steves, Jr.

Albert Steves III

David Pipes Steves

yard war" which featured such magnates as William Cameron of Waco and Henry J. Lutcher of Orange.

A San Antonio newspaper noted, "We can, perhaps, say with safety that there is not a habitation in southwest Texas or northern Mexico which can be reached by rail or wagon that has not got one or more planks about it from the yards of Steves & Sons."

When other large Texas lumber interests began to stock sash and doors supplied from St. Louis, Chicago and Mississippi River points, Albert Steves, Sr., set up a small factory at the Sunset yard in 1904 to manufacture these building materials locally. It was referred to as Steves' "coffee mill."

A fire in February 1913 destroyed the plant and prompted Albert Steves, Sr., to separate the millwork operation from the remainder of the lumber business. He became president of both Ed Steves & Sons and Steves Sash & Door Company in October of that year. His son, Albert Steves, Jr., became vice president and general manager of the new organization with 35 employees.

A new plant was constructed at the intersection of Monterrey and Medina streets. Designed by Albert Steves, Jr., it was approximately 200,000 square feet and consisted of two two-story concrete buildings.

By the time the United States entered World War I, Steves Sash & Door Company had become one of the largest and most modern millwork plants in the Southwest. The plant benefited from the boom in construction caused by the war. It also manufactured "Alamo" propellers used by the Air Service of the Army and secured defense contracts for the construction of a large percent-

"Alamo" airplane propellers were manufactured by the company in 1918 for the war effort.

Steves' "coffee mill" factory was set up in 1904 at the Sunset Railroad Yard.

age of the catonments which housed thousands of soldiers in San Antonio. The company's World War I award for distinguished service and an "Alamo" propeller remain on the walls of the company headquarters today.

By the end of the 1920s, Steves Sash & Door Company had branches in Corpus Christi, Wichita Falls and Fort Worth.

Most of the gains experienced in the 1920s, however, were wiped out in the Great Depression. The company, however, provided a livelihood for between 100 and 300 employees during this period when other firms were failing and laying off workers.

During World War II, Steves Sash & Door Company manufactured wood components that went into "Liberty" and "Victory" merchant ships, as well as lumber products and footlockers for the Quartermaster Corps. In 1943 the company received the U.S. Maritime Commission "M" award with five stars for distinguished service, which is also displayed on the walls of the company headquarters today. Albert Steves, Jr., adamantly refused to per-

mit the company to make a profit from the war boom.

Albert Steves, Jr., died in 1945 while in Baltimore attending the graduation of his son, Marshall

"The plant manufactured 'Alamo' propellers used by the Air Service of the Army."

Steves, from the U.S. Naval Academy.

His sons immediately took over the businesses. Albert Steves III, a graduate of Washington and Lee University and Harvard Business School, was president.

Steves Sash & Door Company at this time engaged primarily in the wholesaling of building materials with its main office and warehouse in San Antonio. Branches continued to operate in Corpus Christi and San

Angelo. A third branch was established in Victoria in 1951 and closed four years later. In addition to Sash & Door and Superior Woodwork, other divisions of Steves Industries by the mid-'50s included Ingram Equipment, Tampo Manufacturing and Steves lumber companies.

Under the management of David P. Steves, Steves Sash & Door Company began concentrating on wholesale distribution rather than manufacturing. Meanwhile, Marshall Steves, having returned from the Navy in 1948, guided Superior Woodwork toward a strong emphasis on stock manufacturing.

In 1955 the five sons of Albert Steves divided Steves Industries. Each of the brothers acquired ownership of one or more of the operations.

Albert Steves III took over Ed Steves & Sons; David P. Steves acquired the separate Steves Sash & Door Company operation in San Angelo; Sam Bell Steves gained possession of Tampo Manufacturing Company; Walter Steves II acquired Ingram Equipment Company; and Marshall Steves acquired Steves Sash & Door Company and Superior

Woodwork Company.

While the Steves name had been associated with wood products for nearly a century in San Antonio, the Sash & Door Company has continuously updated its production methods. By the end of the 1950s, Steves Sash & Door Company

---

"Albert Steves, Jr., adamantly refused to permit the company to make a profit from the war boom."

---

became interested in a then-new product for window manufacturing — aluminum. It acquired the inventory and fixed assets of Coastal Aluminum Window Company in Houston. A Dallas branch of Steves Sash & Door also was established

The Richmond, Virginia, supervisory personnel are, from left, Mark Sly, Robert Lown, Brad Davis, Stewart Waddy, Kraig Bridy, Don McNeill, Margaret Companion, Thomas M. Sykes and Claudia Voight.

in 1960.

By 1970 Steves Sash & Door Company was manufacturing pre-machined and pre-finished plastic door units.

In the late 1960s, Superior Woodwork Division converted from a specialty to a stock door plant. The warehouse in Corpus Christi was sold to Ed Steves & Sons.

Over the next 10 years, door plants were opened in Hannibal, Missouri; Lebanon, Tennessee; Easton, Maryland; and Richmond, Virginia.

The Easton, Maryland, plant was closed in 1971 and its machinery shipped to San Antonio.

In the spring of 1973, flood waters of the Mississippi River rose five feet higher than any time in history

In 1913 a new plant was built at Monterrey and Medina streets.

The San Antonio door plant supervisory personnel are, standing from left, Moises Guerrero, Martin H. Gonzales, Gerardo Leos, Johnny M. Guzman, Linda R. Offer, Edward Willis, David Cruz, Samuel S. Devine, Frank G. Davila, Ruben Garcia, Hilario Perez, Jr., and, seated, Fortunato G. Martinez, Jesse J. Silvas, Jim W. Hashley, Guadalupe De La Garza and Hector L. Lopez.

Guadalupe De La Garza has been a faithful employee since 1922.

and inundated the plant in Hannibal, Missouri. The plant was closed early the next year.

The San Antonio and Lebanon plants were operating at capacity by the spring of 1983, and the plant in Richmond, Virginia, opened July 1 of that year.

In 1985 the company's headquarters were moved from the plant at 203 Humble to the remodeled old Heimann Building in St. Paul Square, and the company's name changed back to Steves & Sons. The new general office building is just across the tracks from the original lumberyard on East Commerce Street founded by Ed Steves in 1866. ⅃

San Antonio headquarters personnel include, standing from left, Arthur J. Williams, Monroe H. Voigt, Wendell C. Stoneham, Jack W. Smith, Gordon E. Osborn and Gene M. Patton, and, seated, Rosy S. Munoz, Anne Day, Janie P. Hernandez and Minnie V. Ortega.

The Lebanon, Tennessee, supervisory personnel are, from left, Homer Leath; Barney Gallagher; Dorris E. Harris; Stella A. Guerrero; Ben E. Thompson; Vickie D. Whited; Kimberly L. Peak; Jesse M. Garcia, Jr.; Jesse M. Garcia, Sr.; Billy J. Arnold; Ruben Herrera; and Mitchell Douglas.

FROST NATIONAL BANK

Always a leader in San Antonio banking, Frost National Bank is the largest bank in San Antonio and South Texas. But its origins go back to a general store on Main Plaza.

Tom C. Frost

Tom C. Frost, a historian in his own right, recounted the bank's beginnings and described its place today in the banking fraternity:

"I read an ad one time for the Irish airline. It said, 'How Would You Like to Walk Down the Street Where Your Great-Grandfather Walked?' I looked at the ad, and I smiled and said, 'I don't have to pay a penny to do that. I do it every day.'

"The founder of what is now the Frost National Bank was my great-grandfather, Col. Tom C. Frost. I am the fourth Tom Frost to be asso-ciated with the enterprise, and there's another one on board today.

"I've often said that if it weren't for Austin College, I would probably be a dirt farmer in Alabama because my great-grandfather came to Texas in 1854, the son of an Alabama farmer. He was the first member of the family, as far as we know at least in this country, to receive a college education.

"After getting his degree, he became an assistant professor of Latin at Austin College when it was in Huntsville. He subsequently be-came a lawyer, his law license sign-ed by Judge R.E.B. Baylor. He be-came county attorney of Comanche County, and at the same time a Texas Ranger, and later a lieutenant colo-nel in McCullough's Mounted Rifles in the War Between the States.

"Then after the war, he could not practice law because he was not a citizen and had fought the Constitu-tion. He went into the freight business, having a wagon freight line hauling from Indianola to San Antonio, living in Gonzales. At some point there, he lost his wife and all but one of his children.

"The colonel moved to San An-tonio with his surviving daughter. Later she married Townsend Wood-hull, who became a vice president of the bank and was a vestryman at St. Mark's Episcopal Church, where a plaque commemorates his service. Col. Frost took up residence in the Menger Hotel and became a partner with his brother, John, who had a trading or mercantile operation here on Main Plaza.

"The colonel and his brother ac-cumulated enough capital to build an inventory, and the trading operation became a general store.

"Later he decided it would be a good business to become a commis-sion agent, sign up the ranchers he was selling supplies to and ask them if he could handle their wool for a commission. That way he could hold the wool until Eastern buyers were

History at a Glance   1868

Founded: *1868 on Main Plaza*
Founder: *Col. Thomas Claiborne Frost*
Original name: *T.C. Frost, Banker; Mercantile Store*
Milestones: **1871** *built two-story building on Main Plaza;* **1887** *built warehouse on North Flores Street;* **1922** *built 12-story building on original site;* **1928** *merged with Lockwood National Bank;* **1961** *established Foreign Department;* **1965** *built six-story Family Bank-ing Center and parking garage;* **1967** *opened banking facility at Kel-ly Air Force Base;* **1968** *offered BankAmericard;* **1972** *'topped out' 21-story Frost Bank Tower at 100 W. Houston St.;* **1973** *joined by Citizens National Bank;* **1974** *opened Liberty National Bank which was formerly Peoples National Bank, added Parkdale State Bank in Corpus Christi as first affiliate bank outside San Antonio, and opened Colonial National Bank under Frost Bank Corporation;* **1977** *merged with Cullen Center Bank & Trust of Houston and Citizens National Bank of Dallas to form Cullen/Frost Bankers, Inc.;* **1982** *opened North Frost Bank*
Owners: *Shareholders of Cullen/Frost Bankers, Inc.*
Officers: *Tom C. Frost, chairman of the board; Fred C. Lepick, vice chairman; Richard W. Evans, president*
Employees: *1,250*
Banks: *Five local affiliates included in 13 member banks*
Assets: *$1.8 billion*

This chapter was based on an interview with Tom C. Frost.

willing to pay a fair market price.

"He built warehouses for the wool as well as pecans, cotton and other commodities, and the warehouse business became an adjunct of his mercantile business.

"From there, he sold merchandise to the ranchers when they had no cash because they got their money once a year when they sold their crops. So he would sell to them on credit. There was a scarcity of capital in the Southwest, and there were no banks. The merchants had to finance their own sales, so it was natural that the colonel would sell on credit and then when the wool crop came in, he'd sell the wool and credit the rancher's account.

"He started receiving slips which ranchers gave to other merchants who had merchandise that the colonel didn't have. The notes directed Col. Frost to pay to so-and-so so much money. Seeing this, the colonel started issuing books of drafts or checks.

"The first checkbooks were drawn on 'T.C. Frost Commission Merchant,' not on him as a banker. The first loans were selling merchandise against the crops and the wool clip that were going to come in later. Then the colonel would lend on the wool on the backs of the animals and take chattel mortgages. From that he evolved into a banker, and the banking business with time came to be more important than the mercantile business.

"In 1899 a national charter was taken out. The ex-Confederate soldier took out a Yankee charter

under federal law because he saw the National Banking Act or the National Banking System as the way to do additional business on a sound basis.

"In more recent times, we've seen the evolution of holding companies, which permitted banks to extend beyond their four walls and own other banks in the state. And just as the colonel made sure that his bank followed the appropriate trend, we set up a holding company in 1973, in-

> "It was natural the colonel would sell on credit, and when the wool crop came in, he'd sell the wool and credit the ranchers' accounts."

corporating into it Citizens Bank, which was founded by my father along with Jess McNeel.

"Our first out-of-town acquisition was Parkdale Bank of Corpus Christi, which also was bought in about 1974. This was the first realization of our desire to expand to many of the other good markets in Texas.

"On July 7, 1977, we merged with

Frost Bank Tower adds to the skyline in San Antonio's downtown financial district.

Cullen Bankers of Houston, and the resulting Cullen/Frost Bankers, Inc. has 13 banks in six major markets.

"More than just a follower of trends, Frost Bank has frequently been a leader in San Antonio banking. As the largest bank in San Antonio and South Texas, with a market share of about 25 percent, we set the pace as often as we follow.

"We became the largest bank in San Antonio when Frost demonstrated its liquidity and strength by surviving a run in the Depression.

"We were the first to issue a credit card in South Texas and in San Antonio, and we were the third bank in Texas to be in the credit card business. For many years here in South Texas, we've been the primary issuer of credit cards, and Frost has the largest credit card system in the region, although there are others larger than we in Texas.

"And Frost Bank was one of the first financial institutions in South Texas to recognize the significant role Mexico would play in our economy. My uncle was one of the first U.S. bankers to attend Mexican bankers' conventions and one of the first to recognize Mexico's potential.

"In summary, you could say that we've all tried to be early in the game on whatever services that should be and could be properly offered. The old motto of the bank was 'Safety, courtesy and promptness.' We still practice those three today." ◾

Two Frost brothers built this general store, out of which grew the banking business based on wool.

JOSKE'S OF TEXAS

When Julius Joske opened his modest dry goods store on Austin Street in 1873, San Antonio was fast becoming a mercantile center meeting the demands of cattlemen, the Army and Mexican trade.

Though the timing was fortuitous, the German immigrant and his three sons, Siegfried, Albert and Alexander, could not have imagined the more than a century of retail history they were launching.

Today Joske's of Texas is San Antonio's largest volume retailer with four stores.

Until recently San Antonio served as division headquarters for stores here, in Austin, Corpus Christi and El Paso. Allied Stores Corporation, one of the nation's largest retailers and owners of Joske's since 1928, consolidated Texas divisional headquarters in Dallas in 1985.

Robert L. Mettler, president of the Texas division, assembled the following colorful history of the retail giant and explained future plans:

In 1867 Julius Joske opened a store on Main Plaza, but closed it and returned to Berlin for his family. Six years later, he and his sons rented the one-room adobe building on Austin Street and opened J. Joske & Sons to a brisk business. In 1875 they moved to Alamo Street on Alamo Plaza and changed the name to Joske Bros.

"Alexander Joske was a 'merchant prince and organizer of the greatest department store south of St. Louis.' "

The new location was so advantageous, Joske's soon occupied 2,400 square feet reaching from a double storefront on the plaza to Losoya Street. To their stock of military and outdoor equipment and men's clothing, the alert merchants added items such as fans, parasols, lace hosiery and corsets.

On January 24, 1887, Joske's advertised a "Grand Clearing Sale on Account of Removal" in local newspapers. The ad promised Joske's would erect "a commodious and magnificent storehouse, larger, in fact, than any in Texas."

The new two-story structure, known as "The Big Store," was opened in 1888 on the site of the current downtown Joske's. St. Joseph's Church was its closest neighbor.

In 1903 Joske's youngest son, Alexander, became the store's guiding force. In 1906 he expanded the store, adding two floors and elevators. Beginning Joske's reputation for fashion, dresses were made by seamstresses in a shop on the second floor.

"French lace and imported buttons were so valuable they were locked up each evening when the store closed," Mettler said.

By the 1920s, Joske's staged style

shows in the Palace Theatre. Mill-end sales caused crowds so great the doors had to be closed to avoid a crush. A 3,000-candlepower searchlight was mounted on top of the store. It guided Lt. James H. Doolittle in 1922 to a landing at Kelly Field for refueling on his first continental flight.

Alexander Joske instituted a first in retail advertising.

"He was quite a literate man and a great letter writer," Mettler said. "He bought space in newspapers to share his opinions on such topics as community affairs, prejudice and politics."

When Alexander Joske died in 1925 at age sixty-six, he was called a "merchant prince and organizer of the greatest department store south of St. Louis."

His son-in-law, Dr. Frederic G. Oppenheimer, became president. In 1928 the store was purchased by Hahn Department Stores, which became Allied Stores in 1932. James H. Calvert, president of Joske's from 1932 to 1960, was responsible for its growth in size and reputation as one of America's leading stores.

In the 1930s, Joske's introduced the escalator to Texas and became the state's first fully air-conditioned store.

In the 1940s, Joske's stressed Texana, the Texas lifestyle and Joske's as a Texas institution. It promoted cowboy paraphernalia including

spurs and saddles. A frontier shop specialized in dude ranch clothes, and the store sponsored the country's first dude ranch fashion show. The idea was so unique, Life Magazine photographed it.

Joske's was known for its promotions. A New Year's Day parade in the late 1940s drew thousands to see more than 50 giant inflated animals. An animated 50-by-50-foot Roping Cowboy, the "world's greatest electric sign," on top of the store was an Alamo Plaza landmark for 30 years.

For decades Christmas season at Joske's meant a 30-foot mechanical Santa sitting on a 20-foot chimney on the store's roof. Inside, an animated Fantasy Land was a major holiday attraction for customers of all ages.

"The Big Store" became "The Largest Store in the Largest State" with a 1953 expansion that more than doubled its size and added almost 20 acres of parking space. The store's facade and interior again were remodeled for HemisFair '68.

While the downtown store grew, Joske's also added branches in suburban San Antonio and South Texas.

The downtown store will be revamped as it becomes an anchor in the Plaza del Rio Mall, also called Tiendas del Rio. The revitalization project will be on Joske's-owned land.

"Downtown San Antonio has so much to offer — the river, the Alamo, lots of historic sites — it would be almost a cardinal sin to abandon the center of the city," Mettler said. ⅃

Sales personnel pose in this early picture, above.

Joske's downtown store today almost surrounds St. Joseph's Church.

The Roping Cowboy sign was dismantled during extensive remodeling soon after this 1938 photo was taken.

ALAMO CEMENT COMPANY

For more than 100 years, Alamo Cement Company has produced cement for hundreds of building projects around the State of Texas.

In San Antonio, its use is evidenced everywhere from the Tower of the Americas, for which the company supplied all the cement, to the expressways, for which the company supplied half the cement.

George Wood, public relations director for the historic business, described the company's most famous project, the State Capitol in Austin.

"It is made out of pink granite and Alamo cement to hold the granite together," Wood explained. "At the time it was built, the Texas Capitol was the largest building in the United States after the national Capitol.

"When William Clements was governor, the chief executive officer of Alamo Cement was Robert Koch. He went to the Capitol in Austin and exchanged with the governor copies of documents proclaiming that Alamo cement would be used as mortar for the pink granite in the construction of the building.

"In exchange, the governor had one of his people go down in the basement and dig out an area where there was some of the granite attached to Alamo cement. He mounted it on a small pedestal and gave it to the company. To this day, those documents hang in the governor's office, and the granite and cement keepsake has a place of honor at Alamo Cement."

Until 1980 when the company was sold, Alamo Cement was strictly a San Antonio-based firm.

Wood told how the company started:

"William Loyd, an Englishman, was on a hunting trip one day near the northern city limits in what now is Brackenridge Park. He literally stumbled over a piece of what he thought was cement rock. He picked it up and took some samples downtown to Kalteyer's Drugstore on Military Plaza. George H. Kalteyer, an expert chemist, heat-tested the

The original company was in what today is the Sunken Gardens in Brackenridge Park.

material and found it was cement rock, probably the finest in this area.

"So they quarried in what today is Brackenridge Park," he continued. "The smokestack and two of the kilns are still left. That big, beautiful place, called the Sunken Gardens, was the original quarry."

When Alamo Cement left the Brackenridge Park area, the company donated the land to the City of San Antonio for the park along with the rest of the land given by George Brackenridge. About five years ago, the Texas Engineering Department erected a plaque on one of the old kilns showing the area as one of the great engineering feats in Texas.

"The company just outgrew the original plant," Wood explained. "They put out 40 barrels of cement a day. That was a very small amount and San Antonio needed far more than that. So the company went out in the country, which now is part of Alamo Heights, and built the plant. It was the second oldest cement plant still operating west of the Mississippi. Now that plant is no longer operating because everything but the office has been moved to the new plant at Loop 1604 and Green Mountain Road."

History at a Glance   1880

Founded: *1880 at Sunken Gardens*
Founder: *Charles Baumberger, Sr.*
Original name: *The Alamo Portland and Roman Cement Company*
Original investment: *$3,100*
Milestones: **1908** *plant moved to Alamo Heights;* **1911** *power plant was largest lignite gas consumer in U.S.;* **1926** *converted from dry to wet process;* **1964** *offices built on Broadway;* **1979** *company sold to Presa S.P.A. and Vigier Cement LTD.;* **1985** *plant moved to Loop 1604 and Green Mountain Road*
Owners: *Robert Koch of Vigier Cement LTD., and Sandro Buzzi of Presa S.P.A.*
Employees: *250*

This chapter was based on an interview with George Wood.

San Antonio Portland Cement Company

WORKS; CEMENTVILLE, TEXAS.

MANUFACTURERS
OF
"ALAMO"
PORTLAND
CEMENT

Early company stationery showed a drawing of Cementville.

When the company moved to what is now Alamo Heights, it was still three miles from where the streetcar line stopped.

"Alamo Cement was two to three miles from there, and it was like a jungle," Wood said. "It was a really wild area and there still were Indian raids at the turn of the century. The people became a little scared, so they built a village.

"The company built a large recreation hall and a church, and then the little houses were constructed of cement. Workers were charged almost no rent. And the company had its own store which charged whatever the people could afford. They had a school, also. Because of the new plant, all of Cementville and the Alamo Heights plant will be torn down. The only thing left will be a machine house that is marked as a Texas Historical Site."

Alamo Cement's new owners are Vigier Cement LTD., the largest producer of cement in Switzerland, and Presa S.P.A. of Italy. The company's market area remains basically Texas.

The new plant is located on the Balcones Fault, which runs from Brackenridge Park, where the com-

"It was the second oldest cement plant still operating west of the Mississippi."

pany originally started, to Austin. Eight cement plants are located along that fault between San Antonio and Austin.

In 1985 Alamo Cement Company completed the second and final phase of construction on its new facility. The first phase, the cement clinker producing facility, was built between 1980 and '82. Since then the company continued to produce its finished products at the Alamo Heights plant.

With the summer '85 start-up, however, all production facilities were located together on the city's northwest side at the most modern, efficient and economical cement plant in the area.

In addition to the new Finish Mill Facility, Alamo Cement Company is building a new clinker storage and reclaim facility, which will increase clinker storage capacity by about 300 percent. Six large cement storage silos will incorporate state-of-the-art innovations including bag-packing facilities over the bulk truck loading area, segmented silos to store different types of cement, and a precast concrete palletizer warehouse building. ▟

Alamo Cement Company completed its new facility in 1985 at Loop 1604 and Green Mountain Road.

SOUTHERN MERCHANDISE & STORAGE CO.

This Federal truck was used in 1917.

In 1880 San Antonio was the largest city in Texas and was the state's center of commerce. The stage lines and railroads enjoyed heavy passenger traffic.

That was the year, too, Southern Merchandise & Storage Co. was founded. Owners Stewart C. Johnson and Henry S. Simms traced their company's history and have developed the following facts:

To meet the transportation needs of early San Antonio, two businessmen formed a partnership in 1880. Henry Carter, operator of a livery stable and a baggage and transfer business, joined with Thomas Mullaly, the leading undertaker who owned horse-drawn omnibuses and handsome hearses.

Their business was centrally located on Alamo Plaza next door to the Menger Hotel and was known as Carter & Mullaly Transfer Line. They advertised their principal services to be "Livery, Sales, Feed Stable, Transfer & Baggage, Undertaker and Funeral Director."

By 1883 they were advertising their services as "Elegant Carriages, Buggies, Saddle Horses, Undertaker & Funeral Director with special attention paid to forwarding bodies to all parts of the United States and Canada."

The need for more space prompted them to move the business in 1898 to 401 E. Houston St., the former site of the downtown J.C. Penney Company.

Carter-Mullaly Transfer Company continued to grow. Between 1903 and 1906, they leased additional warehouses at 523 E. Houston, 114 Blum and 202 Nacogdoches streets. Also during the same period, the company disposed of that portion of their business relating to "Undertaking & Funeral Director," but continued to operate the omnibuses, the livery and feed stable, hack rental and the transfer of freight, baggage and caskets.

H.E. Hildebrand was made president in 1907, and the main location was moved to 801 E. Houston St., one block east of the downtown post office which is the present location of the Central Fire Station.

During World War I, Max Autrey briefly served as president. But in 1920, he joined with J.E. Trimble in purchasing the business and renamed it Southern Transfer Company. Early advertisements featured the services of "Quick Baggage, Heavy Hauling and Furniture Moving & Storage."

Since railroads played such an important part in the company's early history, it was only a natural move when Southern Transfer Company relocated its operation in 1922 to 506 S. Medina St. to be near the International & Great Northern Railroad Depot that is now the Missouri Pacific.

Carter & Mullaly hauled goods in this splendid horse-drawn van in the 1890s.

History at a Glance 1880

Founded: *1880 in Alamo Plaza*
Founders: *Henry Carter and Thomas W. Mullaly*
Original name: *Carter & Mullaly Livery, Sales, Feed Stable, Transfer & Baggage, Undertaker and Funeral Director*
Headquarters: *3232 N. Panam Expressway*
Owners: *Stewart C. Johnson and Henry S. Simms*
Employees: *40*
Motto: *Moving things better since 1880*

This chapter was based on an interview with Stewart C. Johnson and Henry S. Simms.

A Southern-style mansion facade graces the front of the company's headquarters on Panam Expressway.

A.L. Hernandez joined J.E. Trimble in 1924 as a partner. By 1929 A.D. Hood joined the firm and these three men obtained a charter from the State of Texas to incorporate the business for the purpose of "conducting a livery and transfer business with auto and horse-drawn vehicles."

An expansion program began in 1932 with the purchase of American Bonded Warehouse Co. This additional location at 1230 W. Martin St. also provided 25,000 square feet of much needed space.

A tremendous boost in the growth of Southern Transfer Company occurred on May 16, 1933, when an agreement was signed with Aero Mayflower Transit Company, a nationwide company pioneering in the new field of cross-country

Stewart C. Johnson

"We have been slowly changing our own name to replace 'Moving' with 'Merchandise,' which better depicts the storage and distribution services we offer."

household goods moving.

Growth prompted the company in 1937 to purchase adjacent land and construct a modern 32,000-square-foot building at 526 S. Medina St. Also, to better describe its services, Southern Transfer added "Storage" to its name.

In 1939 Trimble and Hernandez sold their interest in Southern to O.E. Latimer and Harry P. Brown with Hood remaining as manager. By 1946 Hood and Latimer had resigned, leaving complete ownership to Brown, who at the time was founder and owner of Brown Express.

Simms joined the company in late 1953 and soon was appointed general manager. Southern's need for further expansion became evident and a 50,000-square-foot warehouse was leased at 1331 S. Flores St. Growing with San Antonio and looking to the future, Southern purchased a 16-acre site on the new Interstate 35 near Coliseum Road.

Henry S. Simms

Desiring to retire to his ranch, Brown sold his entire interest in Southern Transfer & Storage Company in 1961 to a group of San Antonio businessmen.

In addition to Johnson and Simms, the new owners included Fred E. Mueller, Jr., and Hampton Mauze whose interests were later purchased by the company. With the new ownership came a change in the company's name to Southern Moving & Storage Co., and the new management team promptly erected an ultra-modern warehouse and office on the 16-acre site purchased earlier.

"During the next 16 years, from 1962 to 1978, many changes occurred," Johnson related. "In this period, the company completed eight major construction projects, adding warehouse space and new offices for brokers which brought the total of our warehouse complex to almost 300,000 square feet.

"Confronted with the need for additional warehouse space, a deal was made, effective March 1, 1981, to sell our household goods moving department to our employees, and to give them our old name, Southern Transfer & Storage Company. Since that time, we have been slowly changing our own name to replace 'Moving' with 'Merchandise,' which better depicts the storage and distribution services we offer," he said.

"All of us at Southern Merchandise & Storage Co. are proud as we reflect on the past and note that the year 1986 marks 106 years of service to the greater San Antonio community." 🔲

SOUTHWESTERN BELL TELEPHONE CO.

Chet Todd

The history of Southwestern Bell Telephone Co. is the tale of communications advancing from the first telephone in San Antonio's rowdy Old West days to today's newest fiber-optic technology.

With 4,600 employees, Bell impacts the local economy while it looks to the near future, which holds not only telephone communications but new methods of data communications as well.

Today with half a million access lines in the San Antonio metropolitan area, Bell has come a long way from that June day in 1881 when the first line was strung. Eighty percent of San Antonio households now have telephone service.

Chet Todd, former vice president of customer services, spun the telephone company's story from its inception to its latest technological advances:

"In 1881 George W. Brackenridge had the first private line put in in San Antonio," Todd explained, "from his offices downtown to the pumping station at the headwaters of the San Antonio River."

Three black men — stringing wires to 50 subscribers of the new-fangled invention — installed the first lines on poles cut from cedar brakes on the Colorado River in Austin.

Those first few customers were connected to a Gilliland magneto switchboard in the first telephone offices located in a rented space downtown at Soledad and Commerce streets.

When the callers got the attention of "central" by striking a large button which generated current to cause a metal flag to drop at the switchboard, a male operator answered if he were so inclined. As likely as not during this process, the plaster in the wall in the subscriber's home had cracked because of the push.

"The first operators were men because the users of the telephone service were a rather rowdy group such as saloon and resort attendants and hack drivers," Todd said. "But that didn't last too long because the men weren't too courteous."

Soon thereafter the "Hello Girls" of the 1880s, more patient, pleasant female operators, replaced the rude men.

By that time, too, long distance had been established over old telegraph lines between San Antonio, Kerrville and Eagle Pass. And by the late 1880s, Bell's office had moved above a grocery store downtown.

In 1900 Bell boasted 1,236 subscribers, who originated more than 17,000 calls a day. The next year, subscribers peaked 2,000, and by 1905 operators had so many

History at a Glance 1881

Founded: *June 1, 1881*
Founder: *Jasper Keller, owner; J.K. Dunbar, first manager*
Original name: *Southwestern Telegraph & Telephone*
Original location: *Frank Building at Soledad and Commerce streets*
Original investment: *Approximately $25,000*
Original employees: *Approximately 50*
Milestones: 1884 *first long distance established;* **1900** *San Antonio had 1,236 subscribers;* **1932** *Auditorium Circle building completed;* **1950** *greatest expansion in history to 132,775 subscribers;* **1957** *more than 1 million calls originated from San Antonio daily;* **1959** *200,000th phone installed in San Antonio;* **1960** *1010 N. St. Mary's building opened;* **1974** *U.S. Justice Department filed antitrust suit against AT&T and Bell companies charging monopolization;* **1981** *AT&T reached an agreement with the Department of Justice to divest;* **1984** *AT&T divested of 22 operating companies and Southwestern Bell Corporation was formed.*
Lineage of presidents: *Herman Pettengill, Eugene Nims, Albert Elias, Albert Stannard, Victor Cooley, James Crump, Edwin Clark, Richard Goodson, Angus Alston, Zane Barnes*
Headquarters: *4119 Broadway*
Employees: *4,600 in San Antonio*
Access lines: *512,000, involving 365,000 residential and 147,000 business customers*
Assets: *$18 billion for corporation*

This chapter was based on an interview with Chet Todd.

customers they could no longer memorize the numbers. The first directory was a list of names, addresses and phone numbers written by an operator on a school tablet.

"The economy became quite vigorous in the early 1900s," said Todd. "As people became more affluent and the telephone became more inevitable, its popularity rose, although it was not that affordable. The rates were about $1 per month when average wage earners brought in less than a dollar a day."

When the Depression hit, some subscribers disconnected their service to save money. Bell kept employees busy, however, building new company headquarters at 105 Auditorium Circle. The eight-floor building was occupied in 1932 in preparation for conversion to dial phones.

Although before World War II the economy perked up and San Antonio began a building boom, the telephone was used mostly for defense purposes rather than for residences.

"Save 7 to 10 o'clock for the servicemen" became a popular and widely followed slogan for long-distance lines, which were swamped with GIs calling home.

"The circuits in our homes were given a low priority," Todd said. "The company was unable to get materials to build. I personally recall going on inspection tours and stopping four or five times enroute to steal hardware off of existing lines, particularly metallic things like washers and bolts. All our efforts were for defense.

"Because of this void, there was a latent build-up of requirements. Beginning in late 1946, we couldn't keep up with the demand. It took us around 15 years to catch up with the total demand."

By 1950 the company saw the greatest expansion in its history. More than 1 million calls originated from San Antonio each day. Pay phones went up from a nickel to a dime.

As the necessity for and popularity of telephones increased, so did the need for office space. Bell expanded into the building at 1010 N. St. Mary's where electronic data processing of bills replaced the pen-and-ledger system.

In 1890 telephone poles lined Commerce Street looking east from where Groos National Bank Building is today.

Bell employee Pepper McDougald looks over fiber optics on Commerce Street from the same angle as above.

Technology was also advancing and 1-Plus Dialing and Touch-Tone phones were introduced. With the '70s came an Electronic Switching System computer nicknamed Fat Albert, which was smaller and faster. Customers used Speed Calling, Call Waiting, Three-Way Calling and Call Forwarding for the first

"Eighty percent of San Antonio households have telephones."

time.

A few months after Bell celebrated its 100th birthday, AT&T divested of 22 operating companies including Southwestern Bell Telephone Co., and on January 1, 1984, an independent Southwestern Bell Corporation was born. Its telephone subsidiary's headquarters for San Antonio are located at 4119 Broadway.

"We now serve five states, Missouri, Kansas, Arkansas, Oklahoma and Texas, which is by far the largest with 56 percent. Texas is now an operating division," Todd said. "The other corporate subsidiaries are the Southwestern Bell Mobile Systems, Southwestern Bell Telecom and Southwestern Bell Publications."

Todd sees Bell's role in the future "information age" as a "provider of point-to-point communications of every type."

Fiber optics already play a major role in the telephone business. Up to 3,000 circuits can be provided by a fiber the size of a human hair as compared to a minimum of 24 circuits over a pair of copper wires.

Thirty years ago, Todd predicted the future telephone business, and he still believes his prediction today:

"Everyone will have a watch with a video screen with 10 little buttons that will be depressed in certain sequences. At birth each individual will be assigned a number. If you want to speak with someone, you will dial that number on your watch. If you don't reach them, they will be either deceased or in the shower. We're getting very close to that point." ⬛

FRIEDRICH AIR CONDITIONING & REFRIGERATION CO.

A little-known piece of the history of Friedrich Air Conditioning & Refrigeration Co. is that the family started out fashioning furniture from the horns of longhorn cattle, utilizing the curves of the horns to form chairs and settees.

Collections of the Friedrich longhorn furniture are housed in the San Antonio Museum of Art and the Hall of Horns in Lone Star Brewery.

Chuck Tribolet, director of human resources, and Jim Malcolm, director of advertising facilities, assembled other interesting facts of the company's long history:

When Ed Friedrich started his business in 1883, he produced several handcrafted products including store fixtures, wood billiard tables and fine-carved cabinetry. Eventually, these products were phased out, allowing for emphasis on refrigeration.

At the time, ice was a big commodity used for preserving food. To get the most out of each block of ice, Ed Friedrich developed innovative products which were the forerunners of today's refrigeration systems. Salt brine freezer cases employed the natural cooling properties of salt to provide lower temperatures. Bunker-type refrigerators improved product display by concealing the ice from view in side compartments.

After the industry had utilized every method of abstracting the Btu of cooling from ice, it became obvious that there was a need for some type of mechanical refrigeration.

When Ed's sons, George and Richard, joined the family business, the Friedrich plant was located on Cherry Street. After a fire in 1923, the Friedrich business was relocated to East Commerce Street, where Friedrich Plant No. 1 is today. At that plant, Friedrich made food display cases. These products were meaningful to the public and the food industry, for the food remained fresher, looked better and was more nutri-tious, and the stores did not lose as much to spoilage.

As it grew, Friedrich continued to refine its products. Soon George, an engineer, invented the innovative "floating air" principle. This was the concept that all manufacturers use to this day in open frozen food display cases. Revolutionizing refrigeration technology, this principle involved controlling the movement of refrigerated air over the food, thus eliminating the need for doors on most cases.

Richard Friedrich, whose expertise was in sales, conducted post-Depression prosperity tours around the country to commemorate the company's 50th anniversary.

Ed Friedrich stayed active in the business almost to the day he died in 1956. He was well thought of. He knew all his employees and every operation in the plant.

Ed Friedrich instilled in his employees his attention to quality and to detail. Friedrich products became known for superior materials and quality.

In 1947 the Friedrich Company built a warehouse at 3300 Old Seguin Road, which now is an access road to Panam Expressway. It was a two-building complex which functioned as a warehouse for a number of years. Later it was turned into an assembly operation for commercial refrigeration.

The plant was on the elder Friedrich's farm, which stretched from the banks of Salado Creek to San Antonio. Older employees remember if Mr. Friedrich had something to be done on the farm, he would shut down the warehouse and take them out there to work. That explains why the warehouse is located where it is. One of the older workers remembers Friedrich used to stand up in the watchtower of his farmhouse and survey his farm land. The watch-

History at a Glance   1883

Founded: *Feb. 1, 1883, on Cherry Street*
Founder: *Ed Friedrich*
Original employees: *5*
Milestones: 1915 *expanded to 35,000 square feet on Cherry Street;* **1933** *George Friedrich conceived floating air principle;* **1947** *warehouse construction at 3319 N. Panam Expressway;* **1971** *new plant constructed on N. Panam Expressway*
   Headquarters: *4200 N. Panam Expressway*
   Employees: *850*
   Units: *Two manufacturing divisions: Room Air Conditioning and Commercial Refrigeration, San Antonio and Fort Worth, Texas*
   Motto: *Pride in everything we do*

This chapter is based on an interview with Chuck Tribolet and Jim Malcolm.

Friedrich's first location on Cherry Street advertised iceboxes, billiard tables and store fixtures.

tower is still standing.

By 1950 Friedrich had become one of the world's largest manufacturers of commercial refrigeration equipment. To capitalize on this well-deserved reputation, the company entered the field of room air conditioners. The first 500 floating air window units came off the assembly line in 1952 and sales began to climb. Ultimately, this product line would constitute a significant portion of the company's total business.

"The public comes in touch with Friedrich products almost every day without realizing it."

Growth of the domestic and international markets for commercial refrigeration and room air conditioners prompted construction of Friedrich plant No. 3, a two-story 600,000-square-foot facility which also houses the corporate headquarters.

Friedrich moved to its present location on Panam Expressway in January 1971, while the other two plants remained in operation. The new site was once part of Fort Sam Houston.

Today Friedrich manufactures two major product lines of energy efficient products built in the Friedrich tradition of craftmanship. Friedrich has a much larger market than most consumers may recognize.

The public comes in touch with Friedrich products almost every day without realizing it. When people go to the frozen food section in the supermarket and they open a door or reach into a case, it is probably a Friedrich case.

And certainly the most recognizable products are the Friedrich room air conditioners, known for quality and dependability. Quite a few of the original room air conditioners are in operation today.

When Ed Friedrich started business, he thought of ways to conserve energy by building a quality product. He crafted an icebox to better conserve a natural resource — ice. One hundred years later, Friedrich is still conserving energy by paying attention to detail and craftsmanship. Friedrich people embrace the ideals set forth by Ed Friedrich and those ideals are reflected in their attitude and their work.

Many components go into a Friedrich product — condensers, fans, coils, motors. But the essential ingredient is still pride in people, the heritage, the product — Friedrich pride in everything they do. 🔲

Friedrich Plant No. 3 on Panam Expressway houses its corporate headquarters.

LUCCHESE BOOT COMPANY

For more than 100 years, San Antonio's Lucchese Boot Company has stood for quality workmanship, perfect fit and individual attention.

Lucchese boots have been worn by presidents, Hollywood stars, wealthy ranchers and honest-to-goodness cowpokes.

Today the company is owned by Acme Boot Company, Inc., the nation's No. 1 bootmaker.

In a 1971 interview, Sam Lucchese, great-grandson of the company's founder, recalled the family's boot-making past and the evolution of the legendary Lucchese boots:

"My grandfather's father was a shoemaker; his mother's father was a shoemaker on the other side of the family. How much farther shoemaking goes beyond that in our family, I do not know.

"My father had a customer whose hobby was genealogy. He became fascinated with families sticking to one business for a long period of time. He looked our family up in the old country in Sicily and Italy.

"Subsequently, he came back and told my father that he found a record where at one time the Hapsburgs of the German family ruled Sicily. They were disposed of or run out. When they left, they kidnapped a family of shoemakers named Lucchese and took them to Vienna. They held them there for three generations to make shoes for the family. I think he said this was 800 years ago.

"My grandfather was raised in a little village outside of Palermo. When he was sixteen or so, he came with one of his brothers to this country. They landed at Galveston or New Orleans about 1880 or 1883.

"They got to San Antonio primarily because Fort Sam Houston was such a big Army post. There were lots of boots sold.

"My great-grandfather never worked as a shoemaker in this country because he was too old by the time he arrived here. So it was really my grandfather who set up shop — he and his brothers, Joe and Mike.

"My father was born in 1900. I know he was working in the boot shop permanently at age fourteen. He learned the trade from the bench by doing his job. He did not care about the business part of the business. So when I was a young fellow just growing up, he had me do 90 percent of the correspondence.

"He did not care about talking to customers unless it was an old friend or unless they had absolutely decided to buy a pair of boots. Now our boot prices have always been a little bit higher than anyone else's, so there was always someone coming in and saying, 'I want to buy a pair of boots. Measure my feet.' We would have to be very diplomatic about asking if the price mattered because it used to irritate my father if he took somebody's measurements and spent the time to have them pick out every detail on a pair of boots and they decided they were not going to pay the price for them.

"My father knew no grades or classes of people. One of his most magnificent characteristics was that he could treat Rockefeller, Lyndon Johnson or Gene Autry exactly the same as he would treat any beggar.

"His only advertisement was his product. So he became strongly oriented to his product. His boots looked so good that his friends could not stand it until they got a pair. That is what was going to build his business, and we still have that today.

"Everybody liked him. He had the ability to take a man coming in the store screaming mad and have him leave laughing.

"He was always slow and deliberate. I never saw him make a fast move. He liked to work seven days a week. About 12 hours a day suited him just fine.

"I do not like the term 'handmade.' We are in the custom, made-to-measure boot and shoe business. We make a boot that has more handmade work in it than most any boot that is on the market today. We use what we consider to be the best combination of hands and machines to produce the boot. The primary difference is that it is made to individual foot measurements — we make a right and a left.

"We found that feet are like people. They come in all shapes and sizes. We started using a pedograph print, which is the same kind of print they take of a newborn baby. We

History at a Glance   1883

Founded: *1883*
Founder: *Salvatore "Sam" B. Lucchese*
Original name: *Lucchese Brothers Boot Manufacturing*
Original location: *317 E. Houston St.*
Lineage of ownership: *Salvatore B. Lucchese, Cosimo Lucchese, Sam Lucchese, Blue Bell Inc., Acme Boot Company, Inc.*
Headquarters: *1554 Cantrell Drive*
Employees: *200*

This chapter was based on an interview with Sam Lucchese in 1971 by Floyd S. Brandt and Larry Secrest as part of an oral business history project of the Graduate School of Business at The University of Texas at Austin sponsored by the Moody Foundation.

have found this pedograph very helpful because it gives dorsal aspects of the foot's shape. With the use of these two things, we have been able to develop a method of predicting gait and of making lasts that are shaped like men's feet.

"Webster says a boot is an instrument of torture. That is one that does not fit right.

"We figure about 24 man-hours are in a pair of personal boots. Those

"Webster says a boot is an instrument of torture. That is one that does not fit right."

are not the fancy ones. We have made some very, very fancy boots with about 150 man-hours in them. Then we have made some boots with sterling or gold tips.

"In one case, we made some boots for Anne Baxter, and we had to get the tanners to make the leather in certain colors because she wanted butterflies inlaid all over them. To get the authentic colors of the spots on the butterflies, we had to have the leather especially dyed. You could not even get it done today.

"We made some men's dress shoes and at one time women's shoes. That stopped when my grandfather died. My father came home from his father's funeral and announced that there would be no women's shoes made in this place. That was in 1929.

"We have all kinds of foot measurements that go way back. I know we have many measurements of famous generals when they were lieutenants and captains. I know we have the foot measurements of Hap Arnold, who was head of the Air Force in World War II. Gen. MacArthur's are here, too.

"After the war when orders were coming in faster than Papa could fill them, he raised the price until he stopped those orders from coming in.

"He would come in in the morning and say, 'Sam, we are going to raise

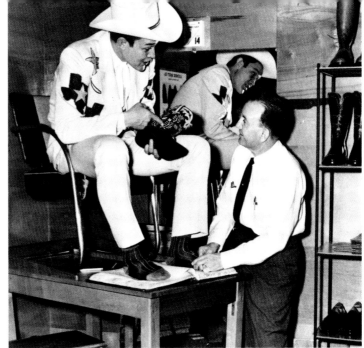

Cowboy singer Jimmy Dean was fitted for custom-made Lucchese boots by Cosimo Lucchese.

the price on our boots. We are selling too many and we cannot watch that many closely enough. We must not be selling them for enough.' Then if they were not selling too good, he would lower the price. He played it like a violin.

"I traveled on the road for the Acme Boot Company out in West Texas from 1957 to 1961. Acme salesmen made the most money of all boot salesmen. They were completely at the other end of the spectrum.

"I just delivered boots this past month to Gene Autry, Dan Blocker and Lorne Greene. Other well-known customers include John Wayne, Bing Crosby, Bob Hope, Joel McCrea, Ethel Kennedy's family, Caroline Kennedy when she was a

little bitty girl, Slim Pickens, Zsa Zsa Gabor, Maureen O'Hara, Sandra Dee, Jimmy Stewart, Clint Walker, Roy Rogers, Fess Parker, Buddy Ebsen. Some others are Ray Milland, Gregory Peck, Fabian, Pat and Mike Wayne who are John's sons, Winthrop Rockefeller, Bud Abbott, and Lou Costello, Phil Harris, Melvin Belli, Shelley Berman, Jimmy Dean and Robert Taylor. And, of course, many of the prominent Texas families.

"I would have to say President Lyndon Johnson is the most interesting customer we have served. It is difficult for anyone to be more interesting than that. We have a customer list that reads like *Who's Who*." [L]

Lucchese . . . 'Always'

Acme Boot Company, Inc. acquired the Lucchese Boot Company in 1984, but a company spokesman pledged, "Lucchese will be Lucchese always."

Tom Duffy, vice president of Acme's advertising and public relations, explained that Acme purchased Lucchese to be even more of a complete boot company. "We are proud to add Lucchese's price range, prestige, image and quality to the quality image Acme already enjoys."

Acme's distribution is nationwide and 22 salesmen from Acme's total sales force now

carry the Lucchese line.

Quoting from a previous Lucchese statement, Duffy said, "What we feel is important is not whether a boot is handmade, but whose hands did the work and by what standards. If handwork was selected because it is the best such as pegging the shanks, or if the machine was selected because it works best such as sewing on the outsole, then the product is honestly the best that can be offered.

"We care about everything from selecting and cutting the leather to polishing, shining and boxing the finished product."

UNION STOCK YARDS

SAN ANTONIO

The Union Stock Yards San Antonio is the largest livestock market in South and Southwest Texas.

Carlton Hagelstein, Jr., president, explained: "In recent years, we have evolved into more than just a stockyard.

"We are also an agriculture center. Other types of businesses are trucking and insurance companies, truck stops and so on. As times changed and urban pressures built, we have been using some of our surplus property for warehouses and other types of businesses that are not directly related to the stockyard's business.

"Through the years, and for various reasons, we've bought and sold some property. At this time, we have about 37 acres.

"The Greater San Antonio Chamber of Commerce ran a survey here several years ago and found that more than 40 percent of the San Antonio economy at that time was made up of agricultural-related activities in the San Antonio trade territory.

"Cattle are a very large percentage of our business. What is visible here is that more than $70 million worth of cattle are sold here each year. In 1984 we sold 266,500 cattle and about 47,200 hogs. Now the hogs are sold at private treaty, but at least 98 percent of the cattle were sold at auction.

"At an auction, there will be in excess of a hundred buyers in the auction arena, and there are a lot of agriculture people — farmers or ranchers — who are present. The cattle are brought into the ring and offered for sale by one of the seven different commission companies on the yard. Bids for the cattle are taken by the auctioneer, and he sells them to the highest bidder.

"The first regular cattle auction was held here in 1958 and the present auction building was completed in 1960. The auctions were held in a tent prior to that. In 1966 we started having auctions four days a week rather than just once a week. Auctions have become more and more popular. We sell primarily stocker and feeder cattle, which have different values to different people.

"The stockyards were built because the railroads were coming into San Antonio. At one time, there were as many as seven different railroads loading and unloading livestock here. Through the years, the different railroads were absorbed into three. It has probably been 10 years since we've shipped any livestock with the railroads.

"Livestock are now shipped by truck. The transporting of livestock by truck started in the early 1930s. Starting at that time and up to the present, all our business comes to the yards by way of truck.

"Everybody knows about the Chisholm Trail and the cattle drives from South Texas to Kansas. That was the way the cattle were

---

History at a Glance   1889

Founded: *1889 at 1716 S. San Marcos St.*
Founders: *Group of South Texas ranchers and trail drivers*
Original name: *San Antonio Stock Yards Company*
Original investment: *$200,000*
Milestones: *1894 company reorganized, changed name and total acreage rose to 41; 1938 Exchange Building constructed; 1940 front loading dock built; 1960 permanent auction building built and regular auctions began*
Lineage of leadership: *Amos Graves; G. Carlton Hagelstein, Sr.; Carlton Hagelstein, Jr.*
Headquarters: *1716 S. San Marcos St.*
Commission companies: *Alamo Livestock Commission Company, John Clay and Company, J.W. Kothman and Sons, A.C. Oefinger Commission Company, Producers Livestock Commission Company, Texas Livestock Marketing Association, Union Livestock Commission Company*
Owners: *Family owned*
Employees: *55*
Company motto: *Your competitive marketplace*

This chapter was based on an interview with Carlton Hagelstein, Jr.

Cattle auctions are held in the auction building built in 1960.

marketed right after the Civil War.

"In the 1880s, the railroads came into San Antonio. Rail transportation created a need for a place for cattle and other livestock to be loaded and unloaded. This area of town was the intersection of all the railroads for San Antonio.

"As the railroads evolved, the need for a market arose. There had been other livestock markets in San Antonio prior to ours. There was the Horse Market right across from the present-day City Hall, and another

The old Exchange Building was built in the late 1800s.

market west of there. Markets were then consolidated into what is now known as Union Stock Yards San Antonio. The word 'union' was used because they all came together in one place at one time.

"In 1889 the stockyards were built on the very edge of town. We were in the country. At that time, 10 or so

> ## "There are ranches all over South Texas which have done business with us through four or five generations. We are very pleased to have their trust."

ranchers got together and started the San Antonio Union Stock Yards Company on this site. The original capitalization rate of the company was $200,000.

"In 1894 that company was

reorganized into the Union Stock Yards San Antonio. My great-grandfather, Dr. Amos Graves, became the owner and had controlling interest in the company. At that time, he was the chief surgeon for the Southern Pacific Railroad, which I'm sure is how he got interested in the stockyards. We've had five generations who have worked and been involved in the company's activities. All three of my daughters at different times have worked down here. At present I have one daughter and a son-in-law working for the stockyards.

"From an agricultural standpoint, which is what we're primarily involved in, agriculture is here to stay. As long as there is land in South Texas, people are going to utilize it for whatever its highest and best use is. That will involve crops and livestock, and we will continue to sell cattle and utilize our particular niche at the stockyards.

"My family has been here five generations. There are ranches all over South Texas which have done business with us through four or five generations. We are very pleased that we have had their trust all this time and hope to continue to have it." ⏹

GREATER SAN ANTONIO CHAMBER OF COMMERCE

San Antonians have long realized the nation's 10th largest city would be a significantly different place to live and work today without the influence over the past 90 years of the Greater San Antonio Chamber of Commerce.

From its early days of purely business promotion to its more recent civic betterment efforts — which have resulted in HemisFair '68, the River Walk improvements, the South Texas Medical Center, military installations, McAllister Freeway and Trinity University — the chamber has been more important to San Antonio than any other single organization in the city's history.

Gen. William V. McBride (USAF Ret), president, collected the following facts about the organization's progress and its contributions through the decades:

"That the chamber has been the catalyst for the city's growth and development this century is rarely disputed," McBride said. "What is subject to question is the date of its founding."

Chamber historians generally regard 1894 as the true beginning of the modern-day Chamber of Commerce, but 1872 and 1910 also are significant.

In 1872, for example, the possible forerunner of today's chamber was chartered by the State of Texas as the San Antonio Board of Trade. It

The chamber held an annual banquet meeting in the St. Anthony Hotel during the 1920s.

worked sporadically for 20 years to promote and protect trade and advance commercial interests in San Antonio.

After its charter expired, business and professional leaders met late in 1894 to create the San Antonio Business Men's Club. By the early 1900s, that club had committees working in areas as diverse as real estate, public improvements, advertising, entertainment, irrigation, transportation and immigration.

By 1908 the club had a membership roster of 862 and a budget — at $12 per member per year — exceeding $9,000. By 1910 the club referred to itself as the "Chamber of Commerce."

"Following that subtle change in names, a not-so-subtle change in organizational direction took place," McBride said. "The new chamber became more aggressive."

Its members joined with eight other organizations to create a 3,000-member Chamber of Commerce that was the largest in Texas. It concentrated on a national publicity program to lure Americans to what the chamber called "a winter paradise, desirable homeland and a

History at a Glance 1894

Founded: *1894*

Founders: *James Slayden, Edwin Chamberlain, August Briam, Charles Kight*

Original name: *San Antonio Board of Trade, 1872; San Antonio Business Men's Club, 1894; San Antonio Chamber of Commerce, 1910*

Milestones: 1872 *incorporated as the Board of Trade;* **1910** *adopted the name Chamber of Commerce;* **1912** *merged with 8 organizations to grow to 3,000 members;* **World War I period** *responsible with local government for locating Kelly Field, Brooks Field and other installations here;* **1927** *raised money with city to donate land for Randolph Air Force Base;* **1942** *encouraged relocation of Trinity University;* **1958** *committee investigated feasibility of international fair;* **1974** *formed independent Economic Development Foundation*

Headquarters: *602 E. Commerce St.; Northside Service Office, Loop 410 and Blanco Road*

Membership: *4,000*

Employees: *41*

Budget: *$2 million annually*

This chapter was based on an interview with Gen. William V. McBride (USAF Ret).

likely place in which to do business." Emphasizing the city as a convention site resulted in 10,000 people attending 23 conventions and spending more than $100,000 in 1912.

"With a stated mission of improving the economy and the quality of life," McBride said, "the chamber embarked on a course that has resulted in achievements in each of its subsequent decades."

"That the chamber has been the catalyst for the city's growth and development this century is rarely disputed."

For example, during the 1920s, the chamber continued the heavy involvement in military affairs it started in World War I in locating Kelly Field, Brooks Field and other installations. With the help of city government, the chamber secured the land and won the location of Randolph Air Force Base.

Fighting the tragic effects of the Depression in the 1930s, the chamber conducted vigorous "Buy at Home" and "Share the Work" campaigns. As the Depression waned, the chamber enjoyed successes in road and highway development, agricultural promotion and city beautification. When the New Deal was implemented, the chamber educated the business community on administering it.

In addition to its obvious importance to the war effort, during the 1940s the chamber was responsible for securing Trinity University. After the war, the chamber concentrated on industrial promotion and development, which resulted in a 50 percent increase in manufacturing employment.

In the 1950s, foreign trade was expanded, particularly with Mexico, and an International Trade Fair was established. The chamber tackled problems of street lighting and public health, worked with Hollywood to attract filming, designed a highly praised master traffic plan, investigated water resources and flood control, and inaugurated extensive downtown development and improvement programs.

Additionally, the chamber succeeded both locally and in the state Legislature in taking the first steps toward creating the South Texas Medical Center.

The 1960s was the HemisFair decade. Following formation of a committee in 1958 to study the possibility of an international world's fair, much of the work of the chamber later revolved around the planning, organizing and staging of HemisFair '68. Coinciding with the fair and the international attention it focused on the city was renewed interest in making further improvements to Paseo del Rio.

More international trade promotion, new approaches to industrial development, increased research services and stepped-up legislative activities dominated the 1970s. The first Mexican Trade Fair, with the chamber as a co-sponsor, was held on HemisFair grounds. The Economic Development Foundation was created to attract new industry and company headquarters to San Antonio. A full Public Affairs Department was created to heighten the chamber's influence in the legislative arena.

In the early 1980s, the chamber's focus turned to helping small businesses, solving transportation problems and improving local education. A Small Business Council was expanded to help small firms, which constituted 85 percent of the chamber's 4,000 members.

The Transportation Department broadened its original highway development efforts to include work in airport and air service improvements, public/mass transit systems and surface streets and roads. And the desire to provide better quality education for San Antonio schoolchildren resulted in the chamber becoming involved in statewide educational reforms and local school district funding.

"As the Greater San Antonio Chamber of Commerce approaches the last half of the 1980s, its mission, which has remained remarkably unchanged in substance over its 90-year history, still calls for its leaders, members and staff to preserve and protect the free enterprise system, to improve the economic well-being for all citizens and to enhance the quality of life for the entire community," McBride said.

"It is a mission the chamber has accomplished well and will undoubtedly continue to do so for the next century." 🔳

Businesses displayed this chamber seal in the 1930s, above.

Today's chamber headquarters are along the River Walk.

NATIONAL BANK OF COMMERCE
OF SAN ANTONIO

Back in 1903 when a group of forward-thinking local businessmen and ranchers pooled their resources to start National Bank of Commerce of San Antonio, little did they envision the 23-bank holding company, National Bancshares Corporation of Texas, of which the bank is today's leader.

At the end of 1984, NBC of Texas boasted an impressive $2.7 billion in assets and the rank of ninth largest banking company in Texas.

Richard W. Calvert, chairman of the board and chief executive officer of National Bancshares Corporation of Texas, further explained:

"We have the largest market share in loans in San Antonio, which came about at the end of 1984. We think to be No. 1 in the loan area is significant. We also have the second largest market share of deposits in San Antonio."

In NBC of San Antonio's fledgling days, San Antonio was a major commercial center in Texas and its largest city. Not only did the railroads make it the transportation hub, its ranching and cattle industries made it an agricultural center as well. Mercantile and manufacturing were on the upswing. Solid merchants and fine old companies based their financial dealings with nine banks and a trust company.

The entrepreneurial founding group including businessmen and ranchers apparently felt San Antonio needed another commercially oriented bank.

Shortly before NBC opened its doors, an announcement ran in the Daily Express. Gen. J.M. Bennett's history book, *Those Who Made It*, recounts that notice:

"The National Bank of Commerce of San Antonio will open its doors on Thursday, October 8, 1903, inviting patronage. Its paid-in capital is $300,000. The stockholders are all local men, thoroughly identified and in harmony with the welfare and progress of Southwest Texas. The directory is composed of well-known public-spirited men, who have aided in and prospered with the varied development of our country. They are in sympathetic knowledge of conditions and requirements in this vicinity.

"In launching the enterprise, they will endeavor and expect to direct and safeguard its management to profitable investment; they will nonetheless strive to maintain the bank as a distinctive public institution and to make it a real benefit to San Antonio and its commercial growth. It will be the intention to be as liberal in management as conservatism and safety will warrant. The bank is well equipped with fire- and burglar-proof facilities and safety deposit box conveniences.

"With earnest desire to merit public favor, we frankly solicit accounts, personal interviews and correspondence. Respectfully, By J.P. Barclay, President."

Bennett, who authored the book, served as chairman of the board in recent years and is the grandson of an original bank founder and the son of John M. Bennett, who was the

History at a Glance 1903

Founded: *1903 on the ground floor of Kampmann Building*
Charter directors: *Robert Lee Ball; Julius P. Barclay, Sr.; John M. Bennett, Sr.; Robert J. Kleberg; Willoughby Williams Lipscomb; William James Moore; George R. Stumberg; Charles Schreiner; Nathan Moses Washer*
Original capital: *$300,000*
Original employees: *7*
Milestones: **1919** *moved to NBC Building;* **1958** *moved to NBC Tower;* **1971** *became part of National Bancshares Corporation of Texas;* **1976** *NBC West completed;* **1980** *traded with NASDAQ;* **1984** *record earnings of $9.46 million and joined National Market System*
Presidents: *Julius P. Barclay, Sr.; Robert Lee Ball; J.K. Beretta; Robert D. Barclay; Forrest M. Smith; Richard W. Calvert; Robert H. Seal; Marvin M. Stetler*
Board chairmen: *Robert Lee Ball; J.K. Beretta; J.M. Bennett; J.M. Bennett, Jr.; Richard W. Calvert, senior chairman of the board; Robert H. Seal, chairman of the board and chief executive officer*
Employees: *700*
Assets: *$1.2 billion, December 1984*

This chapter was based on an interview with Richard W. Calvert.

assistant cashier who helped unlock the doors on opening day.

"The first building was down on the corner of Commerce and Soledad on Main Plaza," Calvert explained. "The next building was immediately across the street. The bank for many years was actually on that corner, just on two different sides of the street. All three of our banking facilities have been on Soledad Street."

With its strategic location, NBC has been a significant factor in the

"A lot of projects downtown have been financed by the bank."

vitality of downtown.

"A lot of the projects downtown have been financed by the bank," Calvert said. "I know a lot of the officers have been involved in downtown activities through the years. I headed Centro 21, the downtown development committee appointed by City Council."

NBC's current building was built

The lovely Kampmann Building at Commerce and Soledad streets was NBC's first home in 1903.

in 1958 and was the first new major structure to grace downtown San Antonio since the Depression.

"I saw it go up and it was quite a deal in those days," Calvert recalled. "It was something so new, so different for the downtown area to have this size of a project at that time. It was really a very bold step on the part of the board because the bank was only about $125 million in total assets when they committed to build this building. That was a big gamble.

"A lot of people thought the bank

was making a mistake. People said, 'They're moving off Commerce Street and that's where most of the banks have traditionally been.' But as it has turned out, the decision was correct and our location today is right in the heart of the financial district."

Known as the NBC Center, the bank's three-block complex includes three buildings connected by underground walkways.

Always in the forefront, NBC of San Antonio was the first local bank to start an instalment loan department for consumers. Another major company milestone was formation of the holding company, National Bancshares Corporation of Texas, in 1971.

"That was a major departure from what we'd been doing," Calvert explained. "We went from owning and operating one bank into a multibank environment, and certainly that has changed the whole character of our company."

The company's character may have changed, but NBC of Texas is known for the longevity of its staff. Calvert said, "This company has the lowest turnover rate of any major banking company in the state. We have some very loyal people here.

"We have been successful," Calvert admitted. "We think our performance financially has been very good, especially when compared to our peers around the state. Over the past several years, our company has had one of the best performance records of all the major holding companies in the state."

Today NBC's third home, NBC Center, still graces Soledad Street.

THE ROEGELEIN COMPANY

A strong tradition of quality at a fair price has made The Roegelein Company the largest full-line meatpacking company in Texas.

Family owned and operated for 80 years, the highly visible operation produces a full line of meats ranging from packaged luncheon meat to fresh beef and pork.

The community-minded firm represents some $100 million to the South Texas economy with a payroll supporting 2,500 people including families.

Directing the company today is the third generation of Roegeleins in the meatpacking business; William Roegelein, Jr., is president and Lawrence Roegelein is vice president. The brothers explained the heritage that has made the Roegelein name a household word:

"In 1905 when the company was founded, San Antonio was a town with dirt streets, and almost everything that we know of San Antonio today didn't exist then. The Roegelein Company then was

nothing but a very small meat market on East Commerce Street, which back in the early days was a wooden street with two streetcar tracks," William Roegelein said.

"Our grandparents, Wilhelm and Anna Roegelein, arrived shortly before 1905 and went into the business. We don't know that our grandfather had a background in butchering, but he must have. Some of the family, still in Germany, are in the sausage business.

"There was no mechanical refrigeration in our grandparents' retail meat market called the Packing House Market. They had small counters or display cases with glass fronts, but the only refrigeration was ice. And they didn't use much of that either.

"They made smoked meats such as ham and bacon and various kinds

William Roegelein, Sr., displayed his company's canned hams.

of sausage that today we might call luncheon meat or processed meat. They salted pork."

"Curing meat is mentioned in the Bible," Lawrence Roegelein explained. "Basic sausage items go back to the Middle Ages."

"Our grandparents had their own favorite recipes, a few of which we're still using today with virtually no change," William Roegelein continued. "We've never changed our Smokets recipe since the day it was developed. We could produce the product at a much cheaper price, but it would reduce quality. It's company policy that if we cannot make it with that formula, then we just don't make it."

The brothers literally grew up in the business.

"We used to live next door to the meat market. Both of us started working in the business when we were about six years old, doing odd

History at a Glance 1905

Founded: *1905 on East Commerce Street*
Founders: *Wilhelm and Anna Roegelein*
Original name: *Packing House Market*
Original employees: *Family*
Milestones: **1936** *second plant opened on South Brazos Street;* **1960** *built San Antonio Cold Storage, office and warehouse;* **1965** *first vacuum-packed franks and full line of luncheon meats produced;* **1970** *byproducts plant started;* **1974** *fresh pork processing major expansion;* **1981** *processed meats major expansion*
Headquarters: *12.5 acres at 1700 S. Brazos St.*
Officers: *William Roegelein, Jr., president; Lawrence Roegelein, vice president; Joe Deres, vice president and general manager; Wayne Wendell, vice president, secretary and treasurer*
Employees: *600*
Market area: *Texas, Louisiana, Europe, Far East, Central and South America*
Owners: *Roegelein Enterprises*
Motto: *Produce a quality product at a fair price*

This chapter was based on an interview with William Roegelein, Jr., and Lawrence Roegelein.

"Our grandparents had their own favorite recipes, a few of which we're still using today with virtually no change."

William Roegelein, Jr., left, and Lawrence Roegelein, the third generation of the Roegelein family, direct the company today.

jobs such as sweeping the floor and later on wrapping bacon and hams," Lawrence Roegelein recalled.

"Our grandmother was involved almost until her death. She would walk through the plant and if she saw people not working, they went to work very quickly or they left. She was very critical of anything that wasn't right. She considered the business a matter of family pride. She had no official position in more recent years, but she still watched things carefully."

"Our grandfather died when our father was sixteen, so our father had to take over the business. Later he was joined by his brother, August," William Roegelein recalled. "Dad told us he used to deliver meat in a little pushcart to his retail customers. He would put whatever the customer had ordered in the customer's icebox — not a refrigerator — on the back porch. On the wall of the screened porch was kept a note pad on which he would write the date and the amount of the purchase. When it came time to collect, he would call on the customer, total up the note pad and collect that amount. It was the only record they had. There were no records kept at the store."

Later William Roegelein, Sr., and August Roegelein expanded and traded the pushcart for a horse and wagon to make more and faster deliveries. "Everyone had to have his meat fresh every day," Lawrence Roegelein added.

A second market was added on East Commerce Street, almost cater-cornered from what is now Joske's department store. Lucchese Boot Company was close by. Though com-

pany records are sketchy, apparently the family had even more than two markets. Old photographs show signs reading "Packing House Market No. 3" and also "Packing House Market No. 4."

Early customers included the Argyle Hotel, which now is the Argyle Club; Bluebonnet Hotel; Bright Shawl; Handy Andy; Hermann Sons; Hong Kong Grocery; Manhattan Cafe; Joske's; Our Lady of the Lake College and Convent; Medical

Arts Hospital; Olmos Dinner Club; Peacock School; Piggly Wiggly; Plaza Hotel; Protestant Orphan's Home; Santa Rosa Hospital; Menger Hotel; Crockett Hotel; and San Antonio Petroleum Club.

The first branching out beyond San Antonio covered the territory from here to Corpus Christi.

"During World War II, the company supplied a lot of products to the military, which went all over the world, and we were awarded the government's award for doing im-

Packing House Market No. 4 displayed meat in glass cases before refrigeration.

This motorized version of the original pushcart delivered fresh meat to customers' doors.

portant defense work," William Roegelein said.

"We became active in the business after the war. We both were in the service, went overseas and got out of the Army in 1946. We've been here ever since. Both of us have worked in every department in the business. Some of them were rather difficult, but our father insisted on it. We now appreciate that very much. Our father stayed in the business from age sixteen until he died at age sixty-six. He worked the day he died.

"Of course, a lot of things have changed," he continued. "Fresh meat has seen a pretty dramatic change. Fresh pork has become a very lean product. Beef has been improved in that same direction. Our processed meats are now in consumer packages. In fact, a number of years ago there was nothing like that. All meats used to be sliced by the retailer and wrapped in a piece of butcher paper.

"The first consumer package we produced was sliced bacon in a one-pound package. We'd slice it, grade it and weigh it to one pound. Then we'd roll it in a cellophane wrapper. It was successful, very successful.

"We were always taught quality. People pay the price for a better product. As far back as we can remember, that's all we've ever known. We learned it from our father and that's the way we've always operated — to produce the best kind of product we can. And we've been successful doing that."

Quality control is still important. Even today an employee from the quality control department daily brings around samples of Roegelein products for company executives to taste. The samples come from supermarket shelves, not from the plant's producing department.

"That's the way we sample our products, just like our father did. Every day he ate sausage," William Roegelein said.

Today the company has six vacuum packaging lines that produce 52 million packages of assorted products annually.

"Vacuum packaging permits us and the retailer to do things we couldn't do before. The meats have a substantially longer shelf life, up to 45 days. This includes virtually all of our consumer products, luncheon meats, bacon, Smokets, franks and so forth," Lawrence Roegelein said. "Frankfurters got their name from Frankfurt, Germany, and Genoa sausage, which is a dry-type sausage, came from Italy. And bologna was from Italy."

In 1960 The Roegelein Company built the San Antonio Cold Storage Company, a public cold storage warehouse. It has a capacity of 3 million pounds with a temperature maintained at a minus 15 degrees Fahrenheit. In 1970 the company added a byproducts plant to manufacture livestock feed, tallow used in soap making, and hides. Hides now are shipped all over the world to finished leather companies. The old plant had produced an inedible beef tallow which was used during World War II to make gunpowder.

''We were always taught quality. People pay the price for a better product. As far back as we can remember, that's all we've ever known.''

The original plant of the Roegelein Packing Co. was located on South Brazos Street.

An early Roegelein photo shows a busy meat business.

"Our original plant goes back to the late 1930s," William Roegelein explained. "But even though it's that old, we have kept it very modern by remodeling at the same time we expand a department. So everything we have in these plants is as modern as a brand new plant.

"In 1981 we doubled our capacity to produce processed meats. At the same time, we put in the most modern, efficient kind of equipment to handle products in the very best way. Again, it was a step to continue our quality."

"Everything is totally automatic today, but it wasn't always so," Lawrence Roegelein explained. "For instance, we used to package lard by hand before we built the lard refinery in 1974. We had a little lard filler that we had to stomp one foot on to put a pound in the package. And we'd stomp the other foot and put a pound in the other package. We handled it all by hand, even making those cartons first.

"Many years ago, Dad was speculating on lard futures and it wound up that the company made a lot of money on that. He bought six tank cars of lard at 60,000 pounds each and I had to put them all into cartons in one-pound packages — 360,000 pounds. Today it's automatic."

"Meat is probably the most viable of all agricultural products," William Roegelein said. "The con-suming public today is health conscious, and there's not another food more nutritious than meat. Almost everyone is a meat eater. It's the most popular food there is.

"Our most popular product is Smokets. While it's not our biggest volume item, it is our most treasured item because of our quality standards. Also popular are our franks — Texas-Size Franks particularly — and our Club hams and sliced luncheon meats. We have a full line of what we refer to as our 'Signature Quality' brand.

"Like our father used to say, we don't make anything we don't eat ourselves. That's a good philosophy." ▯

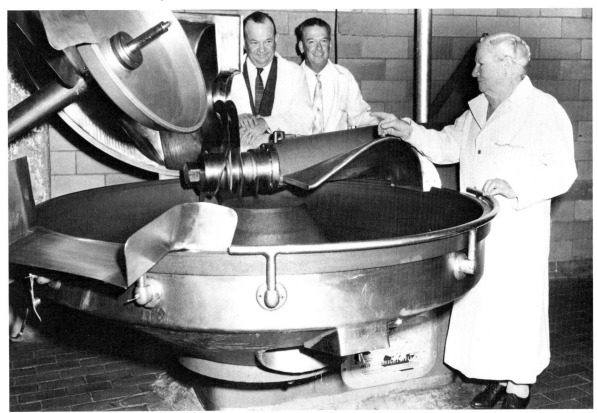

Inspecting a sausage-cutting machine were, from left, William Roegelein, Sr.; his brother, August Roegelein; and their mother, a company founder, Anna Roegelein.

FROST BROS.

For 68 years, the name Frost Bros. has been synonymous with high fashion and quality service.

Frost Bros. family of speciality stores is led by chairman Irving Mathews, left, and Michael Himoff, president.

The San Antonio-based firm with 13 stores maintains a large and loyal carriage trade and more than $125 million in annual sales.

Michael Himoff, president and a member of the family that has provided continuity in leadership for three generations, explained the stores' impeccable reputation and how it was earned:

"Frost Bros. is like a jewel and it cannot be duplicated. Our reputation stems from the top. We carry merchandise that can retail as high as $400,000 including fine jewelry, the finest furs and the very finest dresses that may sell for $12,000 or $15,000. We search the world for exclusive merchandise. But our uniqueness doesn't stop there. We also carry merchandise at lower prices which is as unique as the upper end."

Often compared to Bergdorf Goodman in New York City, Frost Bros. has an ambiance which comes as much from its stores as from its merchandise. The elegant Art Deco decor of its original store is preserved in the downtown store which serves as corporate headquarters. Newer stores feature luxurious interiors ranging from walls covered in suede to artistically appointed salons.

"Frost Bros. is like a jewel and it cannot be duplicated."

Frost Bros. began in 1917 when two dry goods merchants, Jonas Frost and William Frost, bought a dress shop on Houston Street from the Blum sisters.

"It was the first of its kind — a very specialized, service-oriented store that brought high fashion to South Texas. Even during the hard times, the Frost brothers never compromised on quality or service," Himoff said.

The current family leadership began when the founders brought in Sylvan Lang as a partner. Lang soon hired his brother, Gilbert Lang, whose impact on Frost Bros. has become legendary. The next generation included Irving Mathews, an astute businessman from Ohio who married Lang's niece, Jeanne, an interior designer who has designed most of the stores' interiors. Mathews worked his way through the ranks to become chairman of the board. His son-in-law, Himoff, entered the business as a coat buyer 10 years ago.

"One of the reasons Frost Bros. has been so successful is that we've had consistent management all these years. Gilbert Lang preached that the customer is always right and that service is everything. He would drive anywhere to make a sale," Himoff explained.

"We still take merchandise; we still do clinics in people's homes. We believe in educating our customers. The young children eventually become our good customers."

Frost Bros. features the top names in fashion, cosmetics and accents for the home — many of them exclusively.

For instance, when Estee Lauder's cosmetics first came on the market, Frost Bros. was one of the three accounts that launched her company. The "queen" of cosmetics often would stand behind the counter at Frost Bros. and demonstrate her products.

History at a Glance   1917

Founded: *Sept. 5, 1917, at 217 E. Houston St.*
Founders: *Jonas Frost and William Frost*
Original name: *Frost Bros. Ladies Fashion Apparel*
Original employees: *5*
Milestones: **1949** *doubled size of downtown store;* **1963** *opened North Star Mall store;* **1968** *opened boutique in Hilton Hotel;* **1970** *bought by Manhattan Industries;* **1975** *opened in Northcross Mall, Austin;* **1977** *opened two stores in Corpus Christi;* **1978** *opened in the Galleria, Houston, and River Drive Mall, Laredo;* **1980** *opened in Wonderland Mall in San Antonio, and in River Oaks and Memorial City in Houston;* **1981** *opened in Northpark in Dallas and relocated in Sunrise Mall, Corpus Christi;* **1984** *opened Gucci salon in Boston, Mass.*
Officers: *Irving Mathews, chairman of the board; Michael Himoff, president*
Employees: *2,000*
Stores: *13*

This chapter was based on an interview with Michael Himoff.

Renowned designers make frequent visits to the stores. Making appearances in 1984 for Frost Bros. charity fashion shows were Geoffrey Beene, Bill Blass, Liz Claiborne and Bob Mackie.

The stores' prestigious import business was developed by Mathews. Frost Bros. had the first Valentino boutique in the United States and are the only stores to have a complete Gucci salon within a store. Like Estee Lauder once did, Dr. Aldo Gucci himself also "goes behind the counter to sell merchandise" when he visits, Himoff said.

Mathews' philosophy was that if you could sell the best, you could sell anything.

"Price isn't the criteria; it's the look, the value, how you make your customers different. We never have a lot of anything, but we have a lot to choose from."

Frost Bros. continues its early commitment to service.

For customers who want to make a day of shopping, the store will set up a room and furnish a model. Merchandise can be taken into the home and a fashion consultant will put wardrobes together.

"There's really not too much we won't do for a customer," Himoff said.

The store's clientele is as varied as its merchandise.

"We have the very rich, individuals who may come in and spend $20,000 to $30,000 at a sitting. Since I've been here, our largest sale was $340,000, and we had two of

In the 1920s, this scene of Frost's French salon appeared on a post card.

those within a two-week period," Himoff said. "We have people who come in and spend $5,000 or $10,000 at a clip.

"International trade from Mexico, South America and Central America is a very important part of our clientele. Some used to fly in private airplanes and fill steamer trunks to take back to Mexico, especially before the border would close down prior to Christmas.

"In contrast, some customers come in just to buy cosmetics, shoes or a

A couture salon in Frost Bros. provides an elegant setting for high fashion selections.

gift because it has Frost Bros.' name on it.

"When I was a coat buyer, a rancher came in wearing dirty chaps," Himoff continued. "He wanted to buy a coat 'with a little fur on it,' so I showed him a cashmere coat that cost about $149. I showed him jackets, then mink, fox and everything we had. We finally had models show him three sables, one a golden sable worth probably $50,000.

"He said, 'That's what I want. I'll take it.'

"I got worried that he couldn't pay for it. So I asked if he had a Frost's charge card or a check. Then I asked him to wait while I got the credit manager.

"He took $50,000 out of his pocket and paid cash. After that I got the message and we don't prejudge anybody in the stores anymore. That was my indoctrination to Frost Bros.," Himoff related.

On the horizon for Frost Bros. is a store in Fort Worth in 1986 and the possibility of two more stores in San Antonio in the next four years.

"Our view is to stay in Texas. The biggest challenge is to stay the way we are and change with the times without forgetting about our tradition."

AZROCK INDUSTRIES INC.

From its founding in 1912 as a producer of rock asphalt paving materials from mines in Uvalde County, Azrock Industries Inc. has grown into a leading American producer of resilient floor covering with sales and marketing on an international scale.

The San Antonio-based firm is a leader among the five manufacturers of vinyl composition tile located in the United States. Azrock's sales of its flooring products are made through a network of 125 wholesale distributors serving flooring retailers and consumers in all 50 states. International sales of its products extend throughout the world.

In addition, Azrock has become the exclusive marketer in the United States, Puerto Rico, Guam, U.S. Virgin Islands and Mexico of Pegulan Sheet Vinyl Flooring manufactured for Azrock in West Germany and a luxury vinyl tile manufactured in England.

From its corporate headquarters in San Antonio, the firm directs the operations of its tile manufacturing plant in Houston; factory warehouses in Los Angeles and Rutherford, New Jersey; and a staff of 35 field sales representatives based in major metropolitan centers of the United States.

William K. Clark, president, recounted the history of Azrock Industries Inc., which spans almost three-quarters of a century:

"The company was founded in 1912 under the name Uvalde Rock Asphalt Company to produce and mine a natural asphalt deposit in Uvalde County about 100 miles west of San Antonio.

"Two Beaumont businessmen, J. Blewett Smyth and W. Allen Smith, learned of this deposit and were intrigued by its potential as a paving

Genera Marble composition floor tile by Azrock sees use in office flooring.

material. Upon investigation they found they could economically mine this product and furnish a very serviceable paving material.

"They were industrial pioneers who had vision. They started this company with their own funding and it still is a privately held corporation. They formed a mining operation and a town in a remote area 20 miles outside Uvalde. The town was named Blewett after one side of Smyth's family. The company furnished all the services necessary for a happy life — a commissary, hotel, post office and school. Since it was too far to commute from Uvalde, all the employees lived there.

"That village existed until the last person no longer wished to stay. In the 1940s and '50s, transportation was improved and children were bused to schools in Uvalde. People then preferred to live in Uvalde rather than in isolation at the mines. At its peak, probably 150 people

History at a Glance   1920

Founded: *June 13, 1912, in Beaumont*
Moved to San Antonio: *1920*
Founders: *J. Blewett Smyth and W. Allen Smith*
Original name: *Uvalde Rock Asphalt Company*
Original investment: *$150,000*
Original employees: *50*
Milestones: *1920 corporate headquarters moved from Beaumont to City Central Bank Building;* **1926** *moved headquarters to Frost Bank Building;* **1932** *established resilient floor tile plant in Houston;* **1933** *placed sales representatives in key U.S. cities;* **1959** *expanded capacity of Houston plant;* **1963** *established Los Angeles warehouse;* **1971** *established Rutherford, N.J., warehouse;* **1974** *moved headquarters to Century Building, 84 N.E. Loop 410;* **1981** *installed computerized control system in San Antonio and Houston;* **1984** *discontinued rock asphalt division*
Lineage of presidents: *J. Blewett Smyth, Glenn H. Alvey, H. Randolph Brown, William K. Clark*
Employees: *370*
Assets: *Capitalization of more than $10 million*
Motto: *Azrock — covering America's floors*

This chapter was based on an interview with William K. Clark.

President William K. Clark poses with models illustrating high fashion in Azrock flooring products.

lived in Blewett.

"Interestingly, we had a union in our mining operation. At the last union negotiation in January of 1984, the two employee representatives on the union committee were born in Blewett and were third generation employees of Uvalde Rock Asphalt Company and its successor, Azrock Industries Inc.

"**S**imilarly, since our floor tile plant in Houston was established, we have had many people who had their first job there and stayed until retirement."

Asphalt rock comes from a limestone deposit that is permeated with natural asphalt through volcanic action.

"The natural asphalt is within the limestone. The natural asphalt is blasted out, crushed to size and coated with a fluxing material. This material holds the particles together so the asphalt can be laid on a road and rolled over to become paving without being heated. It was a very interesting concept," Clark continued.

"The company really was unique. There have been very few producers of rock asphalt in the United States. And the State of Texas has benefited from the availability of this product as a paving material for highways, streets and roads.

"In 1920 while Smyth was president, he moved the company headquarters to San Antonio, the closest major city to the mining operation;

Azrock's Vinyl Brick composition floor tile is widely used in homes.

the corporate headquarters have been maintained here since.

"In 1932 the company began manufacturing resilient floor tile at a plant that was located in Houston because the city had a port through which we could receive raw materials from abroad and ship products economically to both coasts and around the world."

Clark explained the origin of the company's current name.

"At the time we entered the flooring business, the company wanted to make a floor so durable it would wear as long as rock. Instead of using 'as rock,' they made the trade name 'Azrock.' We adopted that as our corporate name because of our advertising and promotion activities on Azrock flooring products throughout the world. It was simpler if our corporate name coincided with our trade name."

Azrock's original entry into the flooring business was making asphalt plank flooring for industrial use to take advantage of mining byproducts.

"However, this plant was established during the Depression and the company did not find a ready market for the product," Clark continued. "But we discovered a newly developed mineral flooring called asphalt floor tile which launched us as a producer of resilient flooring. So really the mining business led us into the flooring business.

"After World War II, vinyl as a raw material became available, which enabled us to make a more glamorous floor product. We now manufacture no asphalt floor tile but concentrate on the manufacture of vinyl composition floor tile. This fortunately has developed into a high fashion business, which enables us to make a floor of high durability and with style, making our business very exciting for us and our customers."

Azrock discontinued rock asphalt mining in June 1984 to devote all of its efforts to producing floor tile.

"Our business in flooring had developed to such an extent that we believed our future would be better devoted to the flooring business. By that point, flooring represented about 90 percent of the business of this corporation," Clark explained.

"Resilient flooring is a composition material which has resilience. Our product today is a vinyl floor tile which has beauty as well as comfort under foot. It is not a hard tile like ceramic. It is manufactured by a complex process.

"And the State of Texas has benefited from the availability of this product as a paving material for highways, streets and roads."

"The plant in Houston where we manufacture Azrock resilient floor tile has an automated production line that is the length of about three football fields. We manufacture very significant quantities because we must be a major factor to be a success in this business. Of the five producers of vinyl composition floor tile in the United States, we are the only company with headquarters outside the Northeast.

"The market for Azrock floors has expanded tremendously because of the serviceability of the floor and the things it will do from a performance standpoint. Then we have established distributors in major cities throughout the country who stock these products so they're readily available to the consumers. Further, more sophisticated manufacturing processes and advances in technology allowed us to incorporate style and excitement into floors that previously were simply very durable," Clark noted.

"Azrock has been a trend setter in product development in vinyl composition floor tile in many areas. We have originated many new manufacturing concepts, which allowed us to incorporate greater style ahead of our competitors. Our innovation has allowed us to remain an important competitor against some of the major corporations of America. From the standpoint of style, we have been a trend setter and we intend to be even

Houston plant manufactures floor tile using a fully automated assembly line as long as three football fields.

more of one."

He explained the trends in the two markets for Azrock products — commercial and residential.

"In the commercial area, architects specify a product for a building such as a hospital or school which may not be completed for five years or so. We must have styles that will be pleasing for a long time. Many of our floors have been in use for 50 years. But we also must incorporate in our product line new styling that is toned into the colorations and style preference of today and tomorrow."

In San Antonio, large installations of Azrock products are in hospitals, medical buildings, office buildings and department stores such as Joske's. The original Wonderland Mall was floored in Azrock products. Many schools throughout South Texas such as Churchill High School use Azrock floors.

On a larger scale, more than 1 million square feet were installed in the U.S. Air Force Academy in Colorado Springs and the same amount in the Tenneco Building in Houston. Azrock was installed in the U.S. Embassy in Tokyo and in Saks Fifth Avenue in New York City.

Azrock's business is evenly divided between new construction and remodeling. For residential use,

Azrock manufactures do-it-yourself products that are self-adhering.

"The do-it-yourselfer can buy a carton of tile and put the floor in himself. The do-it-yourself market is as important as that installed by flooring specialty dealers," Clark explained.

"The future of Azrock is even more exciting than its past because of the character of the products we manufacture. They have a worldwide market from the standpoint of their performance, value and style. We see great excitement in the products that we manufacture and the breadth of the market.

"Because of new style developments and advanced manufacturing techniques, our products are more competitive in foreign areas where competitors have less sophisticated manufacturing capabilities. As an example, a firm in England produces the same kind of floor products we make. The firm buys and markets throughout the United Kingdom our tile in more sophisticated patterns than they are able to manufacture. So we see our world markets expanding.

"Further, we have an enviable network of marketing distribution in the United States. So there is an interchange in the flooring industry that is extending worldwide, which

means expansion for us through maintaining a position of leadership in technological developments and styling."

Azrock maintains permanent displays of Azrock Floor Products in the Merchandise Mart in Chicago and the Dallas Market Center.

The company continues an ongoing program of national advertising in magazines directed to the flooring trade, architects, interior

"Instead of using 'as rock,' they made the trade name 'Azrock.'"

designers, home builders, ultimate users and consumers. In addition, Azrock makes available to flooring dealers a cooperative advertising program for advertisement of Azrock Floor Products in local markets.

"We will continue our corporate headquarters in San Antonio for a number of reasons. It is an exceedingly pleasant place to live and creates a management atmosphere that has influenced the success of our company in all locations. So we treasure the fact that we are San Antonians. Further, we have taken advantage of our location by having our customers from around the world come to San Antonio. They find it a very pleasant place to visit in contrast to cities where other headquarters are located. Being here also gives us the opportunity to manage because we are not distracted by the manufacturing responsibility we place on those who are in charge of manufacturing," Clark said.

"One of the things that has made me proud to be associated with Azrock Industries is that when I started here in 1948, I found this to be a company with a conscience. Through the years, Azrock has dealt on an honorable basis with employees, suppliers, customers, shareholders and the public. The moral code of this company has been one that every individual can be proud of." ▉

SANTIKOS THEATRES

The motion picture superstar of San Antonio is Santikos Theatres, which has brought entertainment to South Texans for 65 years.

Today Santikos Theatres, Inc. owns and operates 66 screens in 11 local locations with expansion plans for an additional 34 screens and the largest theater complex in the state.

John L. Santikos, the mastermind behind the aggressive firm, traced his business roots back to his father who founded a theater and nickelodeon operation in 1910 in Waco.

The younger Santikos, now chairman of the board, recalled how his father, Louis Santikos, came to the United States from Greece "to find fame and fortune like everybody else."

His first entertainment venture was so successful in Waco, the elder Santikos expanded to San Antonio in 1920 with the purchase of the Rialto Theatre. He then opened the 600-seat Palace Theatre on March 3, 1923, at 325 Alamo Plaza.

The Palace featured silent movies, news weeklies, live comedy and vaudeville acts accompanied by a mammoth pipe organ. Symphony concerts there were conducted by Don Felice from Chicago. The theater was converted exclusively to live acts in 1928 and '29. In 1930 it added film sound capabilities and showed "talkies" until 1954 when it was demolished to make way for a parking lot.

"He had a love for entertainment, vaudeville, classical arts and music," his son remembered. "San Antonio had no outlet for showcasing such entertainment. It was fulfillment of a dream to bring class entertainment to San Antonio."

Louis Santikos took his family back to Athens where his son was born and grew up. There he dealt in film distribution and real estate. After World War II, he returned to San Antonio and opened the Olmos Theatre in 1950. John Santikos entered the business in 1955 after graduating from St. Mary's University.

"I consider myself a self-made man," he explained. "I knew that my family had destined me to do some-

John L. Santikos

thing that should make them proud of me, and since I was the first boy in the family, I felt I should be the first one to do it. I had the responsibility as well as the burning desire to do something successful and to prove myself. The vehicle was the theaters."

His first acquisition was San Pedro Drive-In in 1961. It operated until 1984. Soon it will be replaced with a retail development which will include a multiscreen indoor complex.

Santikos noted the decline in drive-ins in the 1960s and '70s.

"At some point back in the '50s or '60s, the indoor theaters were not doing much business. People wanted to go to the drive-in. Drive-ins would play a picture about six months after the indoor and they'd get three to four times as many people. But for all practical purposes now, drive-ins are on their way out.

History at a Glance 1920

Founded: *1910 in Waco*
Moved to San Antonio: *1920*
Founder: *Louis Santikos*
Milestones: **1920** *Louis Santikos purchased Rialto Theatre in San Antonio;* **1923** *built Palace Theatre across from Alamo;* **1950** *opened Olmos Theatre;* **1961** *John L. Santikos acquired San Pedro Drive-In and organized and presided over Santikos Theatres, Inc.;* **1969** *opened Century South, first multiscreen complex in San Antonio;* **1976** *opened Northwest theater complex;* **1979** *opened Galaxy Theatre;* **1984** *opened Westlakes Theatre*
Headquarters: *85 N.E. Loop 410*
Theaters: *Mission Drive-In 4, Central Park Fox 4, Century South 8, Cinema 4, Galaxy 10, Northwest 10, Southpark 4, Windsor 5, Ingram 6, Wonder 2, Westlakes 9*
Officers of Santikos Theatres, Inc.: *John L. Santikos, chairman of the board; Tom Bridge, president; Tom Higgins, executive vice president and general manager; Jon Wray, vice president of operations; Ken Higgins, vice president of film buying/advertising*
Employees: *500*

This chapter was based on an interview with John L. Santikos.

"We closed a lot of our drive-ins for two reasons: The land became too valuable and the drive-ins were not as popular as they once were."

Santikos made his imprint on the local movie business when he opened Century South Theatre in 1969.

This four-screen theater proved to be a turning point for Santikos Theatres, Inc. with its immediate and immense success. Its first box office hit was "Butch Cassidy and the Sandance Kid." The theater later was expanded to eight screens.

As to why he took the risk of locating his first theater complex on the South Side, he explained, "There were theaters on the North Side. All the major national circuits were here and there were a lot of screens on the North Side while the South Side didn't have any. We knew the economic base was on the North Side, but we also knew that we could get all the first-run pictures we needed for the South Side. In fact, when we opened, we used to draw from the North Side as well. We were the only multiscreen theater here.

"There were only a couple of multiscreen theaters in the United States. I flew to Kansas City to look at one with three or four screens. I liked the idea."

Its advantages were immediately obvious.

"You could operate a four-screen theater with one manager, one ticket taker and one operator, so there was a savings in payroll. But the real advantage is that multiscreen theaters are what people like. The more screens, the more business we do per screen."

Santikos recalled the national premiere of one major motion picture made in San Antonio, "Viva Max," in 1969.

"The star, Peter Ustinov, came to the opening and we had cocktail parties, receptions and dinners in connection with the film's opening. It was a big Hollywood-type event with search lights and a benefit performance. The movie was very successful here."

Santikos' success on the South Side prompted him to build the Northwest 6 complex in 1976 and the Galaxy with six screens three years later. Both have been increased to 10 screens. His newest theater, Westlakes, with nine screens opened in late 1984, making Santikos Theatres almost geographically encircle the city.

Buying other theaters over the past few years has put Santikos in the dominant position in providing film entertainment in San Antonio.

"It was fulfillment of a dream to bring class entertainment to San Antonio."

His future in the movie business appears solid. "When the cable TV and video tapes came out, we were afraid they would affect our business. But instead of hurting our business, they really helped. They have created more interest in movies. Also, filmmakers are making

The Palace Theatre built in 1923 brought class entertainment to San Antonio.

more pictures now because they have other outlets such as pay TV."

Santikos also foresees greater involvement in real estate through Santikos Investments, Inc. His investments company builds theaters and leases them to Santikos Theatres, Inc. The Westlakes and Century South developments, for example, contain multiscreen theaters as well as retail space. Other retail developments with multiscreen theaters are planned along Loop 1604.

But his first love is movies. "I love movies personally. I love to go to the theater and see good pictures." 🔳

The Galaxy complex provides 10 screens for movie-goers in northeast San Antonio.

J.C. PENNEY COMPANY, INC.

James Cash Penney's first store in Kemmerer, Wyoming, in 1902 bore the name The Golden Rule. Repeated on all his early stores, that name summed up the philosophy that launched his retail empire.

Today J.C. Penney Company, Inc. is the No. 3 retailer in the United States. Its more than 2,000 stores are in all 50 states as well as in Puerto Rico and Belgium. In 1983 gross revenues were more than $12 billion.

J.C. Penney is an integral part of the San Antonio economy. With seven stores and a Credit Service Center, the company occupies 685,000 square feet of space and employs more than 1,100 people.

G.R. Bowen, manager of the Windsor Park store, recounted the early history of the company, its mammoth growth, changes with the times and view of the future:

Penney was the seventh of 12 children of a Baptist minister in Hamilton, Missouri, who farmed on weekdays and preached on Sunday without pay. Penney first earned his own money at age eight by raising pigs, horses and watermelons.

After graduation from high school, he worked for $25 a year for the leading dry goods store merchant. Later he saved his earnings and bought a butcher shop in Longmont, Colorado, but lost his business when he refused to bribe the chef at a local

hotel with a bottle of whiskey.

He then clerked in the dry goods store of T.M. Callahan and Company in Longmont and for Callahan and Guy Johnson in the partners' store in Evanston, Wyoming. In 1902 he opened The Golden Rule store in the mining town of Kemmerer as the third partner.

"It was unusual in that he accepted only cash, especially since he was competing with a store operated by the mining company, which offered advance credit against wages. But by selling for cash, he could sell for less," Bowen said. "He built this company on the sale of work clothes."

Soon Penney was outselling his competition. He then supervised the establishment of two more stores in Rock Springs and Cumberland, Wyoming. When the partnership dissolved in 1907, Penney bought all three.

He envisioned a chain of stores covering the mountain states. Crucial to his success would be his employees whom he referred to as associates. He saw them as a chain of

James Cash Penney

partners linked by their adherence to the Golden Rule.

"He initiated The Penney Idea, a statement of philosophy the company still follows today," Bowen explained. "It calls for providing quality merchandise at one price for all, keeping prices as low as possible, allowing his associates to share in earnings, and offering satisfaction to the customer," Bowen said.

By 1909 Penney had established

History at a Glance   1920

Founded: *1902 in Kemmerer, Wyo.*
Opened in San Antonio: *April 17, 1920, at 401-405 E. Houston St.*
Founder: *James Cash Penney*
Original name: *The Golden Rule*
Original investment: *$6,000*
Original employees: *4*
Headquarters: *New York City*
Units: *2,000 stores with 7 in San Antonio*
Assets: *$8.2 billion for company*
Motto: *Honor, confidence, service and cooperation*

This chapter was based on an interview with G.R. Bowen.

headquarters in Salt Lake City, and a year later he had 12 stores with sales of more than $2 million. In 1913 he incorporated the chain under the name of J.C. Penney Company. The headquarters moved to New York City in 1914. Its stock was listed on the New York Stock Exchange in 1929.

The company continued steady expansion from the West to the East Coast.

The first J.C. Penney in San Antonio was one of 115 stores the chain opened in 1920. San Antonio's store was the ninth J.C. Penney in Texas.

James Cash Penney's first store was The Golden Rule in Kemmerer, Wyoming.

The downtown location remained the only J.C. Penney in the city until the suburban shopping trend developed in the 1950s. Subsequently, stores were opened in Terrell Plaza in 1958, Northwest Center in 1960, McCreless Mall in 1962, South Park Mall in 1974, Windsor Park Mall in 1976 and Ingram Park Mall in 1979. A Credit Service Center opened on Nacogdoches Road in 1982. An outlet store is at 2710 Austin Highway. The downtown store was closed in 1984.

The company introduced credit selling in 1958 and soon after broadened its scope of merchandise to include home electronics, furniture and sporting goods. A far cry from selling only work clothes, the company also is the No. 2 fine jewelry merchandiser in the nation. J.C. Penney entered the catalog business in 1962 and has become the second largest marketer of catalog merchandise in the country.

In 1974 a major effort to improve its market share for fashion apparel was launched. This led to increased emphasis on higher taste-level apparel and home accessories. Private designer labels were added in 1983 to attract fashion customers. They include Halston III women's apparel designed exclusively for J.C. Penney by Halston and a men's line designed exclusively by Lee Wright.

"Merchandise in each J.C. Penney store is regionalized," Bowen ex-

plained. "Each store buys what it needs for its customers. What we need in San Antonio is not necessarily what they need in Houston or in Austin. Also, what we need in the Windsor Park store may not be the same as what they need in the South Park store. San Antonio is a more relaxed community and more casual than some cities."

"He built this company on the sale of work clothes."

In 1983 the company announced plans to spend more than $1 billion in the next five years to modernize stores. A new mixture of merchandise and reallocation of space place greater emphasis on family apparel, leisure lines and home accessories. Stores no longer offer auto service, major appliances, hardware, lawn and garden merchandise, and fabrics.

"We are very optimistic about San Antonio," Bowen explained. "I've heard the remark that the '60s were the expansion of Dallas and the '70s of Houston and the '80s could be San Antonio. J.C. Penney wants to be part of it; we have positioned ourselves well for that expansion." ◢

NATIONAL BANK OF FORT SAM HOUSTON

The National Bank of Fort Sam Houston was established in August 1920 as the Sam Houston State Bank and Trust to serve the banking needs of military personnel.

The bank was converted to the National Bank of Fort Sam Houston at San Antonio, Texas, in November 1931. For 65 years, the San Antonio institution has been accepted as the "worldwide, hometown bank" by thousands of Armed Forces members, veterans and families.

Now with more than 100,000 depositors, total assets of more than $500 million, the bank is part of the RepublicBank Corporation, the nation's 18th largest banking organization with assets of more than $22.1 billion.

Satellite communications link the San Antonio bank with military installations around the globe and records are kept current over thousands of miles.

F.R. "Bob" Kirkpatrick, chairman of the board and chief executive officer, and E.P. "Pat" Adcock, president and chief operating officer, both have been with the bank since 1946. They tell the unique story of the bank's beginnings and how the colorful institution continues to serve the military community:

"Men with great foresight started this organization predominantly as an Army bank," Kirkpatrick related. "It was founded on the principle that the military individual was a good credit risk because he was dedicated to serving his country and had character and integrity.

"Unfortunately, there was a time when our military people were treated like second class citizens in terms of credit. This spurred individuals associated with the Army to create an institution to meet the credit needs of military personnel."

The bank, today affectionately referred to as Fort Sam Bank, was located on Grayson Street near other military related enterprises that sprang up across from the historic Fort Sam Houston Quadrangle, built in 1877 as a supply depot. Listed in the National Register of Historic Sites, the Quadrangle also wears a Texas Historical Building marker (south side of the clock tower). United States Army Automobile Insurance Association, now USAA, moved next door at 1406 Grayson in the fall of 1927 from Fort Sam Houston, and the Government Personnel Mutual Life Insurance Co., now GPM, opened at 1506 Grayson in May 1934.

"We're the only one of these three still on Government Hill," Kirkpatrick said. "The others moved away, but we have stayed close to Fort Sam Houston."

While the bank was initiated with

the Army depositor in mind, today's bank accounts are 3-to-1 Air Force personnel. Eighty-five percent of accounts with the bank are held by active duty or retired military or depositors connected with civil service, and approximately 75 percent of those live outside Texas.

Fort Sam Bank's reputation is worldwide because "that's where our customers live," Kirkpatrick said.

A case in point was a letter written by a woman who was stationed with her family in Italy.

"She remarked in her correspondence," Kirkpatrick said, "that there were two things she found as her family traveled around the world: Coca-Cola and the Fort Sam Bank.

"Our chief and most effective advertisement is a satisfied customer who is willing to tell others about our banking services. Military people talk about their banks and compare. It has been a great asset for us

to enjoy that type of advertising."

Fort Sam Bank's success is based on the continuity of management and purpose as well as providing exceptional services for the specific needs of military personnel.

"Just as the military has a mission, this bank has two missions," Kirkpatrick said. "The No. 1 mission is to furnish the most economical, efficient banking services to members of the Armed Forces. The second mission is to make a profit for our shareholders. If we do the first one right, the second one will take care of itself. That has been our philosophy for 65 years."

As a military community, San Antonio was the logical proving ground for such an institution.

"There are more than 280 retired Army and Air Force generals along

Showing its patriotism, the Fort Sam Bank flies a lighted 20-by-30 foot American flag from its fifth story.

History at a Glance 1920

Founded: *Aug. 2, 1920, on Grayson Street*
Original name: *Sam Houston State Bank and Trust Company*
Original capital: *$100,000 from 1,000 shares*
First day's deposits: *$17,521.99 from 100 depositors*
Original employees: *5 plus cashier and president*
Milestones: 1920 *bank rented 1514 Grayson St. for $65 a month;* **1931** *rechartered as National Bank of Fort Sam Houston at San Antonio, Texas;* **1941** *new bank building opened at 1422 E. Grayson St.;* **1973** *eight-lane motor bank opened;* **1974** *stockholders approved formation of holding company, Fort Sam Houston BankShares;* **1975** *lobby expanded;* **1979** *holding company included Northern Hills and Universal City banks;* **1980** *bank began operating military banking facilities in United Kingdom, Iceland and Guam;* **1981** *Fort Sam Houston BankShares merged with RepublicBank Corporation;* **1982** *first stateside military banking facility opened at Fort Irwin, Calif.;* **1983** *opened first embassy support facility in American Embassy in London, England; and five-story, 25,400-square-foot addition completed at local bank*
Lineage of presidents: *W.W. Collier, August 1920 to January 1923; Brig. Gen. William S. "Tex" Scott (USA Ret) to March 1932; J.E. Brinkmeyer to 1934; Gen. H.B. Crosby (USA Ret) to March 1935; Maj. Gen. James F. McKinley (USA Ret) to January 1941; Lt. Gen. Herbert J. Brees (USA Ret) to December 1958; Jess J. Laas to February 1963; William L. Bailey to January 1970; Russell L. Mason to August 1972; John H. Andrews to April 1975; F.R. "Bob" Kirkpatrick to December 1977; E.P. "Pat" Adcock to present*
Lineage of chairmen of the board: *W.W. Collier, January 1923 to March 1932; Brig. Gen. William S. "Tex" Scott (USA Ret) to February 1941; Lt. Gen. Herbert J. Brees (USA Ret) to December 1958; Maj. Gen. Percy W. Clarkson (USA Ret) to February 1963; Jess J. Laas to April 1975; John H. Andrews to April 1976; F.R. "Bob" Kirkpatrick to present*
Board of directors: *F.R. "Bob" Kirkpatrick, chairman; E.P. "Pat" Adcock, president; J.R. Reavis, executive vice president; General Jack J. Catton (USAF Ret); Lt. Gen. Jay T. Robbins (USAF Ret); Lt. Gen. John P. Flynn (USAF Ret); Lt. Gen. John R. McGiffert (USA Ret); Maj. Gen. M.E. Tillery (USAF Ret); Brig. Gen. Lillian Dunlap (ANC Ret); Dr. (Col.) Walter R. Cook (MC, USA Ret); W. Evans Fitch; Peter J. Hennessey; George A. Olson; Dr. Dan C. Peavy, Jr.; George H. Wenglein; Gary V. Woods; Harold D. Herndon, advisory director; Anne Stahl, board secretary*
Holding company: *RepublicBank Corporation*
Employees: *350*
Assets: *Exceeds $0.5 billion*

This chapter was based on an interview with F.R. "Bob" Kirkpatrick and E.P. "Pat" Adcock.

E.P. "Pat" Adcock, left, and F.R. "Bob" Kirkpatrick started their banking careers together in 1946.

Team Management Concept

F.R. "Bob" Kirkpatrick, chairman of the board and chief executive officer, and E.P. "Pat" Adcock, president, did not start their careers at the National Bank of Fort Sam Houston at the top of the ladder.

As young men who returned home to San Antonio from World War II duty, they looked for a job with a future in a peaceful America. Within a short time in 1946, fate led them to the bank. Their careers have paralleled in that institution ever since.

They tell about their rise through the ranks and their team approach to leading the bank:

"I got out of the Marine Corps after fighting in the Pacific and floundered around like a lot of GIs," Kirkpatrick recalled. "But then I met a very fine lady who insisted I have a good respectable job or we could not get married.

"I applied at the bank not knowing a thing about the banking business. They took a chance on me.

"For a while, they let me file checks, the most menial job you can have. Eventually, they trained me to use a hand-operated posting machine, and the next thing you knew, I was an assistant bookkeeper. They let me post the statements then, but not the permanent ledger."

Adcock, a Navy man who also served in the Pacific Theater, began his career at the bank out of curiosity.

"I was a timekeeper on a local construction job when a steel strike prevented the building from continuing its upward progress," Adcock said. "I noticed an advertisement in the paper, and based on the salary they were proposing to pay, I presumed it to be a part-time job.

"They hired me and I started the next week," he continued. "Throughout the remainder of next year, I didn't see the sun. I came to work before it rose and went home after it was down. However, I liked the work.

"My first job was an assistant bookkeeper posting statements on a hand-operated unit."

By 1953 the two men had decided they wanted to stay with the bank, but they realized competition between them could present problems.

"We made a pact that we would work together as a team, and it has worked," Kirkpatrick said.

Throughout the years, the friends have abided by their agreement and at the same time they were promoted to assistant cashiers, assistant vice presidents, vice presidents, senior vice presidents and executive vice presidents.

The day came, however, when only one of them could be appointed to the board of directors. The other would be an adviser to the board. Bank management told them the decision was theirs.

They flipped a coin, and Adcock was appointed to the board. Later Kirkpatrick was named president. When Kirkpatrick was selected to be chairman of the board, Adcock was promoted to president.

The men continue their unique approach to banking.

"This bank is run on a team concept," Kirkpatrick explained. "It's too big a bank for one man to run."

with some 50,000 other military retirees in the San Antonio area," Kirkpatrick said. "At any one time, there are more than 50,000 active duty military here. San Antonio is called the 'Mother-in-Law of the Air Force.' We have more retired military people living in Texas than any other state except California."

The bank works on the "cradle to the grave concept."

"We know the military market," Kirkpatrick said. "We put a great deal of effort into obtaining customers. We seek out senior cadets by making special presentations at the military academies. We visit more than 110 colleges and universities each year where we speak to senior ROTC cadets on the subject of the financial responsibilities of a junior officer.

"If we can get an account and keep it two or three years, we will seldom lose that account to another military bank."

"She found two things as her family traveled around the world: Coca-Cola and the Fort Sam Bank."

The bank has been so devoted to customers that in October 1979, it guaranteed the monthly direct deposit paycheck of its military customers when the federal government wasn't sure funds would be appropriated in time to meet its payroll.

"Congress had not passed the Appropriations Bill to pay the government's bills. It was getting to the eleventh hour and the government had indicated military people were not going to get paid," Kirkpatrick recalled.

"We called a press conference and were the first bank to announce that every customer who was a direct depositor was going to be paid on payday regardless of whether the government had sent the money. We were going to pay them their full pay. And any of those who were traveling and needed advance funds that could not be advanced by the Army or Air Force could get them from us.

"We gave them that assurance. Within the hour, we got a call from the Department of Defense to confirm what had been put on the news wires. Our duplicate deposit tickets were mailed before the Appropriations Bill was signed the following afternoon."

Innovations and a willingness to stand by its customers have kept Fort Sam Bank flourishing.

"We've had to run harder to try to keep ahead of our competition," Kirkpatrick said.

Some of its many "firsts" include being the first bank in San Antonio to have a visual record of checking and savings accounts on a cathode ray tube display, the first bank in the city to have an 800 telephone number for customer use, the first local bank to extend loan officers' hours to accommodate calls from all time zones in the country, the first bank authorized to cross state lines to establish a banking facility on a military installation.

Through the years, the bank has been known for its loans made via telephone to customers with

"Gallant Beginning," one of many art works displayed in the bank, depicts the first U.S. military flight west of the Appalachians over Fort Sam Houston in 1910.

established credit.

"Fifty percent or more of our loans are made over the telephone," Kirkpatrick said. "Established customers can walk into a dealer anywhere, pick out a car, get us on the phone and tell us how much money they need. We work out the arrangements over the phone and tell the dealer, 'Give him the car. The money is here.' The customer is able to get his car serviced and drive it out that afternoon."

One of the most unusual loan requests Kirkpatrick recalled came from "MARS." As a young loan officer, he responded, "OK, this is

Venus." Later he learned MARS stood for Military Affiliated Radio System, which was relaying a loan request call from a customer.

The bank often has been equally accommodating in approving checks delivered in unorthodox ways.

For instance, one check was written on a bar napkin from Seoul, Korea. Another was presented on a piece of tissue paper. Once a customer brought in a check written on a watermelon.

"One time during World War II, the bank received a check written on the backside of a package of Camel cigarettes," Adcock said. "It had

A grand opening on October 26, 1941, saluted the new bank facility.

been processed through a prisoner-of-war camp in Germany and then was processed through the check-clearing channels here."

From time to time, the bank also has received correspondence addressed simply to Fort Sam Bank. One such letter without a city or state address mailed from Istanbul, Turkey, was addressed to "Fort Sam Bank, USA." It arrived in only six days.

Just as unique are customers who have used the bank for years but have never visited it.

"They will come to San Antonio on vacations or will be traveling through the city and come in and say, 'We've been banking with you for 15 or 20 years and we really want to see our bank,' Kirkpatrick said. We look forward to their coming and always take them on a tour of the bank."

While stationed at various installations around the world, customers are linked to Fort Sam Bank through a satellite communications system.

"When we automated in the 1960s, we had the capability of handling large numbers of accounts," Kirkpatrick said. "We developed our data processing programs to meet our particular system in-house.

"So when the opportunity came for us to establish military banking facilities in the United Kingdom, Iceland, the island of Guam and other places, we had to have a means

to maintain those accounts from San Antonio.

"We went to a satellite where we shoot the data from our computer about 22,000 miles in space. For instance, we have complete military

---

"One time during World War II, the bank received a check written on the backside of a package of Camel cigarettes."

---

banking facilities on Guam from which we transmit daily through the satellite back to San Antonio. At the end of the day, all of the data on those accounts are transmitted to our computer. We process it, put it back in the system and when they open at 8 o'clock the next morning, their records are as current as if they were located in San Antonio."

Many famous people have enjoyed Fort Sam Bank's services. They include Gen. Jonathan M. Wainwright, who led the battle against the Japanese invasion of the Philippines and was a prisoner of war for 3 ½ years, and Lt. Gen. Walter Krueger,

who commanded Third U.S. Army at Fort Sam Houston from December 1, 1942, to February 2, 1943. Also, Maj. Gen. Robert M. White, the first winged astronaut who went into outer space in the X-15, and Lt. Gen. Jay Robbins, now a bank director, a P-38 pilot who is credited with shooting down 22 Japanese Zeros in the South Pacific during World War II.

Others include the "soldier's soldier," Gen. Creighton Abrams, who died during the Vietnam War, and Lt. Col. Gus Grissom, the astronaut killed in a launch pad fire. The bank gives scholarships in honor of both heroes.

Famous people also have served and continue to serve on the bank's board of directors. For instance, Maj. Gen. James McKinley, grandson of President William McKinley, was a former bank president. Current board member Lt. Gen. John P. Flynn (USAF Ret) was the highest ranking POW during the Vietnam conflict. Brig. Gen. Lillian Dunlap (ANC Ret) is among the military generals serving on the current board. She was the second chief of the Army Nurse Corps promoted to brigadier general and was among the elite few women in the U.S. military services to earn that rank.

Longevity and devotion to the bank long have been exhibited by board members, customers and bank employees.

For instance, W. Evans Fitch is a second generation director of the bank and follows his father, W.E. Fitch, an initial stockholder and director.

The longest-term military depositor bank management is aware of, Brig. Gen. Noel F. Parrish, has been with the bank 54 years. And the longest-term employee is Adeline "Pete" Peterson, who retired in 1976 after 50 years of service.

She began her career at the bank in 1926 at a salary of $20 a month and worked 12 to 13 hours a day six days a week. She retired as assistant cashier. She trained Kirkpatrick and Adcock and through the years proudly watched them move into leadership positions.

Historically, the bank has been proud of its close proximity to the well-known Fort Sam Houston Quadrangle. The Quadrangle's

From 1941 to the early '70s, this facade faced the historic Fifth Army Head-quarters Quadrangle across the street.

famous 90-foot tower has become a local landmark. In 1886 the Apache warrior, Geronimo; his son, Chappa; Chief Natchez, son of Cochise; and some 30 other Apaches were confined for about 40 days in the Quadrangle while being transferred to Fort Pickens, Florida, after surrendering to Lt. Gen. C.B. Gatewood in Arizona.

Displayed throughout the bank is art work including a scene depicting the Apaches camped in tents on the grounds where Fort Sam Bank now stands. "Gallant Beginning," a painting done by nationally recognized aerospace illustrator Keith Ferris, captures on canvas the first flight of a military aircraft west of the Appalachian Mountains. Piloted by Lt. Benjamin D. Foulois, the flight took place at Fort Sam Houston March 2, 1910. Signed and numbered prints have been displayed throughout the United States and one hangs in the American Embassy in London where the National Bank of Fort Sam Houston opened its first embassy support facility April 5, 1983.

While the bank's locations are far-ranging, the main bank in San Antonio has expanded its facilities to accommodate its many local customers. In 1920 the original bank operated in 700 square feet. The latest addition gives the bank 70,000 square feet in five stories.

Speaking with a potential customer is Col. Ambrose A. Szalwinski (USA Ret), vice president of ROTC Affairs.

On Flag Day in 1983, the bank raised a 20-by-30 foot American flag on a staff on top of the newly built five-story addition. That huge flag, which flies 24 hours a day seven days a week, appropriately symbolizes the bank's dedication to patriotism and its military customers.

The flag inspired Brig. Gen. John E. Rogers, former chief of staff of Headquarters Fifth U.S. Army, to write the bank:

"God bless America and the National Bank of Fort Sam Houston for honoring our nation in such a magnificent way. The large, illuminated flag atop the new building is truly beautiful and most inspiring." 🔲

Bank customers conduct routine checking business in the lobby.

From San Antonio to Borneo

The National Bank of Fort Sam Houston is a worldwide bank with a longstanding reputation of service to its military depositors no matter where they are stationed.

Through the years, many depositors have been so appreciative of the bank's services they have written letters expressing their gratitude.

An excerpt from one such letter is particularly worthy of inclusion in the bank's history:

In 1966 Lt. Col. Ralph S. Johnsen (USAF Ret) of Glasgow Air Force Base, Montana, wrote Jess J. Lass, then chairman of the board, the following story:

"Several years ago while stationed in the Far East, it was my lucky assignment to fly the first jet aircraft to an unnamed airfield in the wild interior of British Borneo. The local natives were not very long out of the real headhunting class, and they looked it.

"I and the other members of my flight, most of whom were ranking full colonels, had been on the go all over Southeast Asia for several weeks and were naturally running very short of hard cash.

"In keeping with the Royal Air Force tradition for hospitality, the local commander designated an old shack as an officers club and we were invited to drink a few toasts to the queen. A grizzled old sergeant was in charge of the

very adequate bar that had been set up in honor of our visit.

"Needless to say, the question arose as to whether it would be possible to cash a check, as none of us were in a position to hold our own without some ready coin of the realm.

"This question was brought up by other members of the flight who had personal checking accounts almost everywhere in the United States from Bank of America and Chase National down to Tucumcari, New Mexico. A few individuals also were carrying American Express Travelers Checks.

"To the absolute incredulity of everyone present, the old NCO boomed out in his most Punjab military voice that he had made it a practice for a good many years not to accept any personal checks from any bloody Yank unless it was from the National Bank of Fort Sam Houston. He added in his wide experience in this cruel world he had learned that Fort Sam was the only American bank that always honored a check in spite of the financial solvency of the individual who cashed it.

"To end the story, when we finally got back to our home base, every officer in the group subsequently opened an account with you."

FIRST FEDERAL SAVINGS AND LOAN ASSOCIATION

OF SAN ANTONIO

Instrumental in the success of First Federal has been the Kampmann family including George Kampmann, Jr., standing; George Kampmann, Sr., seated; and Ike Kampmann, Sr., in portrait.

First Federal Savings and Loan Association of San Antonio is a 63-year-old financial establishment chartered to make home mortgage and improvement loans and to offer savings accounts and certificates.

Today First Federal lends money for a wide range of worthwhile purposes and offers a smorgasbord of checking, savings and investing programs. Building on initial assets of only $2,805, the firm now has assets in excess of $625 million.

First Federal has nine full-service offices in San Antonio and one in Alice. Additionally, two loan agencies are located in Austin, one in Dallas and one in Arlington. Loan agencies make mortgage and installment loans, but do not accept deposits.

Steve E. Holloway, president, characterized the modern institution and traced its growth:

"We focus on identifying the financial services our customers want. Then we specialize in providing the products that meet their needs. Our ultimate goal is customer satisfaction. By building confidence and trust, we encourage our customers to return to transact additional business.

"In 1922 nine prominent San Antonio men met informally to discuss establishing a savings and loan," Holloway continued. "Their final meeting was May 2, 1922, in the office of Ike S. Kampmann, Sr., in the Russell Building at 305 E. Houston St."

Kampmann, an attorney, drew up the necessary documents to file the charter application for the savings and loan, which originally was called Security Building and Loan Association of San Antonio.

"These men believed there was a strong need to promote thrift in home ownership and to encourage people to enjoy financial security through systematic savings," Holloway said.

The Kampmanns are one of San Antonio's oldest and most respected families. The founding Kampmann served as the first president and directed the association during its formative years. Today his son, George A. Kampmann, Sr., is active in the association. He became a director in 1953 and succeeded his father as chairman of the board in 1969. A third generation, George Kampmann, Jr., was elected a director in 1983.

The association opened for busi-

History at a Glance   1922

Founded: *May 2, 1922, in the Russell Building, 305 E. Houston St.*

Founders: *Ike S. Kampmann, Sr.; Herbert J. Hayes; Robert P. Schermerhorn; George D. Campbell; Albert Steves, Jr.; Frank A. Winerich; Dr. E.V. DePew; Sam C. Bell; and Russell C. Hill*

Original name: *Security Building and Loan Association of San Antonio*

Original assets: *$2,805*

Original employees: *4*

Lineage of leadership: *Ike S. Kampmann, Sr.; Herbert Hayes; Charles W. Cart; A. Roane Harwood; Lyle E. Gunderson; Edward D. Hodge III; and Steve E. Holloway*

Headquarters: *1100 N.E. Loop 410*

Employees: *290*

Units: *10 full-service offices and 4 loan agencies*

Assets: *$625 million*

Motto: *Excellence in customer service*

This chapter was based on an interview with Steve E. Holloway.

ness in a three-room suite in the Gunter Hotel. The next year, the office was moved to a storefront at 216 Losoya St. near the Palace Theatre. An oak partition made by Steves Sash & Door divided the room into a lobby and working space. The vault was a large iron safe.

In 1926 the association moved three blocks north to 201 Broadway to elegant quarters decorated in Victorian style. The building later became known as the Security Building. The second floor was inhabited by music teachers and the sounds of practicing students could be heard in the savings and loan

---

"Our first mortgage loan was signed in a swing on the front porch of a customer's home."

---

offices.

"Once, a customer, a tenor in the Beethoven Maennerchor, was making a deposit when a budding contralto faltered over a difficult accompanied solo. Without missing a note, the tenor picked up singing where she left off and finished the song to loud applause from the ground floor audience," Holloway said.

In 1933 the association moved to more spacious offices at 307 E. Pecan, now the office of St. Mark's Episcopal Church. In 1936 the association converted from a state to a federal charter. At that time, the name was changed to First Federal Savings and Loan Association of San Antonio.

Another move occurred in 1959 when the association relocated to 800 Navarro in one of the first modern office buildings built in San Antonio after World War II. First Federal opened its first branch office in 1968 in North Star Mall and thereby started a new era in customer convenience. By the spring of 1978, the growing business had nine branch offices and had built a

10-story corporate headquarters at Loop 410 and Nacogdoches Road.

Being close to the customer has been a First Federal tradition.

"Our first mortgage loan was signed in a swing on the front porch of a customer's home. That loan in June 1922 was for $4,000 for a two-story house on West Mistletoe near Belknap," Holloway said.

"We try to maintain that personal service even now. Our savings customers enjoy our 'branch-in-a-briefcase' program in which account executives go to homes or offices to open accounts. We also have loan representatives perform the same personal service taking loan applications."

First Federal's reputation for service started during the Depression.

"One customer, a destitute house painter, could not pay his loan payments," Holloway said. "Instead of taking his home, the association employed him to paint houses owned by the association. The painter eventually regained financial stability and paid off his mortgage.

"Due to strong leadership which began in 1922, we have established a reputation among our peers and in the community for sound management," he continued. "We are profitable and have substantial reserves. We have a record of planned and controlled growth as well as good community awareness. Our professional personnel offer superior service and products which are structured to offer our customers numerous options. Our locations are convenient and accessible to everyone in San Antonio as well as Alice, Austin, Dallas and Arlington."

Looking ahead, Holloway foresees branches in other growth areas of San Antonio as well as additional loan agencies and full-service branch offices in other cities.

"We are excited about the growth potential of San Antonio," Holloway said. "Our primary goal is to identify and develop financial products and services that meet the needs of our present and future customer base." ⊔

First Federal's headquarters are an impressive 10-story building at Loop 410 and Nacogdoches.

USAA

In 1922 a farsighted group of Army officers realized they needed reliable automobile insurance. What they couldn't have realized then was their efforts to meet that need would result in USAA — a financial conglomerate composed of almost a million and a half members worldwide.

Brig. Gen. Robert F. McDermott (USAF Ret)

Brig. Gen. Robert F. McDermott (USAF Ret), USAA's chairman and chief executive officer, related the early days:

"In the beginning, a group of 25 Army officers met in the Gunter Hotel and discussed their problems insuring their cars with dependable insurance when they were subject to moving around the country. They were led by their founder, Maj. William Henry Garrison. So they formed their own member-owned insurance company with three employees in 1922 and established it in a World War I barracks-type building at Kelly Field No. 1. USAA

has been around ever since.

"Today we have about 1.4 million members. Our employees are approaching 7,000, with 6,000 in our building here and another 1,000 around the United States, Germany and London."

Originally, only Army officers were covered. Later Navy officers also had the privilege, which necessitated the name change from United States Army Automobile Insurance Association to the United Services Automobile Association. The largest group served today is officers, although some State Department Foreign Service and FBI per-

sonnel also are members.

"Ninety-two percent of all officers in all branches of the military on active duty have their automobile insurance with us," McDermott explained. "And that includes, of course, some who don't have automobiles because they're young or stationed behind the Iron Curtain or in Latin America.

"We probably have 98 or 99 percent of our potential market. Once a member always a member. There really is a fantastic record of retention and loyalty to the company.

"The automobile started in about 1905," McDermott said. "By 1922 they were still pretty scarce, but probably a lot of Army officers had them because they had to move around the country.

"It's interesting. I believe the largest insurance company, State Farm Insurance Companies, also started in 1922. So the farmers of that time decided they also needed to have their own insurance company."

McDermott arrived in San Antonio during the summer of HemisFair '68 knowing he would assume his position at USAA in January 1969.

"At that time, there were plans to add to the building at Broadway and Hildebrand and I foresaw that as just a Band-Aid solution," McDermott remembered. "So I decided to cancel that addition and to accommodate the immediate growth by occupying the Rand Building downtown.

"Then I went looking for a long-term solution and found this property out in the boondocks just barely within the city limits and acquired it. I decided we wouldn't landlock our successes. They're not making any

History at a Glance 1922

Founded: *June 20, 1922, in Gunter Hotel*

Founder: *Maj. William Henry Garrison, Jr., U.S. Army Signal Corps*

Original name: *United States Army Automobile Insurance Association*

Original assets: *$85,000 by end of 1924*

Milestones: **1927** *first permanent home purchased at 1406 Grayson St.;* **1952** *first expansion outside San Antonio to Frankfurt, Germany;* **1956** *moved to new home office at Broadway and Hildebrand;* **1976** *present home office dedicated on 286-acre site at 9800 Fredericksburg Road*

Lineage of CEOs: *Maj. Gen. Ernest Hines (USA Ret); Col. Herbert A. White (USA Ret); Col. William F. Jones (USA Ret); Col. Charles E. Cheever (USA Ret); Brig. Gen. Robert F. McDermott (USAF Ret)*

Headquarters: *286-acre site at 9800 Fredericksburg Road with 3.1 million-square-foot building*

Subsidiaries: *Property & Casualty Insurance Division; Life Insurance Division; Financial Services Division; Consumer Services, Inc.; Special Services Co.; Satellite Communications Co.*

Members: *1.4 million worldwide; USAA is the sixth largest private passenger automobile insurer and the 10th largest homeowner insurer in the U.S.*

Assets: *$3.5 billion Dec. 31, 1984*

Employees: *7,000*

This chapter was based on an interview with Brig. Gen. Robert F. McDermott (USAF Ret).

more land, as Will Rogers said. So I acquired 286 acres and started this building in 1971. It was completed in 1975. Because of our new bank which will grow, I think, during my regime, we'll start using up some of the acreage we have here to meet our needs."

Although he admitted he is neither an architect nor an artist, McDermott had had experiences that helped him contribute to the building's concept.

"I was at the U.S. Air Force Academy in Colorado Springs when it was being designed by Skidmore Owings & Merrill, world-famous architects out of Chicago. Those architects started with the academy's programs and then built the building to accommodate what was supposed to happen inside. That taught me a lesson: You don't just build a building and then fill it up on the inside. You start from the inside and relate the building to the purposes it is supposed to serve."

McDermott continued, "They fit the academy's design into the mountain environment just beautifully. They made the buildings accommodate what nature had put there. I thought we ought to do the same thing here. I took two architects from Benham and Blair of Oklahoma City to Mexico City and showed them the Museum of Anthropology,

The Gunter Hotel, shown here after the 1921 flood, was the site of the founding meeting of USAA.

USAA's first headquarters, below, were in the World War I barracks-type building at Kelly Field No. 1.

a massive low-rise which gives you a feeling of strength because it is so massive. On the inside, you go through tunnel-like areas that open up into, all I can say is, a surprise. You go through a narrow space and can see something ahead. You can't wait to get there and see something unusual.

"So I asked them to put those two concepts together for a low-rise building that would be massive and would conform to the land we have

here in color and design. I asked them to put most of the money on the inside rather than the outside.

"That's another concept," McDermott continued. "We spend more of our waking hours at work than we do any other place. So I wasn't as interested in having a building that would impress passersby, but one that would be impressive, suitable and convenient to the people who worked inside.

"That's what we did. The surprises you see in our building are the

Col. Charles Cheever (USA Ret)

five courtyards. People who work in the interior of the building have something as pleasant to see as people who work by the windows. I have a great respect for our employees and they have a great respect for our members and each other. It's a real family atmosphere here. Everybody feels everything is done for their convenience and satisfaction so they can do their jobs and serve other people."

A major concern of USAA is employee benefits.

"We've tried to give our employees as many benefits as we can so they don't have to worry about their health or retirement needs. They have an opportunity to save money and not worry about the risks.

"We started the four-day work week as an experiment," McDermott continued. "I thought this is ideal for a company that has a lot of female workers and working mothers in it. We thought we should give them a day off so they can accommodate the needs of their families on a day when things are available and not crowded. It was an experiment we tried for 90 days and only four people left. Now we couldn't change it back if we wanted to."

Born in Boston, McDermott grew up in the Northeast and graduated from Norwich University in Vermont and the U.S. Military Academy.

"I graduated from West Point in 1943, became a fighter pilot and after the war served on Eisenhower's staff, then the air staff. Next I went to Harvard Business School and then on to West Point to teach. I was just finishing that tour when the Air Force Academy Act was passed. I was selected to go to Colorado Springs as dean. I stayed for 14 years from 1954 to 1968. I've been lucky. The two most desirable places that I've experienced are Colorado Springs and San Antonio, and I've had a good time at both of them."

McDermott met his USAA predecessor, Col. Charles Cheever (USA Ret), when McDermott was a West Point cadet.

"He taught law and I had him when I was a senior. Our paths never crossed again until I was teaching at West Point," he recalled. "In 1953 I wrote a book called *Principles of Insurance* for cadets. In that book, I had chapters on some of the associations serving the military and one of them was, of course, USAA. Col. Cheever asked if he could reprint that chapter and send it out to the members. So that reestablished contact.

"He visited me every year at the Air Force Academy, and in 1963 he asked that I replace him here. I told him I liked what I was doing. So his board gave him an extension until I was ready for a career change. Near his seventieth year, he asked me again and we came out here to San Antonio. He was the most gentle gentleman I've ever known."

McDermott is proud of the fact that Consumer Reports has rated USAA at the top in four consecutive surveys conducted seven years apart. "So just in the last 21 to 25 years, it has had a perfect top rating among all insurers based on consumer surveys," he explained.

Life insurance was started at USAA in 1963.

"It was moving along very slowly with whole life and term life insurance, and then we began to expand it into annuities and then into various interests," McDermott said. "We have, for example, one of the most highly touted universal life programs. Money Magazine has written several times that this is one of the best, most respected products in the trade.

"We started into mutual funds in 1971. My reasoning was that since we had to have an investment department to invest the money for the insurance portfolios, why not use that department's talents and services to provide personal investment opportunities for the membership? We now have 11 mutual funds."

USAA's travel services were started in the early 1970s as an accommodation to members.

"People over fifty-five write or query the company by telephone on

Maj. William Henry Garrison founded USAA along with 24 other Army officers in 1922.

travel more than anything else. A member survey showed they were interested in banking opportunities, home mortgages, automobile financing and automobile purchasing.

"It wasn't until 1982 when deregulation started that we began to look again at the opportunities we might have to broaden our financial services," McDermott continued. "We opened a federal savings bank which is growing so fast it's staggering. It will be the fastest growing bank in Texas, I'm sure.

"In the last year or so, we've added the bank and real estate services for our members. We started a discount brokerage so members could invest in the stock market without paying high commissions. We added what we call a claims replacement service and we also have a consumer buying service.

"We thought, why not give our members an opportunity to buy cars by pooling their demands for automobiles? We made arrangements with dealers so that our members can buy automobiles at about 1 to 3 percent over cost. They now can buy their automobiles, insure them with us and get their automobile financing through our bank."

He continued, "We haven't figured out how to build homes yet, but we do offer home mortgage loans through our banking service."

McDermott relishes anticipating members' needs and desires. "I think

---

"If you focus on the long-term, then you're going to have fewer problems this year than if you'd done it 10 years ago."

---

we've got a pretty good package now, but we've only just begun."

McDermott is responsible for much of USAA's high profile.

"I learned at the Harvard Business School that a business has a respon-

USAA's sprawling headquarters are located on a 286-acre site.

sibility to the community, not just to its customers and stockholders. I got that community feeling in the military because they were always preaching to the senior officers to get out to the wider community so people can understand why we have a military."

Early in his career in San Antonio, McDermott became involved in the Greater San Antonio Chamber of Commerce and later served as its chairman. He was instrumental in starting the Economic Development Foundation, which focuses on the city's economy in a studied, constructive manner.

USAA's name was changed to lessen confusion with companies with similar names.

"We changed our name because there was a United Services Fish and Chips in Los Angeles and in Washington, D.C. There also was a company that had sort of stolen USAA's name, United Services Life Insurance Company. People were confused and bought life insurance there because they thought it was our company.

"We decided to de-emphasize United Services and emphasize USAA. We hired a firm which designed all kinds of logos and put out our first annual report in a magazine format. As an old dean, I believed in information and education. We started a quarterly magazine, the last issue of which was our annual report."

A logo with an eagle and USAA underneath it was selected to represent the company.

"That seems to have captured our membership," McDermott believes. "It's a strong logo. The eagle itself has symbolism for most people. They

identify it with America. We just started using USAA in every sentence that we could and in the strong logo. That got us away then from conflicts with the fish and chips company and the other insurance company. Everybody talks about USAA today."

To McDermott, businesses have three constituencies: the stockholder, customer and community.

"If they put the customer first, then the other constituencies will be better satisfied. But some companies keep thinking in terms of the short run, making sure that earnings per share are good this quarter, this year. If you focus on the long-term, then you're going to have fewer problems this year than if you'd done it 10 years ago. You're going to have better solutions."

McDermott's first priority at USAA was to develop a 10-year plan.

"I just sat down and figured out where I thought things ought to be in 10 years. Then I backed up and said here's where it ought to be in five years and then this is what we ought to be doing this year. And then I took the senior staff to the American Management Association planning center in Hamilton, New York. We just sat there for a whole week and worked out the details for the five-year plan. Now we had control of our destiny.

"We think in terms of customer satisfaction first. It turns out our customers are our owners, so we're satisfying both at the same time. We have an advantage."

McDermott continued, "Service is our way of life. At USAA it's the philosophy that has brought us where we are. And as long as that philosophy continues, USAA is going to continue to grow and expand."

ERNST & WHINNEY

Ernst & Whinney is the city's largest and oldest national accounting firm and is part of the prestigious international public accounting firm that serves its clientele literally around the world.

With a local staff of 215 and responsibility that covers South Texas, the company provides a broad range of accounting, tax and consulting services to a variety of clients in San Antonio, Austin, Corpus Christi, Laredo and the surrounding areas.

"Ernst & Whinney today is a group of dynamic, enthusiastic people who are dedicated to quality service to their clients and serve them with a sincere interest and sense of involvement," explained Sam Bell, managing partner in the San Antonio office.

The San Antonio office is among the largest in the United States. Ernst & Whinney has more individual offices in the country than any other public accounting firm. San Antonio's regional office is in Dallas; the office here serves as headquarters for offices in Austin, Corpus Christi and Laredo. In Laredo it is the only "Big Eight" firm represented.

Originally, Ernst & Whinney, then Ernst & Ernst, opened offices in San Antonio in 1922. Ernst & Ernst, the largest firm in San Antonio in 1964, enhanced its position in both size and quality of clients when it merged with George, Thrift & Cockrell that year.

Bell reflected on the company's early history and explained its growth and current status:

"The company was formed in 1903 in Cleveland, Ohio, by brothers A.C. Ernst and T.C. Ernst," Bell said.

After T.C. Ernst decided early on that public accounting wasn't for him, his brother, A.C. Ernst, built the firm to its international status. Currently, the firm has 115 offices in the United States. An equally large international operation is headquartered in New York.

A.C. Ernst served as the firm's national managing partner until his death in the late 1940s. His successors have been Hassell Tippett, Dick Baker and Ray Groves. Groves is current managing partner of the international firm and also served the profession in 1985 as chairman of the American Institute of Certified

"In no way can one consider the past in isolation from the future."

Public Accountants.

"The San Antonio office was about the 25th office opened by the firm," Bell said. "A very significant impact on the office occurred in 1935 when H.B. Zachry Company moved its offices from Laredo to San Antonio in the process of becoming one of the major general contracting firms in the world. Certainly, the Zachry Company has been a bedrock client since it was founded in 1924," Bell said.

"In no way can one consider the past in isolation from the future," Bell continued. "Our history — the leaders of Ernst & Whinney, their ideas, experiences and contributions — is a springboard for us to continue to progress and take advantage of opportunities the future holds.

"Our partners and staff have a tremendous responsibility to live up to our great legacy. The quality of our people today and the quality of those we will attract give me great confidence in our ability to create a legacy of our own."

In 1979 Ernst & Ernst merged with Whinney Murray & Company, an accounting practice in the United Kingdom, Europe, the East and Australia,

---

History at a Glance   1922

Founded: *June 1903 in Cleveland, Ohio*
Opened in San Antonio: *1922*
Founders: *A.C. Ernst and T.C. Ernst*
Original name: *Ernst & Ernst*
Original employees: *3*
Original San Antonio location: *City National Bank Building*
Texas expansions: *1915 to Dallas; 1917 to Houston; 1959 to Laredo; 1960 to Corpus Christi; 1962 to Austin*
Mergers: *1964 Ernst & Ernst's San Antonio office merged with San Antonio's George, Thrift & Cockrell; 1979 Ernst & Ernst International merged with Whinney Murray & Company*
Lineage of San Antonio managing partners: *Clarence Neville, Thomas Thrasher, Ben Irby, Carl Barlow, Norwood Dixon, Walter Beran, Gordon George, Sam Bell*
San Antonio headquarters: *Frost Bank Tower*
International headquarters: *New York City*
San Antonio employees: *215*
Assets: *Quality people*

This chapter was based on an interview with Sam Bell.

which was as large as the Ernst & Ernst firm based in the United States.

"We had been affiliated with that organization for many years," Bell said. "Ernst & Ernst was 75 years old at the time the name was changed.

"Today our market is literally the world. We merged with a large firm in Tokyo in 1984, so we have offices in every major city in the world including Beijing. We have some 345 offices worldwide."

Among Ernst & Whinney's many prestigious local clients are some of the city's largest companies such as the Zachry Company and some of the city's oldest firms such as Alamo Iron Works. The two companies have been with the public accounting firm longer than any other local clients.

A major reason for Ernst & Whinney's growth was its ability to specialize long before other firms did.

"We have developed specialized practices in many different areas such as financial institutions, health care, and oil and gas," Bell explained. "In addition, we have a dispro-

portionately large tax practice in San Antonio for a 'Big Eight' public accounting firm. This factor alone demonstrates our ability to meet the true needs of the business community in a city such as San Antonio, not

---

"Our reputation earns us new business; our ability to render quality service will enhance that reputation in years to come."

---

someone's preconceived ideas of what the business community should have," Bell said.

"Our specialization efforts have resulted in our services to Cullen/Frost Bankers and Gill Savings, two

very important financial institution clients of our San Antonio office. We have a great health care practice and serve many of the major health care institutions here including Santa Rosa Hospital, Nix Medical Center, Southwest Texas Methodist Hospital and Baptist Memorial Hospital.

"Ernst & Whinney is involved to a major extent in work for the oil and gas industry. This firm's consulting specialists in San Antonio developed computer software packages to serve the oil and gas industry from small operators to major corporations.

"We also take great pride in serving the San Antonio Spurs, a fun client which also has made a great contribution to our community since moving here from Dallas.

"We get new business primarily from rendering quality service to existing clients," Bell continued. "Our reputation earns us new business; our ability to render quality service will enhance that reputation in the years to come."

Bell credits the local office's firm foundation to previous managing partners and "a myriad of others who committed themselves to a

Sam Bell, right, 1986 chairman of the board of the Greater San Antonio Chamber of Commerce, and Chamber President Gen. William McBride, discuss chamber plans.

Jon Sandidge and Jennifer Bray leave the firm's offices in the Frost Bank Tower for a meeting with a client.

quality of excellence which has given us a solid clientele that has been good to us over the years."

"Our alumni have made substantial contributions to the community in terms of their business achievements and their civic commitments. They occupy positions of substance in all areas of the San Antonio business community including chief executive and chief financial officers of many major local companies as well as independent business people and entrepreneurs. Alumni such as Charles Ebrom, executive vice president of the Zachry Company; Morris Wosnig, executive vice president

of Gill Savings; Jim Allen, chairman of the board of San Pedro Bank; Bob Worth, chief financial officer of Robert Callaway Corporation; and Roger Harrison, president of American Century Corporation, have all achieved top levels in San Antonio business.

"We are proud of all our alumni and view them as an extension of our firm and an additional reflection of the contributions Ernst & Whinney has made to the progress of San Antonio.

"Ernst & Whinney attracts the highest quality people and gives them good training," Bell said.

"We've got a bond within our office and within our firm of mutual respect for all the people who work together."

Bell called his firm's greatest asset "our people — human capital."

"We build a base of human capital to do the things that we want to do, and then we do them well," he explained.

"Our success to date can be traced in every aspect to people."

"Our success to date can be traced in every aspect to people," Bell said. "Ernst & Whinney South Texas has a legacy of tremendous leadership and tremendous people. The strength of the firm lies in the interaction of our partners with the staff. Tomorrow our strength will lie with the top quality people we attract and hold.

"It is mandatory that we render the highest quality service available. This requires an extensive knowledge to respond most effectively to the business needs of our clients, whatever the nature of their business."

The company expects community commitment and responsibility from

Financial institutions make up a sizable portion of Ernst & Whinney's clientele. Shown here are Steve Stephens, left, Suzanne Rawlinson, Keith Rollins and Ken Schwartz, financial institution accounting and tax specialists, as they begin an engagement.

The H.B. Zachry Company, one of the major general contracting firms in the world, has been an Ernst & Whinney client for many years. Shown here are Sam Bell, left, and William Schuh, right, with Bartell Zachry at the Zachry headquarters.

its people.

"We were the accountants for and one of the major underwriters of HemisFair '68," Bell pointed out. "We were proud to support our community. It was a major investment for us and has proved to be a great investment for the city and our community. Our managing partner at the time, Walter Beran, put us into HemisFair at a very visible level. We are immensely proud to have been part of it.

"I tell our people that if the highest office we are asked to serve in is treasurer, we flunk. If that's all people think we are able to do, we haven't demonstrated we can contribute other things as well. We want to be more than accountants in our service to our clients and our community; we want to be involved."

A commitment to a standard of service excellence drives the company's professionals to strive for personal goals of competence and expertise. Further motivations stem from a love of what they do and a desire to be the best.

"What we have to do to make ourselves different is be good business people and to render service for our clients from an audit, tax and consulting standpoint. We have to be able to understand their business and be innovative and creative about what we suggest to them to improve their business.

"Throughout time our strength and success have been acquired because we act as partners with our clients and among ourselves." **L**

Don Reeves and Pam Schultz demonstrate Ernst & Whinney's recently developed oil and gas computer system.

Mary Ann Rybacki, left, Ted Popp and Mike Gentry work toward the solution of a client's complicated tax problem.

TRAVIS SAVINGS AND LOAN ASSOCIATION

Travis Savings and Loan Association thrives today — as in the past — on stable, consistent growth and its original philosophy of promoting thrift and home ownership.

Today, of course, with its solid base of $328 million in assets, Travis provides all types of savings investments and commercial lending along with home mortgage lending.

When the association was founded in 1927, San Antonio, like most of the country, was prosperous.

"The economy was on the move and there was a great deal of construction going on. That's probably why the savings and loan business, at that time called building and loans, took off," believes Marvin G. "Jerry" Kelfer, the association's third chief executive officer.

Arthur M. Michael, Sr., who founded Travis, had some family background in the loan business. He also was friends with Walter McAllister, Sr., the founder of San Antonio Savings Association which was formed a few years earlier and was prospering. The original investment for Travis was about $27,000 of Michael's own cash.

"Mr. Michael was a great student of history, especially Texas history,"

Kelfer said. "He became enamored with William Barret Travis and the fall of the Alamo. He believed staunchly in the same principles as Col. Travis. So he named the association after Col. Travis."

Kelfer continued, "The original association was on Travis Street where the current RepublicBank is. It was only about 12 feet by 30 feet and had about four wooden desks in it and a little counter or railing."

A.M. Michael, Sr., was born in Overton, Texas, and his father brought the family to San Antonio in the late 1800s. His father, Louis M. Michael, started the Michael Loan Company on Soledad Street between Houston and Commerce in the vicinity of where Solo Serve is today. Across the street was the town's greatest saloon, hotel and house of pleasure.

"In those days, San Antonio was an open city. All the outlaws of Texas used to come to San Antonio because no one bothered them, a sort

of King's X," Kelfer related. "A.M. Michael, Sr., told the story of the sheriff in Austin who was one of the most renowned outlaws. The sheriff used to come down to San Antonio and rob the stage and then go back to Austin to form the posse to look for himself."

Colorful stories about Louis M. Michael abound. For instance, when the United States went on script during an economic depression in the late 1880s, he put up a sign reading: "we lend real money."

Arthur M. Michael, Sr.

Kelfer related another: "One of his friends was Otto Koehler. Mr. Michael used to tell the story that Otto came to him one day and said he wanted to start a brewery. The closest brewery at that time was St. Louis. Otto asked Louis M. Michael to invest or lend him about $5,000.

"He answered, 'Otto, what the hell do you know about making beer? You're going to fall flat on your face.'

"That later became Pearl Brewery. He could have had a half interest in Pearl Brewery if he'd put up the $5,000."

At about that time, A.M. Michael, Sr., was a student at West Texas Military Academy, a forerunner of Texas Military Academy. There he was friends with Douglas MacArthur, who later became the famous general. After graduation from TMI, A.M. Michael, Sr., went to Sewanee Academy in Tennessee and studied engineering. Upon graduation, he went to Mexico to help develop the silver mines. The Mexican Revolution forced him to walk back to Texas with a mule carrying his belongings. He later went into business with his father at the Michael Loan Company and founded Travis Savings and Loan Association in 1927.

Louis L. Michael

His son, Louis L. Michael, graduated from St. Mary's University in 1931 with a degree in business administration and went straight into the four-year-old family business. He became president in 1957 and then chairman of the board.

When the Depression came along, the savings and loan operations were hurt as were most businesses.

"But there never was a run on Travis Savings," Kelfer explained. "When people were getting nervous, A.M. Michael, Sr., would pull his desk up right by the front door and stack piles of money on it. When people would come in to get their money, he said, 'Now, do you really want to take your money? Where are you going to take it? Are you going to keep it in your house and have it stolen? Here's your money; it's safe.'

"When they saw that their money was there and they knew the reputation of the man, they left their deposits. And during the entire period of the Depression, which ran from about 1930 until World War II, the association never failed to make a profit and pay dividends."

"Being large doesn't mean anything; being stable and sound is the only thing that counts."

Marvin G. Kelfer

During that devastating period, many people couldn't afford to pay for their homes. Many gave up on the payments and abandoned them.

"The association actually sold houses to get someone into them," Kelfer related. "Travis was the first to develop the innovative plan of paying nothing down. Travis set up loans at reasonable interest rates and payments so property could at

The Travis Savings and Loan Association's headquarters are an integral part of the downtown financial district.

least be lived in and maintained. That was revolutionary at that time."

A.M. Michael, Sr., and Louis L. Michael were great believers in the good of people. Their philosophy was, "We will never substitute our stability for size."

"Being large doesn't mean anything; being stable and sound is the only thing that counts," Kelfer remembers Michael believing. "The people of San Antonio knew his creed and his philosophy, and they trusted him just like they trusted the bankers of D. & A. Oppenheimer, Bankers. They were cut from the same cloth."

Travis grew slowly and cautiously under the conservative leadership of Louis L. Michael because he and the association were interested in more than growth.

"We wanted strong reserves and net worth over and above the federal deposit insurance. The rapid growth in the industry came after World War II when the country went into tremendous expansion with returning military people needing housing."

Kelfer continued, "We still like to believe that we're in that banking of yesterday, that we're concerned with people. We try to take care of people and pay attention to what they're saying to us. Above all, our guiding beacon is stability and soundness rather than 'growth for growth's sake.'" **LI**

NIX MEDICAL CENTER

Since 1930 Nix Medical Center has stood as an island of medical excellence towering 24 stories above downtown San Antonio and overlooking the San Antonio River.

The first for-profit hospital in South Texas, the Nix also holds the distinction of being the only institution in the United States with doctors' offices, a hospital and a parking garage housed in one vertical building.

When the Nix opened its doors in mid-November of 1930 as Nix Professional Building, a local newspaper described it as "one of the finest structures in the country, and from a standpoint of services in a particular line, very unique."

Since then the general acute care hospital has been the place for generations of South Texans to be born and cared for.

J. Randolph Harig, current managing general partner; Raymond H. Downs, executive director; and Dr. Duncan Poth, a physician and Nix tenant for more than 50 years; compiled the hospital's history, described its latest renovations and looked ahead to its future:

J.M. Nix

When it was built, the Nix Professional Building was billed as "Your Complete Business Home." One of the most modern structures of its type in the country, the Nix marked a new era in commercial building in San Antonio.

The building was a realization of the faith its builder, J.M. Nix, had demonstrated in San Antonio over 36 years of developing commercial properties. Nix also had built the Majestic Building and Hotel Lanier among many others.

The Nix followed closely the Gothic type of architecture of the Majestic. Its design was based on strong vertical lines with picturesque relief attained in ornamentation reminiscent of early Italian architecture, possessing characteristics of Gothic, Romanesque and Renaissance styles.

In the original building, the basement housed a cafeteria, tailor shop and barber shop. In addition to the elegantly decorated lobby, the first floor included stores and the garage and service department. The next eight floors were for car storage, the next 10 contained offices, and the top five were devoted to what was considered "the most modern hospital in America" at the time.

Nix died a year and a half after the building opened and its management was assumed by his brother, Joe J. Nix.

Upon the building's 10th anniversary, a hospital advertisement proclaimed about the founder: "Founded little more than 10 years ago by the late J.M. Nix, the hospital and building which bear his name stand as a memorial to the man who pioneered in South Texas, a land he loved and where he built always with his eyes to the sky. Establishment of this institution, involving an investment far beyond possible commensurate returns, was a goal toward which he worked for many years. Its achievement came only toward the end of his long and useful career and at great personal sacrifices, for it was completed during a period of extreme economic stress when most men turned back from any untried undertaking."

History at a Glance   1930

Founded: *November 1930*
Founder: *J.M. Nix*
Original names: *Nix Professional Building Corp.; Nix Hospital, Inc.; Nix Garage, Inc.*
Original employees: *25*
Original size: *300,000 square feet*
Original investment: *$1.5 million*
Milestones: 1961 *air conditioning added;* **1984** *acquired by Accord Medical Management, Ltd.*
Lineage of presidents: *J.M. Nix; Joe J. Nix; David Brooks; Richard T. Coiner, Jr.; Richard T. Coiner III; J. Randolph Harig, managing general partner*
Lineage of ownership: *Nix family; Accord Medical Management, Ltd.*
Headquarters: *414 Navarro*
Employees: *450*

This chapter was based on an interview with J. Randolph Harig, Raymond H. Downs and Dr. Duncan Poth.

With the building of the institution, San Antonio had two doctors' buildings — the Nix and the Medical Arts Building, now the Emily Morgan Hotel.

"The Nix has gone beyond the barriers of a downtown hospital and has been the 'carriage trade' hospital of South Texas."

"There were no outlying doctors at all," Poth recalled. "We had a bone and joint man who left the building and went to a neighborhood. He did very, very poorly. You just couldn't exist outside a main medical building. There were only a couple hundred doctors in San Antonio in those days. Now we have more than 3,000."

The type of medicine those physicians practiced was rather unsophisticated by today's standards.

"In those days, we were treating syphilis of the nervous system with

Towering 24 stories, the Nix has been an imposing downtown structure since 1930.

Executive director Raymond H. Downs, left, managing general partner J. Randolph Harig, and radiology specialist Dr. Harold Brannan pose in the newly renovated radiology department.

malaria," he explained. "We gave patients malaria as a treatment because we had no antibiotics. Penicillin did away with all that."

When Poth hospitalized patients, they usually stayed a week. Their bill for food, nursing care, prescription drugs, the room and extras was $35.

Through the years, the Nix has been credited with numerous medical firsts such as the birth of modern orthopedics. Medical textbooks cite the Nix as a pathfinder.

"Back in the '30s, Dr. Charles Venable, Dr. Walter Stuck and Dr. Asa Beech developed vitalium plates for fixing fractures," Poth said. "They were the first to do it and got national recognition. They did animal work before they did human work. The human work was done right here in the Nix."

In 1962 the Nix was the first hospital in San Antonio to offer cobalt radiation therapy. Installed by Dr. Russ Norman, it was the only unit in town for many years.

Poth, a dermatology specialist, has had his own work described in American medical literature.

"In 1936 a patient came in from Corpus Christi with three cherry-sized tumors on the back of his hand. I said they had to be skin cancers, but he insisted they would go away, which cancers won't do. We sent some tissue to the Mayo Clinic and

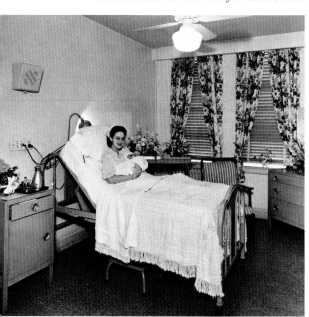

other well-known places and we got back many different diagnoses.

"A doctor by the name of Fred Wideman from the University of Pennsylvania at Philadelphia called it a keratosis, which is a tumor that comes up in the skin from excessive sun. I reported this at the American Medical Association meeting in San Francisco in 1937 and they became known as tumor-like keratosis of Poth. That was the first published account of the keratoic tumor in American literature. Today it is called a keratoacanthoma, which is a descriptive name."

On a lighter side, the 1930s also

begat the Nix Wildcat Softball Team, for which Poth pitched.

"We were famous and we had fun," Poth said. "The Wildcats played the league teams. Whenever we wanted to win a game, we played Groos Bank. We were doing great until we got entangled with the tobacco-chewing boys from Southern Steel.

"The doctors played ball because we had nothing to do. The Alamo Downs races were going at that time and in the afternoon this building closed up. Nobody came here because they were all out at the races. If you saw two or three people a day at $3 or $4 a person, you were doing great."

The Nix always has been known for the best in medical care in pleasant surroundings. Early pictures show ruffled curtains and bedspreads. Poth recalled an example of the hospital's appeal.

"I had a patient come down here from Memphis and spend the winter for four or five years in a row during the Depression," Poth remembered.

"He would check into the Nix Hospital because he could get a room and board for $5 a day. That was a bargain. He loved attention and the nurses gave him a lot of attention

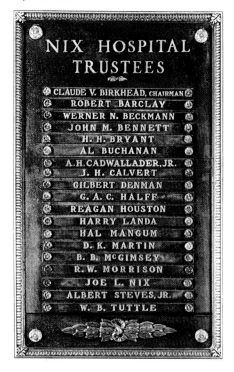
The Nix's decor has changed from the 1940s patient room, left, to modern suite.

because we didn't have many other patients."

By the time World War II came along, however, activity at the Nix was much heavier.

"When the war years came on, we had a place in the basement where we examined draftees," Poth said. "We'd strip them off and go over them. Our problem was with the needles. You'd stick the needle in their arms to take blood and they'd start fainting."

Through the years, Poth has watched as drugs and new procedures have advanced the medical profession.

"The advent of penicillins, antibiotics and steroids has changed medical practice," he said. "I was practicing before the days of insulin.

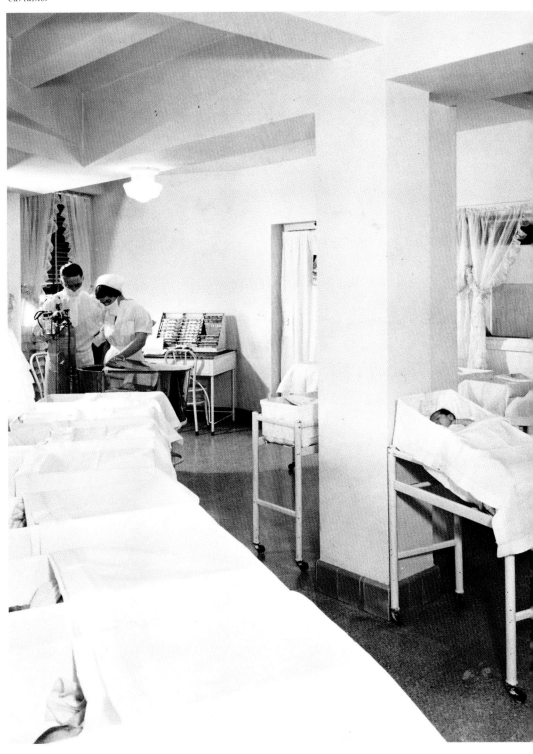

Newborn nursery in the early days was a caring, homey environment complete with white, lacy curtains.

"A hospital is basically a hotel that offers a few more services. The Nix is equivalent to a fine hotel."

I saw babies die from impetigo because we had no specific treatment. Today it's a one-office-visit cure."

Babies always have been big business at the Nix. The hospital estimates 20,000 babies have been born under its care.

During the hospital's 50th anniversary celebration in 1980, a man sent administrators the hospital bill for his birth at the Nix in 1933. Because his father was a government worker, the family got a $2 discount. The bill totaled $13.75.

Today more than 80 physicians have offices in the professional building and more will follow when renovation is completed of offices on the fourth and fifth floors. The hospital now has 180 beds on five floors. The first through third floors are reserved for patient parking.

Owned by Accord Medical Management Ltd., a partnership of five Nix staff physicians and J. Randolph Harig, the Nix is dedicated to its patients and to its place downtown.

"The Nix has been a landmark for downtown," Harig explained. "The people from San Antonio who have been here awhile were either born in or have had someone in their family

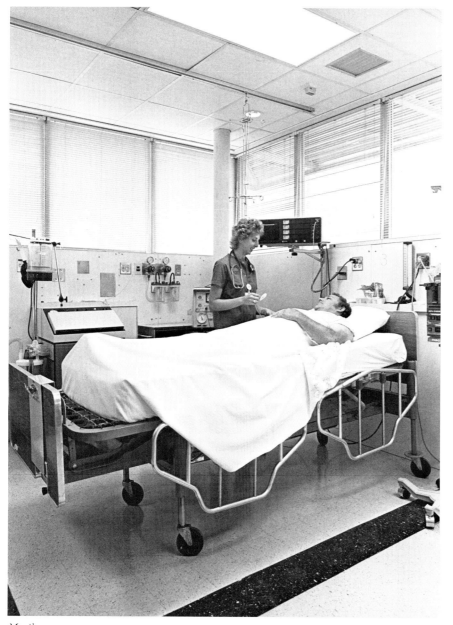

Marilyn Saathoff, R.N., checks a patient in the critical care unit.

segment — businessmen who have their executive physicals done in the Nix. We're also now getting workmen's compensation business from employees who have injuries on the job. And we want to reacquire the Mexican trade that once came here, but for the last 12 or so years has been going to Houston."

"We have a commitment to downtown and to stay right here on the river."

As the Nix actively seeks to attract patients, one drawing card is the hospital's master executive chef.

"In my mind, a hospital is basically a hotel that offers a few more services," Harig said. "The Nix is equivalent to a fine hotel. We now have a master executive chef, who is serving incredible meals such as lobster, scallops, salmon and prime rib. Ninety-five percent of our people here are on regular diets, so they want to eat good meals."

To better serve its patients, the

who was born in the Nix Hospital.

"The Nix has gone beyond the barriers of a downtown hospital in that it has been what I call the 'carriage trade' hospital of South Texas," he continued. "We have third generation rancher families coming up here. We have third generation Alamo Heights, Olmos Park and South Side patients coming here."

Harig believes the Nix is joining the resurgence in downtown vitality.

"We are poised at a good time with San Antonio," he said. "With the growth of downtown and its businesses, we're now getting another

Steak, fresh asparagus and shrimp cocktail are available from the hospital's master executive chef.

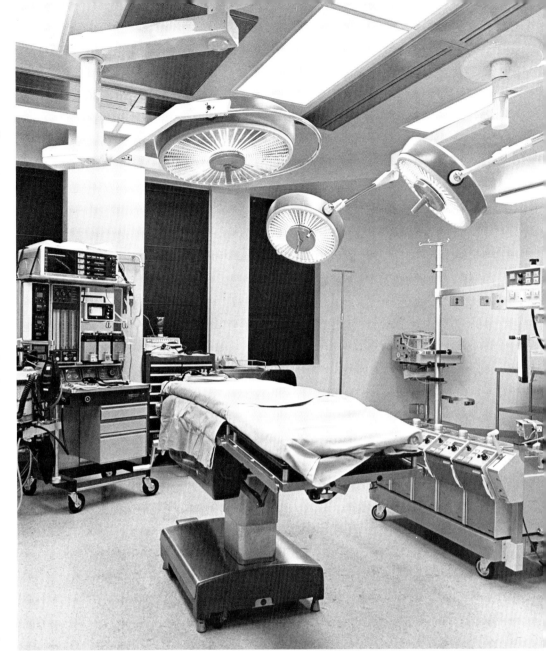

Nix has undergone recent extensive renovation.

"The building has been kept in excellent repair for the 55 years that it has been here. But in the last year, new windows have been put in as well as new wallpaper and paint throughout the building. We have recently purchased $3 million in radiology equipment. The 24th floor, which once housed the 'Top of the Nix' solarium and later an intensive care unit, has been renovated to allow for post-operative treatment of cardiovascular surgery," Harig explained.

"We have a commitment to stay right here on the river. We also have a commitment to downtown to enhance the retail business. Therefore, we have moved our shops and supplies out of the basement. We anticipate we'll have retail activities on the river level which will bring people down to this area of the river."

The Nix's long-time philosophy of providing the best in health care is emphasized by its physicians and surgeons.

Executive director Downs believes San Antonio's health care is divided into four segments: the military hospitals, the South Texas Medical Center, the downtown hospitals and the Nix.

Quality patient care is perpetuated at the Nix because of physician referrals within the building and devotion to primary nursing care, Downs said.

"The doctors scrutinize each other. We have quality care," he explained. "With self-referral the quality is kept here and that quality permeates down through the staff."

With the dedication of Accord Medical Managements, Ltd. to continued downtown medical excellence and the branching into new services, the Nix plans to remain a leader in medicine in San Antonio.

Its place as a unique downtown landmark is assured for today's San Antonians as well as future generations of Texans who will seek its specialized services. ⌶

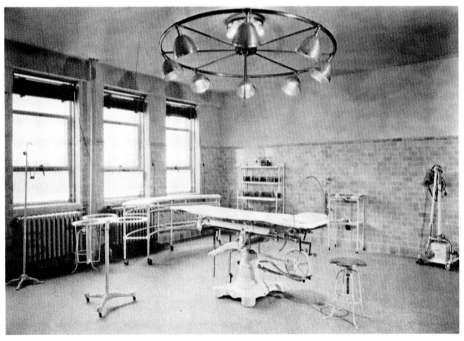

AMERICAN SECURITY LIFE INSURANCE COMPANY

In 1931 most people had never heard of the concept of hospitalization insurance. The man responsible for bringing that idea to San Antonio was Sollie Emmett McCreless, the founder of what today is American Security Life Insurance Company.

His provocative concept of prepaid health care has catapulted into a highly respected insurance company with more than $100 million in assets and in excess of $1.25 billion of life insurance in force. The company operates through more than 200 general agents and is licensed in 24 states. More than 170 people are employed in the company's new headquarters in the American Security Life Building at Trinity Plaza.

Though the company has skyrocketed since its meager beginning during the Great Depression, American Security Life proudly retains the imprint of its founder. His inspiration, philosophies and optimistic business acumen still greatly influence the organization.

The history of American Security Life, in large part, is the story of S.E. McCreless and his wife, Lilla, whose joint devotion to Christian ideals formed the company's cornerstone.

Their son-in-law, Robert B. Sunderland, chairman of the board and chief executive officer, and G. Richard Ferdinandtsen, president and chief operating officer, explained the company's operation today as well as its past:

"Anything to do with insuring people is our business," Ferdinandtsen said. "We insure people against hospitalization expenses. We insure their lives and take care of their families if they die prematurely. We insure them for retirement through

savings if they live."

Helping people help themselves was the life mission of S.E. McCreless.

He met his wife and lifelong business partner, Lilla Marr, while attending Asbury College in Wilmore, Kentucky. After graduation, S.E. McCreless studied for the ministry at Perkins School of Theology at Southern Methodist University and sold life insurance part time.

While in Dallas, he learned of a concept of prepaid hospitalization at the Baylor Hospital called the Baylor Plan. The forerunner of the Blue Cross Plan, it was a contract to pay 50 cents a month in return for a guarantee of paid benefits of up to 21 days a year in a semiprivate room in Baylor Hospital plus routine laboratory and operating room fees.

Enthusiastically, S.E. and Lilla McCreless returned to his hometown of San Antonio to begin a similar venture.

His original plan was to enter into a contract with a hospital in which the company would agree to sell contracts for hospitalization to groups of employed people. These people would pay 75 cents per month to the company, which would in turn pay the hospital 50 cents per month and retain 25 cents.

The company he formed, Hospital Service Company, was a pioneer in the field of prepaid health care — the forerunner of modern group hospitalization insurance.

Robert B. Sunderland, left, and G. Richard Ferdinandtsen direct American Security Life today.

History at a Glance 1931

Founded: *Feb. 27, 1931, in Central Building*
Founders: *Sollie Emmett McCreless and Lilla M. McCreless*
Original name: *Hospital Service Company*
Original investment: *$500 borrowed cash*
Original employees: *2*
Milestones: *1933 moved to Houston Building and opened a branch office in Houston; 1934 took over a floor of Houston building; 1935 incorporated under name American Hospital and Life Insurance Company and became authorized to issue life insurance policies; 1938 opened first out-of-state branch office in Kansas City, Mo.; 1941 issued first life insurance policy; 1942 moved to Builders Exchange Building at Pecan and St. Mary's streets, which was renamed The American Hospital and Life Insurance Company Building; 1972 began operating under name American Security Life Insurance Company; 1973 reached $500 million in life insurance in force; 1974 acquired Western United Life Insurance Company; 1981 acquired Greater Ohio Life Insurance Company; 1983 had $1 billion of life insurance in force; 1984 had more than $1.25 billion life insurance in force; 1985 relocated corporate headquarters to American Security Life Building at Trinity Plaza*

Lineage of presidents: *Sollie Emmett McCreless, Robert B. Sunderland, G. Richard Ferdinandtsen*

Officers: *Robert B. Sunderland, chairman of the board/chief executive officer; G. Richard Ferdinandtsen, president/chief operating officer; Lee Page, executive vice president/chief marketing officer; Lawrence C. Hammer, vice president/general counsel and secretary; Floyd D. Mason, senior vice president/actuary; Billy L. Odam, senior vice president/insurance services; J. Frank Pyle, senior vice president/group insurance; William C. Reed, senior vice president/treasurer; John C. Day, Jr., vice president/field operations; William M. Dennis, Jr., vice president/administrative services; William E. Grayson, vice president/computer systems; Betty Stark, vice president/policy benefits; and John A. Templeton, vice president/controller*

Employees: *170 plus*
Assets: *More than $100 million*
Motto: *Good Americans securing your future*

This chapter was based on an interview with Robert B. Sunderland and G. Richard Ferdinandtsen.

Lilla McCreless, in front, led the 1947 Award Trip to Mexico City.

"In the beginning, he wasn't even operating as an insurance company. He didn't become licensed by the State of Texas and chartered as an insurance company until 1935," Ferdinandtsen said.

"Mr. McCreless looked upon this company as a type of ministry, a way of helping people beyond what he might have been able to do as a minister. He continued to be an active layman in the Methodist Church and became chairman of the board of Asbury College, from which he graduated in 1928. He was a deeply religious man all of his life," Sunderland said. "The best way to sum him up is to use the term 'evangelical businessman.'"

To capitalize the company, S.E. McCreless borrowed cash from a former Sunday School teacher of Lilla McCreless.

> ## "Mr. McCreless looked upon this company as a type of ministry, a way of helping people beyond what he might have been able to do as a minister."

"He started with $500 of borrowed money, an adding machine, desks and chairs. We still have his desk," Ferdinandtsen said.

S.E. McCreless began visiting hospital administrators and handled sales, setting a pattern of leadership he would continue until his death in 1980.

His wife became the actuary. She established tables calculating the maximum and minimum days of hospital care which could be covered by the fee being charged. She set up the office, kept the books and did the administrative work. Initially, she directed its day-to-day operation. She maintained an active involvement in the company until her death in 1985.

"He was not a detail person," Sunderland recalled. "He had huge hands and his fingers were so big he had difficulty dialing a telephone. The office routine such as bookkeeping was not his strength.

"That's where Mrs. McCreless came in. They really complemented and challenged one another. They were business partners and both were active in the company and civic and church-related activities."

S.E. McCreless, center, became an honorary Kiowa Indian chief at a 1951 sales seminar in Ardmore, Oklahoma. With him were Wallace Cantwell, left, and Henry Christopher.

Sales agents
enjoyed a
Western-style
banquet at the
1952 Sales Con-
gress held in
San Antonio.

S.E. McCreless
crowned Bob
and Pat Boon
king and queen
of the
company's 21st
Anniversary
Royal Celebra-
tion in 1957.

The first hopsital to sign up was in Beeville. The first hospital in San Antonio was the Medical and Surgical Hospital. Hospitals were experiencing a low occupancy and financial problems because of the Depression. Many people couldn't afford to go to the hospital, and many who did couldn't afford to pay their bill. Hospitals saw McCreless' plan as a way to develop guaranteed income and to increase the number of patients. Soon his plan was embraced by almost every clinic and hospital in the area. This was the first instance of such a city-wide contract in the nation.

The first large group sale was in 1931 to Wolff & Marx Department Store for its employees. The company grew quickly with little real competition for hospitalization policies until the early 1950s.

The company occupied the American Security Life Building at Pecan and St. Mary's streets 43 years.

In 1933 he opened a branch in Houston. At one point, the company had 32 offices scattered over the south central United States.

In 1935 the company incorporated as The American Hospital and Life Insurance Company and became authorized to sell life insurance. Life insurance, however, did not become a major part of the company until the mid-1950s. The name was changed to American Security Life Insurance Company in 1972 to more accurately reflect the company's direction. Today, however, the company's health insurance premiums still exceed its life insurance premiums.

In 1981 the company was one of the first to have a universal life policy approved by the Texas Department of Insurance. In a universal life policy, the components of risk and accumulation are unbundled and the tax-deferred cash value accumulation competes with high-yield investments.

S.E. McCreless, left and Lilla McCreless, second from right, posed with three owners of early hospitalization and life insurance policies at the company's 25th anniversary celebration.

With his leanings toward the ministry and his positive outlook, S.E. McCreless was an excellent sales motivator.

"Mr. McCreless was a very strong-willed man. He was under tremendous conviction in terms of his faith and he was an eternal optimist. He was such a positive force he put a heavy influence on whatever he was involved in," Sunderland said. "He had tremendous stamina with great physical energy to carry on his business and his life.

"He respected people and he never asked anybody to do anything he wouldn't do himself. He loved people around him and drew a crowd wherever he went. He was the most optimistic person I've ever had the privilege of meeting," Ferdinandtsen said. "He could will things to be and they would be."

S.E. McCreless even challenged the Federal Trade Commission and won in a landmark decision before the U.S. Supreme Court. He led a winning battle for insurance companies to advertise without interference from the FTC. The 1958 Supreme Court ruling said the federal agency had no jurisdiction over insurance advertising "in those states which are regulating those practices under their own laws."

His positive attitude helped him cope with serious health problems in his later years.

"He was so positive, he simply wouldn't accept 'no.' People did the things he asked because of their respect for him," Ferdinandtsen said.

"He had a tremendous stamina with great physical energy to carry on his business and his life."

Lilla McCreless was equally inspiring. She conducted sales meetings and could deliver a motivational speech as well as her husband.

"Mr. McCreless' influence still is very much with us. The things we do today are an extension of him and the way he conducted business,"

Ferdinandtsen said.

For example, the company still begins executive meetings with devotionals and does not serve alcohol at company-related functions such as sales conventions.

The McCreless family influence continues through the leadership of Sunderland, who has been with the firm since 1957.

"It's unusual for an insurance company our size to remain in the control of one family," Sunderland explained. "The McCreless and Sunderland families control about 95 percent of our stock. The remaining 5 percent mostly is owned by small shareholders who are employees, former employees or persons closely associated with this company.

"Private ownership means that we're not going to wake up tomorrow being owned by someone else. And it enables us to commit to a growth strategy; funds that otherwise would be divided among stockholders can be used for growth capital."

A change in signs accompanied the company's name change in 1972.

Though the style has changed with the new generation of leadership, American Security Life still operates on the basis of what is fair for the customer, the employee and the company.

"That is something we inherited," Ferdinandtsten said. "We have a medium-sized company, but we're still very personable. We're not an IBM, Xerox Corporation or General Motors. We have attitudes that are more representative of a small company. We provide individual recognition of performance and personalized incentive.

"We develop loyalty. For example, our No. 1 salesman is an independent agent in Abilene who has sold our products for some 15 years. He sells only our products because they benefit his clients. That man is a testimonial to this company, to the way we do business and to the way we've helped him develop as his market has changed.

"We retain good people like this by

doing a better job of matching the product to the needs of the public. Then we provide the agent with a way to present the product and sell it. We're consumer-oriented and take care of our agents," Ferdinandtsen said.

"Another example that indicates the fairness of this company is my career here," he continued. "I started in the data processing department as a machine operator. The company has afforded me the opportunity to move up to president."

S.E. McCreless' altruism and concern for providing the best medical care led him to be a major force behind the creation of the South Texas Medical Center in northwest San Antonio. He was instrumental in the development and donated land for the first hospital there, Southwest Texas Methodist Hospital. Lilla McCreless was influential in the direction of the hospital, serving for years as secretary of its board of trustees.

Uncannily, S.E. McCreless also was responsible for choosing the site of the new American Security Life Building which was occupied in 1985.

"A new home office building was always on his mind," Ferdinandtsen explained. "We had been in our downtown location at Pecan and St. Mary's since 1942. Before he died, Mr. McCreless planned to build a new headquarters, but the company couldn't justify expansion at the time.

"We determined about four years ago that we wanted to relocate along the McAllister Freeway corridor between the airport and downtown," Sunderland explained. "We had to have access to the freeway in both directions and we needed an area suitable for commercial development. We picked the site of Trinity Plaza and became venture partners with Embrey Investments, Inc. Ironically, this location was the spot Mr. McCreless had pinpointed years before."

The beautiful nine-story building is one of the city's outstanding office buildings. American Security Life presently occupies five floors with spacious and elegantly appointed offices.

The building boasts such exceptional features as thermal-insulated

glass, a sophisticated security system and an energy management system with multiple sensors to monitor temperatures for greater efficiency.

The stately exterior is composed of precast panels and Napoleon red

"The McCrelesses left us a fine example to follow."

granite from Sweden, which is polished, honed or flame-cut to bring out varying depths of color. An arched entrance, fountain and landscaping add to the building's pleasing design.

"We wanted to make a statement with our corporate headquarters," Sunderland explained. "We wanted it to be representative of this company."

When S.E. McCreless went to Austin to apply for a state insurance charter in 1935, his attorney asked how many years he wanted the charter to be in effect.

The attorney explained that an insurance company can be chartered by the state for as long as 500 years.

Without hesitating, S.E. McCreless replied, "Let it be 500 years."

"He never thought in terms of short-range goals or objectives," Sunderland said. "He would have liked to have used 'Alamo' in the name of the company, but he thought it might be identified only with San Antonio and, therefore, too limiting.

"Like an individual, an organization has character and personality. This is developed from the way it is created, the people it employs, the nature and scope of the business venture and the commitment to the community.

"At American Security Life, the McCrelesses left us a fine example to follow, a legacy of loyal employees, a tradition of sound business practices and top-quality products, an obligation to continue the support of community endeavors, and a strong Christian commitment."

Looking to the future, Sunderland predicts "continuing success." **LJ**

REDLAND WORTH CORPORATION

One of the largest quarries in the United States — 3,000 acres — is located 15 miles northwest of San Antonio and is the property of Redland Worth Corporation.

The second generation of McDonoughs were Jim, second from left, John, center, and Dan, second from right.

With approximately 500 employees and around-the-clock, seven-days-a-week work schedules, the company provides thousands of tons of limestone materials a year for the construction industry across Texas.

Although based in San Antonio, the company owns a total of 11,000 acres around the state, where it employs an additional 800 workers.

Owners are Redland PLC and Bill Worth, who is a descendant of the founders of McDonough Brothers, Incorporated, the company's name before it was changed to Redland Worth Corporation in 1983. Worth grew up at the San Antonio quarry site. He recalled the company's vivid history:

"The original McDonough brothers were my grandfather and great-uncle. They came from Alabama in the early 1930s. My grandfather was in the construction materials business there. His was one of the largest in Alabama.

"The Depression got him and he came out here with just the shirt on his back. He had been one of the most prominent men in Alabama from the turn of the century to the late '20s, and then he lost everything. There was no risk in starting a new business because he didn't have anything to lose.

"I don't know how he picked this location. He was just looking for areas of the country with growth possibilities. He couldn't see any real future in the Mississippi-Alabama area. He never got to see any of our success here because he died in the late '30s.

"My mother's two brothers came out here when they were very young, seventeen or eighteen years old, and were working in the business then. I mean hard physical labor. They later took it over. They were in their early twenties when their father died.

"When both were drafted into the service during World War II, they got one of my older uncles, who was living in New York, to run the business until they got out. Then it was the three of them: Jim, Dan and John McDonough.

"We moved here in 1945 and lived on the place. It was remote and all the workers lived together in a little village with one street. At one time, we had 20 or 30 families here. We had a little store and most of us went to school at Lockehill.

"Once you're in the rock business, you can formulate pretty much your own plans. You know how to find it yourself; you don't have to be a geologist. We are in the Edwards Plateau formation in the Balcones Fault that extends from west of San Antonio to Austin. Everybody knew rock was here.

History at a Glance 1934

Founded: *October 1934 15 miles northwest of San Antonio*
Founders: *R.N. "Nute" McDonough and Joe McDonough*
Original name: *McDonough Brothers, Incorporated*
Milestones: **1952** *began production of crushed rock;* **1954** *opened asphalt plant;* **1963** *opened concrete batching plant;* **1964** *purchased 4,000 acres in Poteet for silica sand;* **1968** *completed lime plant;* **1968** *supplied aggregates for construction in HemisFair;* **1983** *changed name to Redland Worth Corporation*
Lineage of ownership: *R.N. "Nute" McDonough and Joe McDonough; John McDonough, Jim McDonough and Dan McDonough; Bill Worth, Jim McDonough, Jr., and Larry Irvin; Bill Worth and Redland PLC*
Headquarters: *Interstate 10 West at Beckmann exit*
Subsidiaries: *Manco Prestress Company, South Texas Construction and Waco Ready Mix*
Employees: *1,300 including 500 in San Antonio*

This chapter was based on an interview with Bill Worth.

Holes are drilled into the rock and exploded out with amonium nitrate.

"We've grown through the years, but originally they just mined big hunks of limestone and shipped it by rail to the Gulf Coast for jetty stone. Now we further refine the limestone.

"I can remember when I was a kid this was just an old gravel road out here. It's unbelievable how it has grown. I had a normal childhood. We were required to work at an early age. I've been working here since I was six years old. My first job was cleaning the office after school each day. I shined shoes, went to the store for soda waters, washed cars, whatever needed to be done. But it was fun. I enjoyed it.

"I've worked in the quarry all my life. I gradually evolved in it as I got bigger and older and started running some of the equipment.

"I was the only boy in the family and it was just expected of me to do it. That's why taking over the company never really bothered me. I actually ran this operation when I was twenty-three years old. My three uncles were active, but basically I ran it on a day-to-day basis. That's a big advantage in growing up in a business. I love the business; I love the people.

"The company is very dedicated to our people and our people are very dedicated to us. That is our asset — our people. We've got third generation people here now. I actually grew up with a lot of the superintendents and foremen here. We were kids together; we grew up together. The old-timers were tough. It's a pretty dangerous occupation and they were all tough, big men.

"Our growth came from the utilization of our product. We went into the asphalt business in the 1950s, into the ready-mix concrete business in the 1960s and into the prestress concrete and lime business in the late 1960s. We bought an existing construction company headquartered in Corpus Christi, South Texas Construction Company, in the mid-'70s.

"Our new mobile impact crusher on walking feet will be the largest in the world. It will weigh 830 tons."

We grew by building the business.

"The limestone here is one of the finest deposits in the world. It's chemically good so it can be used in chemical plants. And it is hard and durable, so it can be used in construction materials. We've got the best of both worlds.

"We excavated the mountain here

The largest hot mix plant in Texas is owned by Redland Worth.

Redland Worth headquarters are located 15 miles northwest of San Antonio.

at road elevation, and we have reserves here which will last 100 years. We refer to this as home base, but we have other quarries throughout the state. We're presently relocating the Interstate 10 plants into the quarry floor on the east side of the highway.

"Today we furnish materials all over the state. We provide materials for the interstate highway system, state roads and farm-to-market system. We did the Tower of the Americas and a lot of other work at HemisFair. Our products are in the USAA headquarters, and we did housing work at Lackland Air Force Base. We helped build Calaveras Dam and the Deely Power Plant.

"**O**utside of San Antonio, we've done the ARCO Chemical Plant and Intercontinental Airport in Houston, Exxon Refinery in Baytown, the hurricane protection levy around Port Arthur and the Texaco Refinery there, and Pittsburgh Plate Glass in Corpus Christi.

"Although we've done work for The University of Texas, we're all Aggies here. We did all the precast work for the baseball stadium at Texas A&M University and for The University of Texas Memorial Stadium.

"Mining is a sophisticated business now. We drill a series of holes and explode it out with amonium nitrate. It's not like it was 30 or 40

Limestone base is loaded into a continuous flow of trucks.

years ago. We monitor all of our blasts; we have to make sure we don't do any damage or blow any dust on anybody or create any excessive noise. It is a sophisticated blasting technique. Basically, we drill and then explode the material off the face, load it and put it into a crushing plant. It's refined from there, screened, washed and dried and then it goes into the other products we make.

"While a lot of our plant is automated, we're in the process of putting in a new plant here. We're spending about $25 million to relocate, and everything will be fully automated and computerized.

"I have English partners, a large conglomerate called Redland PLC, which has plants all over the world. We're putting in a very sophisticated

Limestone is run through the crushing plant on conveyor belts.

"You have to look forward to coming to work in the morning."

plant, something that can exist here and the public won't even know it is here.

"We are building the largest asphalt plant in Texas and putting in a new mobile impact crusher on walking feet. It weighs 830 tons and will be the largest mobile crusher in the world. It is being made in Germany and will be operational in 1986. Instead of taking the rock to the crusher as we do now, we'll walk the crusher over to the rock.

"The railroads have come out here since the late 1800s. The Southern Pacific main line gives us a direct single route into the Gulf Coast market area. We're shipping unit trains now into that market area. They've depleted their shell and a lot of their natural river gravel deposits all along the Gulf Coast. Every month we're shipping more than 25 unit trains that are dedicated to this. Sixty to 75 cars come out here, we load them and they go to material yards, unload and make another run out here. The material is used for roads, bridges, streets and buildings.

"Because of our proximity to San Antonio, we can provide materials for use here very economically. We provide a good source of reasonably priced building materials, which we have to have if our city is going to grow and be maintained.

"We're going to continue to acquire other companies and expand. That's our goal: to keep going.

"Our philosophy is if you see an opportunity, take it. We expect a day's work. We pay well. We don't like to argue. We work hard, but we have fun. My wife, Darolyn, handles all the social activities. We have a couple of parties a year for all the employees. We're just like a football team; we have to work together. You have to look forward to coming to work in the morning." L

The lime plant produces thousands of tons of lime each year.

The ready-mix plant is located inside the quarry.

H.B. ZACHRY COMPANY

The H.B. Zachry Company's record of challenges and accomplishments stretches from San Antonio to the far corners of the earth.

Behind this giant company was an industry giant and community leader — H.B. "Pat" Zachry.

"He was an extraordinary man — a leader," H. Bartell Zachry, Jr., said of H.B. "Pat" Zachry upon his death in 1984. "That the world might be a little better for his having lived and that he made a difference were essential for living to him. In my mind, there is no doubt that he succeeded."

Today the H.B. Zachry Company continues the tradition of making a difference and accepting challenging assignments close to home as well as around the world.

For the past several years, the Zachry Company has been listed among the top 50 construction companies in the United States by the Engineering News Record, the contracting-engineering fraternity's foremost publication. To be thus included requires an annual volume of business in the $500 million range.

Datelines on stories of Zachry Company's accomplishments range from Small Town, U.S.A., to such distant places as Kwajalein Atoll, the Sinai Desert and to company office locations in Santurce, Puerto Rico; Riyadh, Saudi Arabia; and Honolulu, Hawaii. Other offices are in Dallas, Houston, Henderson and Longview, Texas; and Durham, North Carolina.

"San Antonio is home to us," Bartell Zachry explained. "There is very little that we haven't somehow touched here in the city. A great deal of anything that anybody either touches or sees or comes in contact with here has had some of our involvement."

Headquartered in San Antonio for more than 40 years, the company, although concentrating in heavy and industrial construction around the world, has put its mark on the Alamo City. Its many construction projects range from the Hilton Palacio del Rio Hotel to numerous public utility projects, highways, dams, buildings and a hospital.

Zachry Company's construction of the Interstate Highway 35 Interchange near downtown San Antonio and the construction and early completion of the Fratt Interchange in northeast San Antonio (largest dollar volume contract — more than $64 million — ever let by the Texas Department of Highways and Public Transportation) is an example of this involvement.

More than one-half of the generated power in San Antonio has been built by the company for City Public Service. This includes the four 415-megawatt units at the J.T.

History at a Glance   1935

Founded: *Aug. 23, 1924, in Laredo*
Moved to San Antonio: *April 8, 1935*
Founder: *Henry Bartell "Pat" Zachry*
Original name: *H.B. Zachry Company*
Original assets: *$17,000*
Original employees: *16*
Original address: *Ramos Building, Laredo*
Milestones: **1925** *first bridge job;* **1940** *first defense project;* **1941-'45** *wartime projects including defense installations at Harlingen, Laredo, Fort Hood, Eagle Pass, Hondo, El Paso, Brownsville;* **1946-'49** *first large dam, gas recycling plant and sewage treatment plant;* **1952** *first large pipeline;* **1953** *first power plant;* **1959** *first large overseas project*
Significant 1960s projects: *Built Atlas ICBM Facility area in Abilene for U.S. Air Force; constructed Nike-Zeus Anti-Ballistic Missile System in Marshall Islands; built highway project in Amazon Basin of Peru; constructed Twin Buttes Dam, San Angelo; was general contractor for Zorita Power Plant, Spain's first nuclear power plant; completed Hilton Palacio del Rio Hotel in 202 working days; built Palo Seco Power Plant, Puerto Rico*
Significant 1970s projects: *Built largest U.S. olefin plant in Taft, La.; built Texas' largest lignite-fueled generating station near Longview; built sanitary and storm sewers in Riyadh, Saudi Arabia; built U.N. base camp in Sinai Desert as part of Camp David Accords; constructed world's largest concrete paving project, Dallas-Fort Worth International Airport; participated in construction of 208 miles of Alaska pipeline project*
1980s projects: *Fratt Interchange; Capitol Cogeneration (engineer, purchase, construct, finance); Capitol Cement plant expansion; initiation of offshore marine services; Sri Lanka irrigation canals*
Lineage of presidents: *Henry Bartell "Pat" Zachry, Wayne Tiner, Delbert Ward, H. Bartell Zachry, Jr.*
Headquarters: *527 Logwood*
Employees: *8,500 in the U.S.*

This chapter was based on an interview with H. Bartell Zachry, Jr.

Deely Power Plant. Two are gas-fired and two are western coal-fired.

The company ventured into the dam construction field in the 1930s and built Calaveras Dam, a power plant cooling water reservoir for City Public Service.

Construction of airfields was begun in the early 1940s. Paving and repair of runways, taxiways and aprons have been performed at San Antonio International Airport and Kelly Air Force Base.

Not visible to the eye is the local underground utility work performed by the Zachry Company. Water and sewer lines and a sewage treatment plant have been constructed for the City of San Antonio; telephone communication services have been constructed for Southwestern Bell Telephone Co.

Commercial construction projects in San Antonio include the equipment manufacturing plant for Friedrich Air Conditioning & Refrigeration Co., buildings at Trinity University and St. Mary's University, Air Force Village, the SASA Center Office Building and parking garage, The Dominion Country Club and Taft High School.

Now at the helm of the firm with more than 8,500 employees, Bartell Zachry measures its success:

H.B. "Pat" Zachry oversaw his multidimensional company from the Tower Life Building.

"It was my father's character that attracted people to him; it was his character that was the company and endures."

"If success means having attained a measure of respect professionally in terms of what you do and also being considered as an asset to the community, then I think we have achieved those two things because of the caliber of people we have.

"My father was a leader who created the kind of climate that attracted good people. We have a great number of employees who are almost entrepreneurs in their own right. It was my father's character that attracted people to him; it was his character that was the company and endures."

The company's first major large-diameter, long-distance pipeline project — a 100-mile, 24-inch job — was for Transco in South Texas. Today more than 5,300 miles of large-diameter projects lie behind the Zachry Company.

These include participation in building the northernmost 208 miles of the Alaska pipeline. Construction of the 48-inch crude oil pipeline from the North Slope through the Brooks Mountain Range was accomplished under varying climatic conditions that often saw the temperature dip to minus 60 degrees Fahrenheit.

"The Alaska pipeline clearly captures the imagination," Zachry admitted.

Closer to home, in 1973 Zachry Company performed construction of the largest concrete paving project in the world — the Dallas-Fort Worth International Airport. The runways and taxiways were the first in the world to be constructed using a 50-foot-wide slip-form paving technique. Bridges were built to permit jets to cross an automotive expressway.

Zachry called the airport project "a major landmark in the State of Texas."

Major landmarks, however, are not uncommon for the Zachry Company. In the 1960s, the company built the Highway of the Incas, which crosses the Andes Mountains where rainfall is measured in meters. It was also during that period that the company participated in the construction of Spain's first nuclear reactor.

An undertaking in Houston, Capitol Cogeneration Project, is the one Zachry points to as the example of his company's far-ranging "scope, depth and maturity."

The Zachry Company was fully responsible for the design, procurement and construction of the 375-megawatt power plant by a date certain, guaranteeing its output and arranging interim and permanent financing. The company also handled the insurance, fuel contracts, electricity sales, steam sales and hydrogen purchase contracts, lease of the plant site and operation of the facilities.

To H.B. "Pat" Zachry, creating was the most fascinating element of his work.

"The creation of a company or the construction of something physical was the same to him in the sense of a challenge to be done," Bartell Zachry said.

One example of H.B. "Pat" Zachry's creative risk-taking was the creation of Capitol Cement. A lithium plant which closed in 1960 is today a cement manufacturing facility making a significant contribution to the economy of South Texas and its labor market. The facility has a work force of more than 250 people. Another example is Metropolitan General Hospital, now Humana Metropolitan Hospital. Initially constructing the building, he later owned and successfully managed the hospital.

Modular construction was an idea that intrigued the company founder. His use of this construction technique enhanced the company's reputation for having the ability to build quickly and meet deadlines. Locally manufactured modular concrete room units were used in the construction of the Hilton Palacio del Rio Hotel and Metropolitan General Hospital and as far away as the Sinai Desert in Egypt and Jubail, Saudi Arabia.

Bartell Zachry summarized his father's philosophy:

"Whatever needed to be done, he approached it with the idea that if the job is worth doing, then find something interesting and challenging in it and do it."

Early Days

Amado Cavazos went to work for the H.B. Zachry Company in 1928 as a clerk in the Laredo office.

Fifty-seven years later, the faithful employee and confidant of H.B. "Pat" Zachry is semi-retired from his post as senior vice president. He recalled the company's early days:

"Mr. Zachry started his business in Laredo by accident. When he graduated from Texas A&M University as a civil engineer in 1922, he accepted a position with the U.S. Coast and Geodetic Survey in Panama. However, his mother became ill in Laredo and he stayed with her until her death, thus missing out on the promised job.

"He then worked as a surveyor and engineer for Webb County and as an engineer for the Texas Highway Department. By August 1924, he had saved enough to start a modest construction company.

"His first job was a small bridge near Laredo. He bought a small concrete mixer, surplus World War I wagons, wheelbarrows, fresno scrapers and tools. The mules used to move dirt were rented. His first crew consisted of 16 men who earned 17½ cents to 20 cents an hour. He kept track of the payroll himself on a small pocket diary from a cement company. When he finished the job, he had lost a few dollars, but had gained enough experience and self-confidence to continue as a small contractor.

"The greatest challenge H.B. Zachry faced was having the full weight of the Depression hit him in 1929 just when he was getting started. Many lesser men faltered and gave up. He fought on for 10 long years. He never let an unsuccessful bid bother him; he just tried harder. He planned his work and worked his plan. He had the courage to take calculated risks and the perseverance and stamina to proceed full steam ahead.

"In the early days, he stayed in a tent at the construction camp and ate frijoles and guisado with the workmen in the cook tent. He knew every employee by his first name."

J.T. Deely Power Plant is an example of the Zachry Company's involvement in San Antonio.

Fratt Interchange in northeast San Antonio was constructed by the Zachry Company.

The Palacio del Rio was completed in record time with the use of modular construction.

The Hilton has undergone $11.5 million in renovations.

Hilton Palacio del Rio Hotel

The Hilton name commands worldwide respect from the hospitality industry, and in San Antonio its story is one of challenge and success prompted by HemisFair '68.

"At the time we were contemplating the building of a hotel complex, H.B. Zachry and I decided we weren't hotel people," remembered Nic Catalani, Hilton co-owner. "Of the major hotels interested in this project, we thought the Hilton Hotels Corporation was the best qualified to manage it.

"Of the more than 300 Hilton hotels in the United States, ours is the most unique because of its construction," Catalani continued. "This 498-room complex is the only hotel completely fireproof, soundproof and explosion-proof. The ceilings, walls and floors are solid concrete.

"San Antonio was planning HemisFair '68 without adequate housing accommodations. We decided to build a hotel to help make the fair a success, but time was of the essence. This was 1967 and we had 10 months at most.

"Mr. Zachry converted his equipment yards into an assembly line for modular construction similar to the way General Motors produces automobiles. They cast six rooms at once.

"After the rooms were cast, a track, similar to a little railroad, and a gantry crane were used to move them to other areas where different installations such as plumbing and electrical were made and into the area where furnishings were assembled. The carpet, air conditioning, televisions and bathrooms were assembled in the rooms, making them ready for occupancy.

"Each room was elevated by crane. One room was stacked on top of another room. Helicopter rotors kept the rooms level and steady during the hoisting. In fact, when we elevated our first room, we had guests in there. Even Mr. Zachry went up in one of the modules.

"Conrad Hilton came during construction. Barron and Eric Hilton also worked diligently with us because this hotel had to be functional in such a short time.

"I'll never forget the remark Conrad Hilton made. He said, 'I've been in the hotel business all my life, but I've never sold rooms when a hotel wasn't complete.' We were selling rooms while we were in the process of construction.

"There was no city or federal funding; this was all private enterprise, which is another reason for our pride. When Mr. Zachry pursued anything, he wanted to do it on his own. The Catalani family owned two-thirds of the land and the rest was acquired.

"This construction helped San Antonio receive front-page publicity around the country. People began to realize that here was a city on the go. As a 'people' place and business generator, the Hilton had a great impact on subsequent river development."

San Antonio continues that on-the-go image first initiated by HemisFair. As the city has grown, so has the Hilton. Today's general manager is Siegfried Richter, whose responsibilities have included $11.5 million in renovations.

"I see great things for the future," Richter predicted. "I think the Hilton, whose developers had the foresight to risk placing it on the river, now has an outstanding location in the center of everything.

"Today we host more than 350 conventions a year. San Antonio is also a tourist Mecca, and we needed to expand," he continued. "We created meeting rooms, a beautiful lobby, an executive office complex and a very attractive bar on the river. One of the greatest advantages was building the ballroom over our driveway. The gorgeous roof garden blends Mediterranean, Spanish, Mexican and contemporary decor and architecture.

"The name of Palacio del Rio, which is 'palace on the river,' actually identifies what the hotel is — a palace."

BROADWAY NATIONAL BANK

Broadway National Bank founder Col. Charles Cheever (USA Ret), left, instilled in his son and current board chairman, Charles Cheever, Jr., a love for the banking business.

The Broadway National Bank is a commercial bank of approximately $340 million in assets and $300 million in deposits.

It was originally opened in the 5000 block of Broadway in the present location of The Broadway 5050 in Alamo Heights, which was somewhat remote from San Antonio.

Charles E. Cheever, Jr., chairman of Broadway National Bank, recalled the bank's history:

"In 1938 my parents lived on Carnahan Avenue near the Witte Museum. They would take evening walks in the Alamo Heights area. My dad got the idea that Alamo Heights was growing to the point where it ought to have its own bank.

"At that time, my father was a captain in the U.S. Army, a judge advocate with no banking connections. He was a self-taught person, so he went to the library and read all the books he could find on banking and started the ball rolling. He got some friends, other Army officers, and they all agreed to put up some money. But in the summer of 1939 he was ordered to West Point to teach law.

"The organizers had a difficult time getting the bank open but did so in February 1941. What is amazing is that it opened with $65,000 in capital, surplus and undivided profits. That was all, and most of that was borrowed.

"This was just prior to World War II and in those days there were only a half dozen banks in San Antonio. And it was rare — and quite an accomplishment — to get one opened.

"It was a modest opening and the beginning of a very difficult time. During the 1941-'45 period, they had six presidents. It was wartime and most men were entering the service. The bank went through some traumatic experiences. My mother was on the board of directors during the war, trying to hold things together until 'the boys came marching home again.'

"My parents were first stationed in San Antonio in 1936 at Fort Sam Houston. They liked it. They came from the poor Irish part of Boston where there was limited opportunity and they thought this was the great frontier. After the war, my dad stayed for the war crimes trials in Nuremberg as a prosecutor and returned to Fort Sam Houston in late 1946 as judge advocate for the Fourth Army. He retired in 1948 and went with USAA, where he was elected chief executive officer in 1953. He retired from that position in 1969. He then moved into the bank as an active part-time board chairman.

"The turning point for the bank was 1952 when we moved into a modern structure which now houses InterFirst Alamo Heights. In 1946 the bank had moved from its original location into an old wooden building which was the old St. Peter's School. The location is the site on which Satel's is now located.

"They made a big step when they moved across the street into this new building and it strained them financially. Cost overruns caused them to exceed their fixed assets limitations and they got quite a bit of criticism from the regulatory authorities. But in the eyes of the public, they got a lot of credibility and were finally recognized as a 'real' bank.

"Most of the customers were Alamo Heights residents. It was strictly a neighborhood suburban bank drawing from a two- to three-mile radius.

History at a Glance   1941

Founded: *1941 at 5044 Broadway*
Founder: *Charles E. Cheever, Sr.*
Original name: *Broadway National Bank of Alamo Heights*
Original employees: *5*
Original investment: *$65,000*
Milestones: 1952 *moved to 5201 Broadway;* **1961** *extended hours and expelled from San Antonio Clearing House Association;* **1964** *opened affiliate Northeast National Bank on Loop 410;* **1968** *moved to Nacogdoches and Loop 410;* **1982** *formed Broadway Bancshares Inc.*
Headquarters: *1177 N.E. Loop 410*
Owners: *Cheever family and 180 shareholders*
Employees: *258*

This chapter was based on an interview with Charles E. Cheever, Jr.

The bank got its modest start in Alamo Heights during wartime.

"I got out of law school in January of 1957 with a wife and two children and not a decent job offer. An El Paso firm offered me $275 a month and I was about to take it. My parents said, 'If you're going to starve that way, we can starve you.' So I became a banker then.

"In 1961 our motor banks were open the same hours as our bank lobby. We had traffic counts of all these people pouring down Broadway to San Antonio and going home each evening the same way. Of course, we didn't have Interstate 35 or the McAllister Freeway then. We decided that we were going to open the motor banks from 7 a.m. to 6 p.m.

"Our new hours really upset the banking fraternity. We were expelled from the Clearing House for violating its rules. The rules were violations of antitrust statutes and were later changed.

"The longer hours put us on the map. We were renegades in those days; maybe we still are by just trying to do the customer-oriented thing, not the bank-oriented thing.

"The thing that really changed us was the idea of switching locations of the banks.

"In 1964 we applied for and received a charter for a new bank to be located on Loop 410 and Nacogdoches called the Northeast National Bank. It was the first time that anybody had applied for a charter where there were exactly the same shareholders in the new and the old banks. People thought that was branch banking, but it was perfectly legal and we got the charter. It started a trend that might have started the holding company movement in Texas. But it was 'affiliate' banking.

"So in 1964, we opened that bank in a temporary building next to the Petroleum Center. We had acquired a beautiful nine-acre site at the northwest corner of Loop 410 and Nacogdoches. We tried to plan the nine acres for a little 5,000-square-foot bank that could only cost $250,000 because of Northeast Bank's small capital. At the same time, the Broadway had bought property in Alamo Heights where the Tree House Apartments are now, and we were trying to build a six- or seven-story building there and move across the street.

"I came up with the idea that we just needed to flip the two banks. The board of directors asked, 'Why didn't you think of that before?'

"So we got authority to switch banks. We contracted to build a $3.5 million building on Loop 410. On one weekend, just after HemisFair opened, April 29, 1968, we moved the Broadway Bank from Alamo Heights to Loop 410 and on the same weekend Northeast Bank moved into our old location. On Monday morning, we were both in business at new locations.

"In 1974 we applied for another affiliate bank, this time on Fort Sam

---

"**Somehow my dad got the idea that Alamo Heights was growing to the point where it ought to have its own bank.**"

Houston. We had a big debate as to what to name it. Since it was to be a military bank on an Army post, we considered Pershing, Bradley, Patton and Eisenhower. Dad pushed for Patton, for whom he had served as staff judge advocate in World War II.

"Eisenhower won because besides being a famous military person, he had been president of the United States. And early in his career, he had met his wife in San Antonio and they lived on Fort Sam Houston in 1941.

"At the last minute, the Comptroller of the Currency said that we needed the family's permission to use the name. So I made contact with an old family friend whose husband had been military aide to President Eisenhower in the White House. She arranged an appointment with John Eisenhower and he graciously gave the family consent. He wrote a letter of approval which hangs in the Eisenhower Bank lobby, and he and his wife came down for the opening.

"At the Broadway, we cater to the customer. We were the first to extend motor bank hours, to create a mortgage servicing operation, to start a bank discount brokerage operation, to start true affiliate banking and to switch two banks' locations over a weekend. And when savings rates were deregulated, we were the first to raise savings rates when authorized. I give my dad a lot of credit for that. He was from Boston where the Five Cent Savings Bank grew into a mammoth institution because they made it clear they wanted your nickels. He always believed that interest bearing savings, not the 'free' checking balances, were the true core deposit. It's proving true right now.

"The Broadway will always strive to stay ahead of the pack by concentrating on customer needs." ▉

TRINITY UNIVERSITY

Dr. Ronald K. Calgaard

One of the oldest institutions of higher learning in the Southwest, prestigious Trinity University started in 1869 as a tiny Presbyterian college operated in an eight-room farmhouse in the unlikely location of Tehuacana, Texas.

Nationally recognized for academic excellence, the Trinity of the 1980s sits atop Trinity Hill — one of the most beautiful locations in San Antonio.

The primarily undergraduate liberal arts and sciences university with approximately 3,000 students is headed by Dr. Ronald K. Calgaard, president.

Calgaard described Trinity today and recalled its colorful past and its move to San Antonio:

"In the main, we're an undergraduate residential institution with selective admissions, offering what we think is a superb educational experience for high-ability students. We also offer master's degree programs in a few selected disciplines," Calgaard said.

By most standards, Trinity is one of the most selective institutions in this part of the country. For example, Calgaard expects that in 1986, out of 2,200 applications, the university will enroll a freshman class of approximately 650.

"Sixty-five to 70 percent of these students," he explained, "will have graduated in the upper 10 percent of their high school classes. Their average grade point in high school will be in the neighborhood of 3.7. We also expect their average S.A.T. scores will be approximately 1,200. Around 100 of those 650 will be National Merit Scholars."

The origins of this dynamic university are far from San Antonio.

"Founded as a successor to three Presbyterian colleges which closed during the Civil War, Trinity was chartered in Tehuacana," said Calgaard. "Its original purpose was to prepare people for church service careers, as was the purpose of most early church-related colleges.

"In the latter part of the 19th century, the Trinity trustees thought a Presbyterian-related college would do better in another location. The choice was between Waxahachie and what now is downtown Dallas. The trustees thought the prospects in Waxahachie were superior to Dallas.

"In 1902 Trinity moved to Waxahachie, where it spent the next 40 years. In the early 1940s, Trinity's trustees received a proposal from the Chamber of Commerce to relocate here.

"This proposal called for Trinity and Austin College, another Presbyterian-related college in North Texas, to merge and move to San Antonio. The Trinity board approved that proposed merger.

History at a Glance   1942

Founded: *Sept. 23, 1869, in Tehuacana, Texas*
Moved to San Antonio: *1942*
Founders: *Presbyterian Church of Texas; Rev. Richard Overton Watkins, Willis Burgess, R.R. Dunlap, N.P. Mondrall, Rev. Jacob Henry Woffard, Rev. W.G.L. Quaite, Alpha Young, W.M. Dillard and Alfred Smith*
  Original name: *Trinity University*
  Original employees: *President and four faculty*
  Original investment: *$30,000 and 1,700 acres*
  Milestones: *1950 construction began on Trinity Hill;* **1968** *became independent university;* **1969** *celebration of centennial year;* **1974** *Phi Beta Kappa chapter established;* **1984** *$48.5 million Second Century Capital Campaign completed;* **1984** *ranked 10th in nation in number of National Merit Scholars*
  Headquarters: *715 Stadium Drive*
  Lineage of presidents: *Rev. W.E. Beeson, B.G. McLeskey, Luther Apples Johnson, Rev. J.L. Dickens, B.D. Cockrill, Jesse Anderson, Rev. L.C. Kirkes, Archelaus E. Turner, Samuel L. Hornbeak, John Harmon Burma, Raymond Hotchkiss Leach, Frank L. Wear, Monroe G. Everett, James Woodin Laurie, Duncan Wimpress, Ronald K. Calgaard*
  Lineage of chairmen of the board: *Dr. J.S. Wills; H.L. Prendergast; L.B. Prendergast; D.M. Prendergast; Rev. P.M. Riley; Frank N. Drane; Royal R. Watkins; Rev. R.E. Joiner; Rev. Rasmus Thomson; Clint C. Small; C.W. Miller; Robert R. Witt; James H. Calvert; Forrest M. Smith; Gilbert M. Denman, Jr.; Joseph N. Sherrill, Jr.; Flora C. Atherton; Harold D. Herndon; William H. Bell*
  Assets: *$150 million endowment*
  Employees: *700*
  Motto: *E Tribus Unum*

This chapter was based on an interview with Dr. Ronald K. Calgaard.

"Legend has it that because of a snowstorm in North Texas, which prevented several Austin College trustees from attending their board meeting, the merger failed by one vote. Trinity, nevertheless, moved to San Antonio in 1942.

"For a decade, the university occupied an old campus on the west side of town which had previously been known as Westmoorland College and then as the University of San Antonio.

"Our current 107-acre site was one of several possibilities. Because it was a quarry, some board members thought it unsuitable. But a few strong personalities led the argument that this site had enormous topographical advantages.

"Trinity trustees, who originally envisioned traditional Gothic buildings, first contracted with a well-known architect at Massachusetts Institute of Technology. He advised that the campus should relate to its site. Subsequently, the trustees employed two local architects, O'Neil Ford and Bartlett Cocke, whose firms either jointly or separately became the Trinity architects and over a period of 30 years designed the 50 buildings on campus. The campus has low, red brick buildings that blend ideally with their setting.

"It is unusual, especially in private colleges, to have retained the architectural integrity that this campus has. Trinity is generally regarded around the country as one of the most physically attractive campuses. And the campus fits its surroundings. Furthermore, the virtually worthless land to which Trinity moved in 1952 is now probably among the most valuable 107 acres in the near North Side of San Antonio."

"What we wish to be is one of the best liberal arts and sciences universities in the country."

In 1969 ownership and legal control passed from the Presbyterian Church to an independent, self-perpetuating board of trustees. Today, although the church has no legal authority, Trinity maintains a covenant relationship with the Presbyterian Church U.S.A.

Calgaard continued, "Trinity is one of the remarkable success stories of American higher education: In the early 1950s, it was an institution in a serious and precarious financial position. Yet, within a 30-year period, it built one of America's most attractive physical campuses and emerged as one of the universities in the United States best endowed on a per-student basis."

Many of Trinity's graduates have chosen to make San Antonio their home and have become extensively involved in many aspects of the community. The university also plays an important role as a center for cultural and intellectual life for the broader San Antonio community. Lectures, concerts and special events series — most of them free and all open to the public — bring in some of the most influential individuals and outstanding performers in the country. There are literally hundreds of community events on campus each year sponsored or co-sponsored by the university as well as other organizations.

Having firmly established its role as a primarily liberal arts and sciences university, Trinity intends to continue to focus its attention on academic excellence.

"We do not expect to grow much," Calgaard said. "We don't want to be large. We don't expect to start new academic degree programs. No institution can try to be all things to all people. What we wish to be is one of the best liberal arts and sciences universities in the country." L

Trinity University students and faculty helped move from the Woodlawn campus in 1952 to the present site on Trinity Hill.

GUY CHIPMAN COMPANY, REALTORS

Guy Chipman Company, Realtors is a privately and locally owned general real estate brokerage company which is responsible for approximately 10 to 15 percent of the sales in San Antonio.

Founder Guy Chipman, Jr., now chairman of the board, explained his company's status in the local marketplace and how it got there:

"The last time I saw a figure, there were around 5,200 real estate agents here and we represent a little more than 200 of those. Like most other things you run into, 20 percent do 80 percent of the business."

His highly visible company started out as a family enterprise.

"My family goes back to the Mayflower. The wife of the first Chipman in the United States, Hope Howland, came over on the Mayflower.

"My mother and father bought a home here in 1945 after he retired from the Army. He still lives in that same home today and is one of the oldest living graduates of West Point.

"After studying pre-law in college, I received a degree in 1941 and went to active military duty. I had intended to go to law school, but reservists were being called out of school to do a year's duty and I had a reserve commission. So I volunteered for a year's active duty in the Army, which due to Pearl Harbor and the war became a lot longer. Four and a half years later, I decided I'd try the civilian business world, thinking I could always go back to law school.

"In 1945 when I moved to San Antonio, this was a beautiful little town like Austin was four or five years ago. San Antonio was hot in the summertime and a little dusty, but very pleasant. Our population was about 325,000 and all of the major businesses were downtown. San Antonio just seemed such a nice charming town and I enjoyed my family. I've been here ever since and never been sorry.

"Real estate then was a business you could get into fairly easily. The idea of sales interested me, and what really appealed to me was that it was a business where you earned whatever you could make. You had a chance to really go as far as you wanted to and that intrigued me. So I thought, 'I ought to give it a try and if I don't like it, I'll go on to something else.'

The leaders behind the Guy Chipman Company, Realtors today are Guy Chipman, Jr., left, and John H. Drought.

"I went to work on the first of January in 1946 for the Arthur E. Baird Company. They were the largest in town by far. Arthur Baird was a very smart man, a very good promoter and salesman.

"In the meantime, my mother wanted something to supplement their income. She obtained her real estate license and started advertising in the Army Times and the Army/Navy Journal and places like that, primarily to serve military retirees.

History at a Glance 1946

Founded: *1946 at 215 Elizabeth Road*
Founders: *Guy Chipman, Jr., and Mrs. Guy Chipman, Sr.*
Original Name: *Guy Chipman Realty Company*
Milestones: 1948 *moved to 3930 Broadway;* **1959** *moved to 535 Busby Drive;* **1967** *moved to 8546 Broadway;* **1970** *largest volume of listings and sales in Multiple Listings Service;* **1972** *converted gas station to office;* **1973** *formed corporation;* **1973** *moved to current headquarters at 7911 Broadway;* **1983** *Guy Chipman, Jr., named president of Texas Association of Realtors;* **1984** *sales of more than $220 million;* **1985** *John H. Drought named president by Guy Chipman, Jr., chairman of the board*
Services: *Residential and commercial real estate sales, farm and ranch sales, property management, new home sales, relocation and referral*
Employees: *235 sales agents, 65 employees*
Offices: *10*
Motto: *Guy Chipman sold signs are everywhere.*

This chapter was based on an interview with Guy Chipman, Jr.

"By February of 1947, I decided to join her. My father was never really active in the business. I was the 'outside man,' did all the selling and all the listing, returned all the calls, made the appointments and showed the houses, wrote up the contracts, got the property financed and did whatever else had to be done.

"We put in a telephone in the garage apartment of my parents' home and operated from there. I did not hire any salespeople for about a year. I wanted to learn more about the business and I knew you learn it best when you do it yourself.

"In our company I wanted people to be treated fairly. I wanted to have knowledge, I wanted to be able to find my clients the right financing and to have contracts drawn so they wouldn't fall through and everyone would be as satisfied as humanly possible. My object was to have a financially successful real estate business in which I rendered service that I could be proud of.

"In the early days, I did a lot of the showing of properties and the city was small enough to where I knew every street by name, which was better than most taxi drivers."

"A funny thing — I have many times thought about sitting around the fraternity house at Northwestern University and talking about what we wanted to do when we got out. I was going to be a lawyer. I said, 'Well, if I can earn what a federal judge earns, I'll be very satisfied.' In 1939 and 1940, a federal judge earned about $10,000. That was my horizon.

"In the early days, I did a lot of showing of properties and the city was small enough to where I knew

Even in the early days, Guy Chipman was putting sold signs everywhere.

every street by name, which was better than most taxi drivers.

"At first you had to have 50 percent down payment to buy the average house. The average house in those days ranged from $7,000 to $12,000. The biggest house I sold my first year in real estate was a house in Olmos Park at $39,500. That house today would probably be worth at least 10 times that amount.

"It has been predicted that within five years the real estate industry will be made up of three groups. First, there will be the big national franchise companies with branches around the country. Then there will be large local chains — privately owned firms with branch offices like ours. The third large factor will be specialty groups which specialize in areas such as commercial sales, property management or a certain geographic area or price range. Today in San Antonio, we are the only

major large local chain.

"The local companies have a personal touch. As time goes on, we will promote much more heavily the fact that we are locally owned. We don't have to wait for decisions from some headquarters some place else; our management is here. We do it all more expeditiously with less expense, and all the money stays here.

"We've always grown on a solid financial basis. We've lived through seven or eight recessions and we've had to go to the bank — thank God for some friendly bankers.

"We've seen a number of our competitors rise up and fall down and some that have not had the organization to continue their company. I'm very fortunate. January 1, 1985, I appointed John Drought president of my firm and I took over the duties as chairman of the board. He will continue our growth and continue our traditions." ⅃

LUBY'S CAFETERIAS, INC.

The concept of cafeteria-style dining was revolutionary in 1911 when an enterprising young businessman named Harry Luby opened the New England Dairy Lunch in Springfield, Missouri.

His freshly prepared, home-style foods and buffet-style service marked the beginning of a new era in dining out. Almost 75 years later, his innovative ideas have been refined into the operating philosophy behind the country's premier cafeteria company, Luby's Cafeterias, Inc.

Harry Luby's son, Robert M. Luby, co-founder of the modern Luby's chain which now numbers 89 units in three states, recalled the beginning of the cafeteria business and how it has progressed:

"The first New England Dairy Lunch was a small room with a few tables and a 12-foot counter, all built by his own hands. It was a start.

"The Dairy Lunch was a modification of an eating establishment he had frequented as a young man in Chicago. It was a place for working people to get a wholesome, practical meal at an inexpensive price.

"He called his version of this Chicago eatery the New England Dairy Lunch, which featured a New England boiled dinner. He kept the

The New England Dairy Lunch featured home-cooked food at popular prices.

menu short and simple. He hired a couple of good cooks, and, of course, my mother was an excellent cook. She helped develop the initial food setup. So with the good food and the good prices and someone who didn't

have the experience to know what he shouldn't do, the Dairy Lunch was successful.

"Over the years, Dad opened a number of these eating places, which he called New England Cafeterias, between 1914 and 1916. He brought his idea to Texas in 1920 when he opened a cafeteria in Waco.

"But he was anxious to get out of active management. Eventually, he started helping others, usually relatives and friends, develop cafeterias and accepted an interest in their businesses in return.

"I grew up in the business. Unfortunately, I never worked with my father. He retired in his late thirties, as soon as he thought he could live comfortably for the rest of his life. You see, Dad never really liked the business. He got into it because it was the only venture he could think of where he could make a nice profit with a minimum amount of capital.

"How he succeeded with so little

History at a Glance 1947

Founded: *Jan. 28, 1947, at 517 N. Presa St.*
Founders: *Robert M. Luby and Charles R. Johnston*
Original employees: 25
Milestones: **1948** *opened cafeteria at 4902 Broadway;* **1949** *opened in Tyler;* **1959** *incorporated;* **1973** *first public offering of stock;* **1981** *name changed;* **1982** *listed on New York Stock Exchange*
Lineage of presidents: *Robert M. Luby, George H. Wenglein, John B. Lahourcade*
Headquarters: *2211 N.E. Loop 410*
Current employees: *5,700 with more than 1,100 in San Antonio*
Cafeterias: *89 including 15 in San Antonio*
Company motto: *Good food from good people*

This chapter was based on an interview with Robert M. Luby.

---

experience and knowledge about restaurant operations, I'll never understand. He had lots of guts, good luck and perseverance. He had a terrific sense of ethics and responsibility.

"Dad opted to retire in San Antonio. I graduated from Main Avenue High School and studied business administration at The University of Texas at Austin. I finished my degree in 1934 and opened my own cafeteria in Dallas. By that time, the name New England Cafeteria had been replaced with Luby's Cafeteria. The units were in Texas and a few other states and mostly were owned by relatives and friends who had been helped by my father.

"It cost about $5,000 to open a cafeteria then, and I could make around $10,000 a year. That was a heck of a markup. In those days, we served two or three times as much lunch as dinner because the only people who ate out in the evening were either single or traveling. Of course, you could buy a nice meal for 25 cents. The entree cost from 8 to 15 cents, vegetables 3 to 7 cents and a dessert 5 to 8 cents.

"My mother tried her best to talk me out of going into this business since she knew how hard you have to work. We opened at 7 o'clock in the morning, closed around 8:30 at night and were back for half a day on Sunday to clean up.

"When World War II broke out, I

volunteered. But I used those years in the Air Corps to think, to make contacts for the business I hoped to start. I envisioned a cafeteria that would serve the highest quality food, pay good wages and not require working from dawn to dark.

"While attending intelligence training in Florida, I ran into Charles Johnston whom I had known for many years and had worked with in

---

"My mother tried her best to talk me out of going into this business since she knew how hard you have to work."

Dallas. We talked about my ideas and agreed to get together after the war.

"Charles and I opened our first cafeteria in San Antonio in 1947 on the lower floor of a hotel at the corner of College and Presa streets. Joining us were George Wenglein and John Lee, who had also worked in a Luby's Cafeteria in Dallas, and Norwood Jones, whom I had been stationed with at Santa Anna Army Air Base in California. We didn't have much money. It cost about $70,000 to open, which was shocking.

"The location at Presa seemed huge. In the past, 100 seats was a big cafeteria, and we were looking at a space that would seat about 180. Equipping and remodeling the building were especially difficult in the early postwar years. Materials and some ingredients were still rationed or in short supply. But none of us could believe our sales once those doors were open.

"We realized we were providing a much-needed service to the community. San Antonio was crowded with servicemen and their families looking for places to live. A lot of people were living in downtown hotels or were coming down at night for dinner or a movie. I expected the evening business to wane after a year or so, but the volume remained high.

"Soon after opening that first cafeteria, we debated about the value of moving into a suburban area. We bought property on Broadway in Alamo Heights and opened our second cafeteria in 1948. By 1959 we were operating nine cafeterias in Texas, all partnerships owned by a group of men Charles and I brought together.

"Each cafeteria was paid for and subsidized by the men running it. Some of the partners supported interests in one or two of the other units, and, of course, Charles and I owned an interest in all of the stores.

"This group of 14 also became our original board of directors. Our philosophy was to share the work, share the risks and share the money. You have to put money in before you can grow, and we were all willing to do that.

"The best thing I did was to get an outstanding group of people together. None of us really worried about who was responsible for what idea. The ideas were based on what was good for the company. And as others came in, we maintained a continuing sense of cooperation and mutual gain.

"Those early years were great learning experiences. John Lee once said one of the prerequisites for a new cafeteria should be its proximity to a grocery store. You never knew when we might need to run over for a box of salt. Our accounting system wasn't all that sophisticated either. We paid for everything in cash — deliveries, bills — right out of the

Modern Luby's cafeterias offer good food and plenty of free parking.

cash register. The outgo was recorded in a little book kept beside the register.

"There was no question about the customers' confidence in us. We checked the trays and took money at the end of the serving line, adding up the items in our heads. The food was priced so that most totals came out in

and San Pedro, we had to subsidize the bus service to get our employees to work.

"But it was a landmark for us. One Sunday we stopped by and the place was jumping. But no one else was open. That's when we realized it wasn't the mall that necessarily drew customers, but the parking.

prepared just prior to each meal. Plus we cook only in small portions. That's expensive, but we think it's worth it.

"I wrote the opening menu for years, but it's been a long time since I've done it. The number of entrees now stands at about 12, and we're continually refining and upgrading.

"The menus now are regionalized. If you opened without rice in Beaumont, the public would close you down. The East Texas area favors more Creole cooking whereas El Paso is much like San Antonio with a heavy Hispanic influence and a penchant for enchiladas.

"In the beginning, we didn't serve much chicken or fish. The quality of chicken has improved over the years. Quite a few people in our organization are responsible for our seafood entrees evolving into what they are today. The fish is shipped exclusively from Iceland and distributed to each of our locations. Henry Jones developed the batter that makes it so popular.

Harry Luby started the first cafeteria in 1911 in Springfield, Missouri.

multiples of five or 10 to keep the arithmetic simple — 3 cents for a roll, 2 cents for butter.

"We paid our employees once a week by totaling the payroll and putting the money out on a table — loose change in vegetable bowls — and dividing it up envelope by envelope.

"The turning point in our growth occurred in 1959 when we incorporated. Since then we've added 80 cafeterias to those original nine; 15 of those are in San Antonio.

"Our headquarters are here because we like San Antonio. When we began to plan our new home office building, we considered that it might be more logical to relocate in Houston or Dallas. But after much thought, we decided San Antonio is a very pleasant city to work and live in.

"Our first mall cafeteria was in North Star Mall. Some people thought we had lost our minds because it was so far out. Since the city bus service stopped at Oblate

From that time on, we have made sure each cafeteria has a maximum number of parking spaces. Parking was important to us in the development of our free-standing units.

"During our development, we have never strayed from our founding premise: to serve top quality food at a fair price.

"The fresher anything is, the better it is. We let our vendors know that we won't accept anything but the freshest produce and the best in meats and poultry, and then we train our management to recognize it. Almost every item on the menu is

"To talk about our servings, Virgil Hill decided we should give bigger portions — larger, at least, than I was in favor of serving. But the public likes big orders. I was wrong; he was right.

"Our recipes have been collected throughout the years from managers, employees or someone's mother or grandmother. About half of the soft pies are my mother's recipes. We've worked hard on their development. Although hundreds of employees and managers have access to the recipes, we still make it a policy not to give them out.

"In the fiscal year ending August 31, 1984, our sales were just short of

Early customers enjoyed entrees for 8 to 15 cents and vegetables for 3 to 7 cents.

$175 million. I was looking over a poster produced by the Rice Council which said Luby's sells 182 tons of rice a year. I thought that was ridiculous. But it isn't. At a little more than $4 per meal, $175 million amounts to more than 40 million people eating in our cafeterias in one year. That's a lot of meals.

"Looking ahead, we see no reason why we can't continue to grow and maintain a strong position in the food service industry. Today we're operating cafeterias in Texas, New Mexico and Oklahoma and soon will open our first store in Arizona. We've established an excellent reputation throughout the Southwest, an area that still offers many opportunities for this company.

Family dining in a pleasant atmosphere is a Luby's tradition continued today.

"During our development, we have never strayed from our founding premise: to serve top quality food at a fair price."

"We keep a close eye on what's behind us. If we see a weakness, we are perfectly happy to stop, evaluate the weakness and correct it. We grow only as fast as we can place well-trained managers in each new location.

"All of our managers begin their careers with a three-month course in our training school in San Antonio. Following that is a rigorous on-the-job training period which lasts from five to seven years. We pay our managers very well, giving them an incentive for moving up. Each month they share in the profits shown by their own individual cafeteria.

"A large part of our success is due to the fact we have been blessed with some of the nicest people. Life is too short to put up with someone who may be very bright but just a little mean. We train our people to learn this is a successful organization; it's a house of high standards. We do everything possible to be fair to everyone — the customer, the employee and the business. And we try to enjoy life as we go.

"Our company gets stronger every year. If we continue to remain flexible with the times — remembering where we came from and how we got here — our potential growth and prosperity are unlimited." **LJ**

Harry Luby, second from right, posed with his staff in one of his early cafeterias.

ELLISON INDUSTRIES, INC.

The No. 1 home builder in San Antonio, Ray Ellison, began his empire 36 years ago building one house at a time.

Today Ray Ellison Homes, a division of Ellison Industries, Inc., is the largest individually owned home building and development company in the United States. With more than $250 million annual sales volume, the company garners 40 percent of the San Antonio housing market, more than the next 10 local builders combined.

A conservative estimate is that in San Antonio one family out of every 10 lives in a Ray Ellison home. The company annually builds approximately 3,500 houses ranging in price from the mid-$40s to $130,000 and above.

In addition, Ellison founded and owns Lackland City Water Company, the largest privately owned utility in Texas. His well-managed organization also has interests in land development, lumber, banking, component manufacturing, real estate, title search, mortgage lending and a relocation center.

The man behind the company is a legend in the industry and the San Antonio community. Ellison has received almost every award given for leadership, innovation and service. He recalled his humble beginning, his business risks and his secret of success:

"We're known for building the first homes many young couples can afford, although now a lot of families we've sold to are moving up and buying a larger house from us. We're very proud of that.

"I went through the same thing, so I know what it is like to work for a house. Normally a house is the only thing of value most people have when they retire.

"I always thought ahead. I worked 12 hours a day seven days a week on my first job. After studying auto mechanics at Fox Tech High School, I worked at Wagner's Garage by the railroad tracks on Ashby. I made $10 a week. By the middle of the week when my co-workers' money had run out, I loaned them a dollar. They paid me back $1.25.

"A friend talked me into going into home building and we started building one house at a time. The market was tough in 1949; the rash of home buying after World War II was over.

"The tight market helped us be more careful on our bidding. On our first house, however, we failed to in-

Ray Ellison, right, chairman of the board, checks blueprints with Jack Willome, president.

History at a Glance   1949

Founded: *1949*
Founder: *Ray Ellison*
Original name: *Ray Ellison Homes*
Original employees: *5*
Milestones: **1955** *purchased B.B. Smith Company including Richmond Lumber Company and ranch land;* **late 1950s** *built Valley-Hi enclosed mall and bank and started Lackland City Water Company;* **1972** *exceeded 2,000 unit sales for first time;* **1973** *moved corporate office to Fredericksburg Road and Loop 410;* **1984** *set record with 3,500 homes sold*
Subsidiaries: *Richmond Lumber Company, Ray Ellison Properties, Ray Ellison Homes, Ray Ellison and Associates, Component Manufacturing Plant, San Antonio Title Company, World Wide Realty, Texas Homestead Mortgage Company, Lackland City Water Company, San Antonio Relocation Center and Valley-Hi Bank*
Owner: *Ray Ellison*
Officers: *Ray Ellison, chairman of the board; Jack Willome, president*
Employees: *1,000*
Assets: *12,000 acres undeveloped land and $75 million in residential inventory*

This chapter was based on an interview with Ray Ellison.

clude the garage in the bid from our subcontractor, so we ended up building it ourselves. We never forgot again.

"Our first house was on Lullwood and the second on the corner of Gramercy and St. Cloud. We got into volume building in 1953 when we built about 100 houses in Loma Park," Ellison said.

Even in the early days, Ellison kept land purchases ahead of building operations. The land gave him a strong asset base on which he could draw in leaner times.

His next development was 125 houses on the West Side between Acme Road and Commerce Street followed by 100 houses in Billy Mitchell Terrace. He then started Valley-Hi near Kelly and Lackland Air Force bases. That venture proved to be the turning point.

"People say we don't build houses like we used to. I'm glad we don't."

"People have asked me if I thought when I bought the land in Valley-Hi and Heritage Northwest that those areas would grow as much as they have. I wouldn't have bought all that property if I didn't," he said.

"In Valley-Hi I built eight houses in the middle of a field. People thought I had lost my mind and I thought so, too, for a while. But I knew we were sitting next to those bases and I knew people wanted to live close to their jobs. But we had no water or sewer systems, so I put in my own water and sewer plants.

"I go where people want to go. We've built more houses in recent years on the South Side than any other builder. But most people want to live in the north, northwest or northeast portions of San Antonio, so that's where we build. We don't try to swim upstream."

Ellison leads the industry in offering innovative financial plans. He also keeps housing prices low

A Ray Ellison model home complex in Heritage Northwest is among 3,500 homes the company built in 1984.

through incisive land purchases, volume building and sound management.

"We were among the first to offer 100 percent financing, which helped sell houses when people didn't have the money for a down payment," he explained. "The monthly payment is more important than the price of the house.

"We also try to make the price as low as possible by using land we bought 25 or 30 years ago. I'm able to pass along that low price to individuals. The real profit comes from commercial property, but you have to have people on the land in the area to sell that commercial property. So we have found that giving good deals on homes to individuals makes it easier to sell our commercial property," he explained.

Ellison's assembly line approach to building places a premium on money-saving techniques such as manufacturing prefabricated panels and trusses.

"You can get a better and more accurate house if you build it on a bench in a shop where you have constant weather.

"People say we don't build houses like we used to. I'm glad we don't because utility bills would be so high no one could afford them. Homes now are much better insulated and have double-paned windows, thick batts in the walls, and slab foundations."

Ellison credits much of his success to the people who belong to his organization.

"I mention every time I win an award that it is not Ray Ellison who is doing this. It's the people we have here and they do a great job."

Among his most prestigious awards are the Builder of the Year and induction into the Housing Hall of Fame from the National Home Builders Association. In addition, he received the 1984 Dealmaker Award given in Dallas on the recommendation of a selection panel of Texas business and civic leaders. He has received the President's Builders Award from the Greater San Antonio Builders Association as well as many grand prizes and awards for model homes, merchandising and marketing achievements.

Ellison's innovative approach to understanding target market segments through application of continuing research in values and lifestyles has put his organization at the forefront of the national home-building industry in the 1980s. Surveys, questionnaires and focus groups of buyers provide a continuing source of information about customers' perceived values. This information enables his management team to design and build homes with features that are attuned to the changing needs and desires of contemporary home buyers.

"If you treat people right, it will come back to you whether you're dealing with customers, employees or peers," Ellison said. "That's our philosophy and it's the reason we're selling as many houses as we are today." □

KMOL-TV 4

"On the first day, December 11, 1949, Channel 4 was dedicated at 11 a.m. and everybody in San Antonio who was anybody — the mayor, county and city leaders, civic leaders and the CEOs of San Antonio's leading corporations — was here.

"Television was a whole new dimension to San Antonio life, to its businesses and to the advertising industry. So everybody came, and they pushed the button and we went on the air with very limited programming and very few television sets in San Antonio. No one then knew what we had begun on that day."

Thus Edward V. Cheviot, president of KMOL-TV 4, described the day San Antonio's first television station went on the air. Cheviot, who has been with Channel 4 since 1952, traced the station's colorful history:

"**W**e were the first and only television station on the air in San Antonio. There were 47 stations on in the country and there were only 1 million TV sets in America. We were NBC, ABC and Dumont Network-affiliated at the time. There was no other station in San Antonio. CBS came on six months later. The Spanish independent became the third commercial station in 1955, followed in 1957 by the ABC station.

"Today we're a major-market NBC

station, and we reach 1.5 million viewers in our market area, which is roughly a 75-mile radius from San Antonio.

"But in 1949 on December 11, there were probably only 25 TV sets in the city. We kept track of the number of sets being sold every week through the major department and retail appliance stores that would give us weekly sales figures. This became the source of our audience data base during the early years.

"Television was first tested in the New York World's Fair in 1939. When it became commercially feasible, the Halff family, who also owned WOAI Radio, applied to the Federal Communications Commission for a construction permit in 1949. With no TV sets in the marketplace, it was a big gamble. But it caught on fast, and the history of television has proved the wisdom of G.A. Halff, the founder.

"**I**n 1949 we didn't have the vaguest idea of the unlimited opportunities in entertainment and news in television or the importance of programming in the public interest. As a matter of fact, most of the people who worked in television in the early '50s came from radio and most of the early programs came from radio as

History at a Glance   1949

Founded: *Dec. 11, 1949, at 1031 Navarro St.*
Founders: *G.A. Halff and Hugh Halff, Sr., Southland Corporation*
Original name: *WOAI-TV*
Original employees: *50*
Milestones: **1965** *sold to AVCO;* **1975** *sold to Twentieth Century Fox;* **1975** *changed call letters to KMOL-TV;* **1981** *became a separate publicly owned company, United Television, Inc.*
Lineage of leadership: *Hugh Halff, Sr., chairman of the board; James M. Gaines, president; Hugh Halff, Jr., chairman of the board; Edward V. Cheviot, president*
Headquarters: *Los Angeles, Calif.*
Employees: *110 full time*
Units: *6*
Assets: *$8 million*
Motto: *Be sensitive to community needs*

This chapter was based on an interview with Edward V. Cheviot.

well such as 'Fibber McGee and Molly,' Jack Benny, Roy Rogers and so on.

"Television news was actually a radio newscast on television in the beginning. It had no support in terms of graphics or pictures. It was strictly a newsman reading the news while sitting in front of a microphone and a television camera.

"During the first few years, we were on the air from 11 a.m. until 10:15 p.m. Most of our programming came from NBC by mail on Kinescope, which was a method of making a motion picture off a television screen. It was on black-and-white film. These programs were scheduled throughout the broadcast day along with our local live programming. We also ran movies that we bought from Hollywood producers.

"Justin Duncan was an engineer who helped put the station on the air and helped people tune their sets properly. He came on the air every Sunday night the first few years for 15 minutes and told you how to adjust your set. He was very popular because he was helpful.

"We produced and programmed shows like 'On the Alamo,' which was a half-hour variety show. There was 'Tip the Scales,' a game show in prime time and a one-hour country-western program called 'Hayride.' We produced 'TV Dude Ranch,' the most popular half-hour show in our prime time. We also had a live cooking show in the daytime called 'Menu Matinee.' We had some other shows. Some were hits; some were misses. It was the golden years of local live programming.

Red River Dave crooned his way through "The Hoffman Hayride" on the Saturday prime time show.

Square dancing was a popular activity on "On the Alamo."

Puppet Johnny Duggan starred on the Saturday morning "Tree House" along with host Perry Dickey in 1949.

Aunt Rosie, left, and Carmen Phelps stirred up dishes on "Menu Matinee" from 1949 until the late '50s.

"Then in the mid-'50s, we became interconnected live by way of telephone lines with NBC Television. We received the picture on a live basis. Then in the '60s and early '70s, the telephone lines changed to microwave, which is a direct signal

Roy Rogers and Dale Evans guest-starred on "TV Dude Ranch" in 1954.

"We had to sell the sizzle to cause people to spend $500 to $600 for a black-and-white 10-inch screen set, which was the largest screen then."

sent through the air from tower to tower. Today all NBC affiliates are on a live basis by way of satellite. The microwave and land lines are gone. NBC is the first network to have this satellite feed capability for all network programming.

"Because television in the '50s was so new, we had to make an extra ef-

Dennis James hosted San Antonio's first telethon in 1952 for cerebral palsy.

fort to promote the desire to have a TV set. We had to sell the sizzle to cause people to spend $500 to $600 for a black-and-white 10-inch screen set, which was the largest screen

then. The newspapers at first didn't want to publish our television logs. One newspaper yanked the logs because they felt they were promoting a competitor, but the logs were reinstated quickly when viewers demanded them.

"We had ratings as a measure of performance and audience back in the '50s. But we had difficult times because television rating was an early technique to ascertain who was watching when and was not as scientific or as sophisticated as it is now.

"For instance, when Dwight D. Eisenhower ran for president in 1952, he came to San Antonio and spoke in front of the Alamo. We televised this appearance live. The next week the rating service came out and said there was no measurable audience watching Gen. Eisenhower. But at 5:30 p.m. on Saturday, we had a test pattern with a 21 rating. Something was wrong!

"In the days of black-and-white television, it was difficult for the retailer to advertise on television. There was no production house available in town and all commercials had to be presented live — no film or video tape. It took a different skill to write for television as opposed to writing for radio or creating a printed ad. But they learned along with us how to use television effectively.

"Some of the major stores like Joske's, along with Lone Star and Pearl breweries, used television early on. They knew what it could do. And then when color came in 1956, it changed everything again. Lone Star Beer actually changed its label, as others did, so that it could be used with color television to the maximum advantage.

"We were the first station with color in San Antonio and probably the second in the entire Southwest. We did a half-hour Sunday evening show designed just to show off all the colors of the rainbow. It was gawdy, but it highlighted color television and created color TV set sales.

"The first color I saw in a home was on an eight-inch color set. It was the play 'The Women,' and it convinced me that color would be a viable technology and that it would add an important dimension to our industry.

"In those days, the greens looked blue-green, and all the colors flared. The RCA color cameras were in the development stage when they were put into commercial use. Everybody was trying to scramble on board and

The Lone Ranger visited San Antonio fans at the station.

capture the advantage. But after a year of experimenting with color locally, we shut it down. The colors were causing fuzziness on the black-and-white sets. There might have been 500 color sets to 25,000 black-and-white sets. So until the technology was fine-tuned a couple of years later, we put color in mothballs to protect our black-and-

white audience.

"There were some great shows early on like 'Milton Berle's Texaco Star Theatre.' In 1948 he owned television on the East Coast. For about two years, he dominated Tuesday nights at 7 to 8 o'clock New York time. Bishop Sheen came on against him on the Dumont Network two years later. He was the only one who really put a dent in Milton Berle's ratings.

"There were other great shows in the early days — Sid Caesar and Imogene Coca on 'The Show of Shows,' 'The Philco Playhouse' and 'I Love Lucy.' The 'Ed Sullivan Show' was on CBS for 20 years. Then there was 'Gunsmoke,' 'Wagon Train' and 'Bonanza.' 'All in the Family' was the first program that broke some of the taboos in sensitive areas. Now we have almost an open door on what can be said and what can be produced for television.

"With all the research that is done in this industry, all the pre-testing of programs and formats and scripts, we still don't know how the viewers are going to react in many cases. For example, about 85 percent of all the

Starting in 1953, Phil Hemphil predicted the weather from this original weather set.

network programming that premieres every fall is canceled in the first year.

"Groucho Marx is part of our station's history because a young man by the name of Pedro Gonzalez-Gonzalez was the station's messenger. He also had a gig. He used his hands to play pots and pans that were sewn into his pants. The first telethon ever televised in San Antonio was for cerebral palsy. We did it in 1952 in the Municipal Auditorium, and the emcee was Dennis James from New York.

"We had to fill over 20 hours, so we put everybody on we could in order to use local talent. One of the people who volunteered was Pedro Gonzalez-Gonzalez. One of the Hollywood people in town invited him to come on 'You Bet Your Life' as a contestant. When he went on, he was a great success. Because he was so outstanding and funny, Hollywood picked him up, and John Wayne put him under contract. He has appeared in a great number of Hollywood films these past 30 years.

"The hottest show in this market back then was live wrestling. We ran it Wednesday nights from 8 to 10 o'clock in the mid-'50s, and it got a 55 to 60 share of all the audience. We pre-empted the 'Kraft Theatre' to present wrestling, and Kraft would call us, 'You've got to clear for our show.' We told them we'd get run out of town if we did. A few years later, we did clear for Kraft.

"Some of our other firsts included being the first station to use Hollywood films. We televised the Texas Open Golf Tournament in 1950. We broadcast the first live church service.

"We did the first news simulcast in 1953 with WOAI Radio, and we did that at 10 o'clock Monday through Friday for about four years. It was the highest rated television newscast in Texas in terms of percent of viewers watching in a given market. It was just a newsman reading a radio script while sitting at a desk.

For video we used still news photos.

"In 1957 Channel 12 came on the air with local news film and had a format of blood and guts that achieved high numbers of viewers. Within six months, they took over the leadership at 10 p.m. We had to convert to the new 16 mm black-and-white film to compete.

"In 1953 we went to 100,000 watts, the maximum power allowed by the FCC. We built the tall tower in 1957, 17 miles southeast of San Antonio in Elmendorf. It is taller than the Empire State Building or the Eiffel

The station's black-and-white remote mobile unit was used for sports, church services and parades.

Live music was provided for local programming by musicians, from left, Spud Goodall, Tony Rozance and Curly Williams.

Tower and was the tallest man-made structure in the world at that time.

"Then in the late '50s, this station revolutionized television news in Texas. We developed the format of a half-hour with three different people presenting the news — one did news, one did weather and one did sports. Prior to that time, the news was presented usually by one newsman.

"We found out early on that news, information and public affairs were becoming, probably the most important functions of television. We were using film and were doing a better job on presenting the news as we entered our second decade.

"But it took us hours then to get a film story ready for the air. Today we're electronic in terms of our cameras, and we can do the story live on the scene or we can do it within five minutes fully edited. Today we have 52 people in our news department and are still growing. In the '50s, we had 12 people in our news staff.

"News is critical. It creates an image for the station. News is where we do our best in terms of programming in the public interest and in serving the community. News is where we have the most challenges. Since 68 percent of our programming comes from network, the news is a big part of the balance. News

has become the flagship program of television stations and will continue to be the centerpiece of local programming.

"Henry Guerra, Frank Matthews and Jim Metcalf were the early news anchors on our station. They were all journalists and they all came from radio. Back then there was no chitchat or happy talk.

"The first woman we ever had on camera doing news was Martha Buchanan, and she was the first female anchor in the State of Texas. This was in the mid-'60s. She did a 5 o'clock news show called 'Early Evening Report.' It was soft news, interviews, brief headlines and human interest stories. It was the first early news on San Antonio television. For years we were the only station with news at 5 o'clock.

And then we moved Martha to 6 o'clock and she became the first prime time female co-anchor newsperson in this part of the country.

"We were sold to AVCO Broadcasting of Cincinnati in 1965 and later sold to Twentieth Century Fox in 1975. In 1981 we became part of the United Television Broadcast Group.

"We developed the format of a half-hour with three different people presenting the news — one did news, one did weather and one did sports."

"Our commitment made some 35 years ago to broadcast in the public interest remains irrevocable and is the basis for our programming and our community involvement.

"A broadcaster's responsibility to the community is very clear, and the presentation of local news in an unbiased fashion is the No. 1 priority of this station.

"That has been the history of Channel 4, and this priority and community involvement touch all aspects of South Texas and San Antonio life."

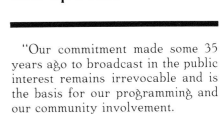

Martha Buchanan Lucero was San Antonio's first on-camera newswoman and the first female anchor in Texas.

McCOMBS ENTERPRISES

New car sales were the cornerstone of entrepreneur Red McCombs' multimillion dollar business empire which now ranges from commercial real estate to professional sports.

The colorful and community-spirited businessman described his rise from commission-only auto salesman 35 years ago to entrepreneur extraordinaire:

"New car sales was my first job out of college in 1950. I hadn't planned that because my father was an auto mechanic and my image of the automobile business was not something that I would have selected to go into. It meant long hours and hard work and not much pay.

"**B**ut when I got a job through the placement office at The University of Texas, I wanted a commission-type selling job because I felt that was the best way to receive compensation based on performance.

"So my first job actually was to have involved a company that manufactured cotton gin equipment. I had six weeks before that training class opened and I was going back to work on a drilling rig where I had worked during holidays and summers. A friend encouraged me to sell cars because it was easy, you didn't have to work very hard and they gave you a new car to drive. So my interest in the car business was with

the intention of being in it six weeks.

"Once I got into it, I found that there weren't too many steps from the bottom to the top. The average car salesman sells about 10 cars a month, and I set a goal to sell a car a day. For the three years I sold cars, I averaged 31½ cars a month.

"I married the most beautiful girl

Getting the feel of a new 1960 Thunderbird were, from left, Lynda, Connie, Charline and Marsha McCombs.

in Corpus Christi, Charline Hamblin, a few months after I started selling cars. She is — and always has been — my biggest supporter and loving partner. Our three daughters, Lynda, Marsha and Connie, were born in Corpus Christi but grew up in San Antonio. All my activities have involved Charline and 'the girls.'

"I don't think I worked any longer

hours than the others. I worked smarter. To me the use of time was and still is a very precious gift. Each day when I awaken, that's a gift. I like to see that when a day is over that I've made some good use of it.

"In 1953 I left that job and entered business for myself and formed Red McCombs Enterprises. I started the business with $7,500, the bulk of which came from equity that I had in a house, and $25,000 I had borrowed from a bank. The first business in that enterprise was a used car lot in

Corpus Christi. About a year later, I opened a second car lot. At the same time, I began on a partnership basis building GI homes and formed an insurance agency and a loan company, which I operated myself.

"In 1957 I made my first move into the franchised auto business when I became the youngest Edsel dealer in the United States. I operated that business for four months until it was obvious that although we had the most successful Edsel operation in Texas, the car was not going to be acceptable to the public.

"So I disposed of that business and in January of 1958 I came to San Antonio where I became a partner of Austin Hemphill in Hemphill-McCombs Ford. I became the sole owner in 1970 and continued my involvement in other businesses. First, we expanded the automotive business with operations in Houston and Dallas. And beginning in the early '60s, other businesses that came under the enterprise involved investments and operations, oil and

---

History at a Glance   1958

Founded: *1953 in Corpus Christi*
Moved to San Antonio: *1958*
Founder: *Red McCombs*
Original employees: *3*
Original investment: *$32,500*
Headquarters: *8333 Interstate 10 West*
Areas of interest: *Automobile sales, investments, commercial real estate, oil and gas, cattle ranching, broadcasting and professional sports*

This chapter was based on an interview with Red McCombs.

gas, real estate, broadcasting, banking and additional automotive dealerships.

"I've never had any one business that I favor over the others except possibly the automobile business.

"I have always felt that sports was a great common denominator. My first entry in the professional sports business was in 1953 when a former classmate of mine and I purchased the Corpus Christi Clippers, which was a professional minor league baseball team in the Big State League.

"My first involvement in professional sports in San Antonio involved a few professional prizefighters and some racing cars. But my interest in the Spurs was a little

---

"To me the use of time was and still is a very precious gift. Each day when I awaken, that's a gift. I like to see that when a day is over that I've made some good use of it."

---

different from that.

"When I was on the executive committee of HemisFair, we were trying to encourage industrial exhibitors to qualify for the Bureau of International Expositions. San Antonio was terribly hard to sell to these national corporations. There's a certain identity that comes through major league sports that cannot come any other way, and it goes far beyond the activity of the sport itself.

"I sold my interest in the San Antonio Spurs because there was a business opportunity in Denver where I would be the sole owner of a club, the Denver Nuggets.

"What measure of success I've had comes from some very basic areas. One, I'm a risk taker. Secondly, I have had such a tremendous amount of help and assistance from business

associates. I don't consider the people who are involved with me employees.

"I consider success to be the journey, not the destination. And I've had a lot of help from a lot of people. I have respect for everyone, but I don't have awe of anyone. And I think that has served me well.

"Maybe one of the keys is that I don't consider what I do as work. Another thing that probably would figure in what success we've had is not fearing failure. I had a failure, for example, with my Edsel business.

"But in a way, I am a quitter because I like to get into something and give it my best shot. And if it doesn't work, then I want to push that one over to the side and out of mind and go to something else.

"My ranching interest involves a registered seed stock business. I come from two bases. I have a registered Texas longhorn operation and then I am a partner in Brinks Brangus, one of the noted Brangus operations in the country.

"In the longhorn business, I put the syndication together on the first $1 million bull in the longhorn breed. There had never been a bull in the breed that had even been sold for as much as $100,000. In the Brinks Brangus business, our January bull sale for four years in a

row has grown from more than $1 million in sales to an excess of $4 million. To give you a benchmark, there's not a registered bull sale in any breed that has ever done $1 million.

"Primarily, we're dealing in genetics. We've extensively used embryo transfer methods. That has been the basis of both of those breeding programs.

"As to what I'm the proudest of in my career, I came to San Antonio in 1958 because of a recession in the automobile business. So it was very exciting to me to come into this company as a partner, take a business that was suffering, within a matter of months turn it into a profitable operation, and then build it to where over the next 15 years or so it was one of the most outstanding Ford facilities in the country. The pleasure of doing that was a thrilling and outstanding feeling for me and very satisfying.

"Just as exciting was going to Philadelphia with Charline and the girls for the San Antonio Spurs' first game in the NBA, which we won 121-to-118, which I will never forget. Those instances stand out as being very memorable, but they were yesterday. What I am most excited about is today." ⬛

Of all his endeavors, Red McCombs favors the automobile business.

PEAT, MARWICK, MITCHELL & CO.

With more than 300 offices worldwide and gross fees of approximately $1.5 billion annually, Peat, Marwick, Mitchell & Co. is one of the largest certified public accounting firms in the world.

It provides a broad range of auditing and consulting services to such prestigious clients as Xerox Corporation, General Electric Company, Twentieth Century Fox Film Corporation and Lloyds Bank, Ltd.

The local office of Peat Marwick also is impressive. Formed in 1958, it was the second of the "Big Eight" national accounting firms to enter the San Antonio market. It continues as one of the dominant accounting firms in the Alamo City and boasts an impressive list of local clients and a reputation for high standards.

Paul W. Reddy, managing partner of the local office since 1978, explained how the international firm started, its merger with a San Antonio firm and consequent growth, and the range of services it offers to keep it in the forefront of public accounting:

"Peat Marwick began in 1897 with the partnership of Marwick, Mitchell & Co. of New York City when S. Roger Mitchell and Sir James Marwick joined forces," Reddy said. "Sir William Peat, founder and senior partner of W.B. Peat & Co. in England, and Sir James Marwick met on a boat while both were crisscrossing the Atlantic to service clients internationally. They decided it would be better to join together and this was accomplished on October 1, 1911.

"Accounting firms were just beginning at that time," he continued. "For many of the early years, the English practice of Peat Marwick developed areas of the world where there was significant English influence, and the United States practice developed the remainder of the free world. As the firm grew and U.S. influence increased around the world, this pattern of development changed and resulted in the formation of Peat Marwick International, the organization we have today that directs our worldwide operations.

"One prestigious client in England is the Queen's Privy, for which our firm is the auditor. In England most people refer to us as Peat's. The firm there is very old; its offices used to be on Ironmonger Lane, which had pieces of a tile floor in its basement from a Roman house built in 200 A.D. On the same site were found 14th century relics from the residence of Prince Edward, the Black Prince. Now, however, the firm is in a new building in the financial district beside the Thames River," Reddy said.

One relative of the founders is still in the United Kingdom practice. Sir Gerald Peat is a partner in the London office of Peat Marwick. Nepotism policies now prohibit relatives from joining the firm.

In the 1950s and 1960s, Peat Marwick merged with numerous local CPA firms to build its size and structure to be able to service a wide variety of clients.

"One of the mergers that was particularly beneficial to the firm was with Barrow, Wade, Guthrie & Co. in 1950. That firm is acknowledged to have been the first accounting firm organized in the United States. Its founding date was 1883.

"Peat Marwick began operations in San Antonio on July 1, 1958, with the merger of a prestigious local firm, Eaton & Huddle. The roots of Eaton & Huddle dated to 1942 when Marquis G. Eaton and Thornton C. Huddle joined forces as oil and gas tax specialists serving San Antonio," Reddy explained.

The 1958 merger resulted in four new partners for Peat Marwick who would someday assume leadership positions with the firm. New Peat

---

History at a Glance   1958

Founded: *1897 in New York City*
Opened in San Antonio: *July 1, 1958*
Founders: *S. Roger Mitchell and James Marwick*
Original San Antonio employees: *30*
Lineage of local managing partners: *Thomas L. Holton, John K. Kramer, Russell H. Kyse, James E. Windlinger, Paul W. Reddy*
Headquarters: *NBC Building*
San Antonio partners: *Paul W. Reddy, managing partner; George F. Golder, PIC-audit; Joseph D. Crawford, Jr., PIC-tax; William C. Nussbaum, PIC-PBAS; Philip W. Barnes, PIC-management consulting; Walter E. Belt III, Michael T. McClellan, John C. O'Rourke, Park E. Pearson and Bill K. Wisecarver, audit; Ronald R. Bryant and S. Fred Bartz, tax*
Local employees: *120*
Motto: *Service to the client that is timely and has value*

This chapter was based on an interview with Paul W. Reddy.

Paul W. Reddy is managing partner of the San Antonio office.

Marwick partners were Thomas L. Holton, John F. Kramer, Russell H. Kyse and Neal Y.R. Sheffield. Thornton C. Huddle retired. Eaton, who had been president of the American Institute of Certified Public Accountants in 1957, died five months before

"From inception, the office has had high standards for professional excellence."

the merger.

"From inception, the office has had high standards for professional excellence, which is proved by the number of San Antonio alumni who have served and are presently serving as partners in other offices," Reddy said.

Holton, past senior partner and chairman of Peat Marwick-U.S., currently serves as chairman of Peat Marwick International. Kramer retired as managing partner of Atlanta, Kyse retired as managing partner in San Antonio and Sheffield retired as partner-in-charge-tax of San Antonio.

Also, James E. Windlinger is managing partner of Denver. Walter P. Schuetze is a partner with the Department of Professional Practice-Executive in New York. Gerald R. Heep is managing partner of Shreveport and Albert H. Coldewey is managing partner of Amarillo-Lubbock. Gregory B. Tomlinson is partner-in-charge-audit of Midland, Robert D. Whitlow is an audit partner in Indianapolis, John G. Louden is a tax partner in Midland and Tim E. Bentsen is an audit partner in Los Angeles. All of these partners served major portions of their careers in the San Antonio office.

Some of the firm's local major clients include Datapoint Corporation; USAA; La Quinta Motor Inns, Inc.; National Bancshares; and Church's Fried Chicken, Inc.

The firm started in the Alamo National Bank Building and moved to the National Bank of Commerce Building in 1962.

Today the San Antonio office occupies 2½ floors of the downtown bank building. The Audit Department is on the ninth floor, the Tax Department fills the 10th floor, and Private Business Advisory Services and Management Consulting share one-half of the 11th floor.

"We have a policy in our firm to be located in the financial center of the city. Our firm serves all of San Antonio. Most of our auditing is done at the client's office, so our employees are out of the office a great deal. We're in a much better position if we're working from the hub of the city," Reddy said.

Competition for clients has changed significantly. "It changed several years ago when the federal government sued the AICPA for antitrust.

Ethics were rewritten to allow advertising and competitive bidding. But actually, a firm develops successfully because it has satisfied clients who recommend it to new clients."

Services offered by the firm's local office are extensive.

The office's Audit Department provides services that include Securities and Exchange Commission filings, litigation support, acquisition audits and special purpose examinations in addition to the usual annual audit.

The Tax Department provides complete tax services for both corporate and individual clients, which include tax planning, estate planning and representation before the Internal Revenue Service in addition to the usual preparation of federal income tax returns.

The Private Business Advisory Services Department offers both audit and tax services to the small to medium-size, closely held business. In addition, this department assists clients with business planning and strategy, budgeting and obtaining financing.

The Management Consulting Department provides services that primarily center around electronic data processing and accounting systems. In addition, services such as employee benefits consulting, executive compensation, actuarial consulting, strategy and organizational planning and executive search are offered through the Dallas and Houston offices of the firm.

As to what lies ahead, Reddy predicts "continued growth." ∎

LYDA, INC.

Only five years into his own construction business, Gerald Lyda, Sr., took on one of the most ambitious — and most politically visible — jobs in San Antonio history: the Tower of the Americas.

The University of Texas' Memorial Stadium upper deck was the most challenging project in Lyda's history.

Today the company is listed among the top 400 contractors in the country, according to the prestigious Engineering News Record construction magazine.

The San Antonio-based firm with more than 400 employees made its first major mark in the commercial construction field before HemisFair in 1968 with the erection of the Tower. Now the company has an annual volume of business in the multimillions.

Lyda, founder and president, recalled his early days in construction and the pitfalls his company overcame in such challenging projects as the Tower and Memorial Stadium at The University of Texas:

"I've been in this type of business since I was 18. I started out carrying lumber and digging ditches, and I have had lots of opportunities come my way. After working for other people for 20 years, I'd learned how the machine worked. I couldn't see any point in working for somebody else if I understood contracting well enough to do my own. So I organized Lyda, Inc., started doing small jobs and gradually built up.

"The Tower of the Americas and the Convention Center were my first major jobs. They were the largest in San Antonio at that time. Our company first became interested in the Convention Center, which was three large buildings. The project's architect, Tom Noonan, requested I bid the job since I had supervised the construction of a number of the larger projects in the San Antonio area for others.

"I'd been in business about five years. My first job was for $9,000, and this was up in the millions. I hadn't intended to go into a job that size that quickly. But with the encouragement I had received and not wanting to destroy the confidence shown in me by a former partner, Steinmetz Darragh, who had died, and along with ambition, I decided to make a run at it.

"To bond this $10 million to $12 million job, I went to an old friend, Alvin Lott, whom I had worked under with one of the nation's largest contractors and who had a lot of confidence in me. He probably taught me more than anybody else. He had become successful; his first major job was the Astrodome in Houston. We went 50-50 on the Convention Center job, and did all the construction and a large part of the worrying with Lyda, Inc. personnel.

"When the Tower of the Americas, designed by architects Ford, Powell & Carson, came along, we were the lowest bidder. Of course, politics got into the project and delayed things until it was almost too late to go ahead, but we told City Manager Jack Shelly and the HemisFair planners if they'd remove the penalty clause, which was $1,000 a day, we'd do the job. They did and we did."

Lyda explained how the San Antonio landmark was constructed.

"It took one year to build. The foundation went 65 feet in the ground with 55 big piers. We cut large bells on the bottom of each pier and installed a couple of thousand tons of reinforcing steel in those shafts. Then we poured concrete up to ground level and put a big cap on those 55 piers and made a uniform, one-piece pad underneath the tower.

"We slip-formed the concrete core,

History at a Glance   1960

Founded: *1960*

Founders: *Gerald Lyda, Sr., Steinmetz Darragh*

Original name: *Darragh & Lyda*

Original location: *6224 Bandera Road*

Original investment: *$11,000, experience, ability and good reputation*

Original employees: *3*

Milestones: **1961** *incorporated;* **1964** *first $1 million job, Biosystems Lab, Aviation School of Medicine, Brooks Air Force Base;* **1968** *built Convention Center Hall, Performing Arts Theater, Sports Arena, Tower of the Americas, river extension and parking garage for HemisFair '68;* **1969** *name changed to Lyda, Inc.;* **1975** *ranked among 400 leading construction companies for the first time, according to Engineering News Record;* **1981, 1984** *Gerald Lyda, Sr., served as president of San Antonio Chapter of Associated General Contractors of America*

Officers: *Gerald Lyda, Sr., president; J.C. Renfrow, executive vice president; Bobbie Lyda, secretary/treasurer; James Lyda, vice president; H.O. Ritchie, vice president*

Headquarters: *6228 Bandera Road*

Owners: *Gerald Lyda, Sr.; James M. Lyda; Bobbie Lyda; J.C. Renfrow; A.V. Polansky, H.O. Ritchie; Jack Janicke, Jr.; Floyd Braune*

Employees: *350*

Assets: *More than $12 million*

Motto: *Integrity, quality and speedy production*

This chapter was based on an interview with Gerald Lyda, Sr.

starting from the ground with a four-foot-high concrete form made of wood and stainless steel. As we lifted this steel-lined form upward, we placed concrete in it slowly and slipped it all the way to the top, 628 feet high. We had chemicals to retard or accelerate the setting of the concrete. Lifting was accomplished with hydraulic jacks climbing on jack rods which projected from the concrete as we placed it.

"It was a unit-type operation that virtually went from top to bottom. After we got the concrete core slipped to the top, we constructed the structural steel frame that makes the frame of the house. We constructed it around the core, connected hydraulic jack rods to the frame, which weighed 650 tons, constructed the rough floors for the steel deck and raised the frame for the top house as well as the restaurant equipment by hydraulic jacks."

Hurricane Carla interrupted the progress.

"Those high winds crystalized the rods. We had three rods break one time and four rods another time, but the building was close enough to the ground to be salvaged. We had bought safety rods with twice the capacity recommended for safety.

"So there we were with 650 tons hanging on it. I couldn't have stayed in San Antonio if I had let it drop. We got oil well drill stems, which were made of the toughest material I could think of. We threw away the engineered rods and put drill stems on it. We went up to the top and keyed it off with big steel keys.

"The most chilling incident during the building of the Tower concerned my brother, James, a dedicated Lyda, Inc. man. During those winds of 80 miles an hour, I called the Tower to tell them to get down if the storm got any worse. James said, 'We can hardly talk on this phone because I've got a rope tied around me letting a man down over the side to tie those broken rods off.' Earlier in the job, we had the rods hanging underneath the slip-form table. Somebody had to go down and cut all the rods loose. We found people short on nerve for that. My brother tied a rope around his feet and they put him upside down through a hole

in the work deck with a cutting torch in his hand. He cut those rods loose and it was 600-plus feet to the ground.

"When I think of all the courage and dedication the people put into it, naturally, I feel proud of the Tower. The Tower, along with HemisFair, was the turning point of San Antonio becoming a city rather than a big country town," Lyda said.

"We accepted the challenge and accomplished what we set out to do."

The Tower was the most unusual job for Lyda, Inc., but not the most difficult.

"The University of Texas football stadium was our most challenging," Lyda explained. "We built the upper deck and the physical education center. It's an enormous structure of architectural concrete. The configurations and the design made it ultra-difficult. Architects design something like that and they don't worry about how you're going to build it. They can design you almost out of business sometimes and that was one of those cases, except we did make money.

"We accepted the challenge and accomplished what we set out to do. Some of our competitors told me if we could do that job, there wouldn't be anything else we needed to turn back on.

"From a monetary standpoint, Fort Hood was our biggest job, about $22 or $23 million. We built a complex of 40 or more military buildings."

Other projects of Lyda, Inc. include GPM Office Towers, the Greater San Antonio Chamber of Commerce Building, Lincoln Center, Forum Office, Riverbend Parking Garage, Air Force Village, San Antonio State Hospital, Mercantile Bank Building, North Frost Building, Gill Plaza, Alamo Savings Association Towers I and II and Uranga Towers.

Lyda summed up the secret of his success:

"If you know what you're doing and can give a service to an owner, architect or developer and can turn out quality work within a time frame at a price that's within his budget and he doesn't have to worry about your integrity, everything works out fine.

"I have no college education. I took the long road. I really think I may have gotten a better education than a lot of people who went to school.

"Every one of our jobs was a joy, and most all of them were profitable. Knowing your work well and being honest are important factors of success." [LI]

Gerald Lyda, Sr., stands before his most famous project, the Tower of the Americas.

TRAMMELL CROW COMPANY

Trammell Crow Company is the largest privately held real estate development company in the United States, and its program locally makes it one of the largest commercial real estate developers in San Antonio.

The company owns, leases and manages more than 3 million square feet of space in San Antonio composed of office, retail, office showroom, office service center and distribution properties.

"Trammell Crow came to San Antonio and built his first warehouse here in the early 1960s on Kraft Street, and he still owns it," explained Mike Birnbaum, regional partner in San Antonio.

With major projects in office buildings, both downtown high rise and suburban; retail development such as shopping centers and restaurants; and industrial developments which include office/showroom, service center, distribution and warehouse space; Trammell Crow Company has grown to become a significant factor in real estate development in San Antonio.

One of the central controlling philosophies of the company is long-term ownership and appreciation.

"We build not to sell, but to keep," Birnbaum explained. "Our customer is the tenant. I would distinguish that from developments which are built to sell. Generally, if you are building to keep, you build differently from the way you would if you were building to sell. Our ultimate customer is not a buyer for the development, but the tenant."

Central to the success of the Trammell Crow Company is that it is market driven. Commitment to being knowledgeable about its properties and the market in general is part of the ongoing process of being market responsive and sensitive to its customers.

The Trammell Crow Company has perpetuated its national reputation for excellence in San Antonio with several noteworthy projects. The 28-story InterFirst Plaza completed in 1983 was designed by the nationally renowned architectural firm of Skidmore, Owings & Merrill. Its design includes three skyward vaulted forms at staggered heights which are reminiscent of Gothic-style towers.

"InterFirst Plaza is the result of a great effort to blend what was San Antonio's past to its present and future," explained Birnbaum. "It is a significant contribution to downtown San Antonio, a downtown that has a great future."

The company set the standard for suburban development in San Antonio with the construction of The Colonnade, a mixed-use complex on a 66-acre site along the rapidly growing Interstate 10 corridor. At this point, The Colonnade features mid- and high-rise office buildings offering more than 300,000 square feet, along with restaurants, fashion retail stores, an athletic club, and the 19-story luxury Wyndham Hotel. "Colonnade," the dramatic sculpture by noted San Antonio artist Richard Harrell Rogers, is the focal point of the project. Approximately 30 acres

History at a Glance   1960

Founded: *1948 in Dallas*
Opened in San Antonio: *1960*
Founder: *Trammell Crow*
Headquarters: *InterFirst Plaza*
Regional partner: *Mike Birnbaum*
San Antonio employees: *57*
Units: *18 projects including 3 million square feet of space*

This chapter was based on an interview with Mike Birnbaum.

enhance the environment for tenants and visitors. Its proximity and access to Interstate 10, the complete range of amenities, and the aesthetics produced by a well thought out master plan, attractively designed buildings, dramatic public art and complementary landscaping combine to make The Colonnade a prestigious business address.

The company also has recently completed Phase I of Interpark, a mixed-use business park in north central San Antonio on McAllister Freeway four minutes from the San Antonio International Airport and 12 minutes from downtown.

"We believe it is the nicest business park in the city," stated Birnbaum.

Phase I of Interpark is composed of 12 buildings featuring 60,000 square feet of offices and showrooms, 60,000 square feet of office/service center space and 150,000 square feet of office/distribution facilities. Future phases of the Interpark development will include additional retail, garden office facilities and restaurants.

The Trammell Crow Company is a series of partnerships, and the partner in each city or each area is responsible for creating development opportunities. The development decisions, beginning with site selection and continuing through design, marketing, financing and property management, are made by the partners in their respective cities. Their active involvement in the communities in which they build enables the partners to keep their fingers on the pulse of the local real estate market.

The company hires entry level positions primarily from the major M.B.A. programs or law schools across the country. They enter the company as leasing agents and learn the development business by leasing and responding to the space needs of the tenants.

Trammell Crow once wrote, "I began my career in real estate almost by accident more than 35 years ago. My idea and my motives were simple: to provide space to growing businesses."

In San Antonio, Birnbaum has succeeded in developing projects throughout the Alamo City that are reflective of Trammell Crow Company's central philosophy: to provide the highest quality of space and service to its customers. ⬛

of The Colonnade project remain available for future office and retail development.

The Colonnade was designed to provide the many amenities that make an office building, retail and hotel environment more functional, attractive, productive and enjoyable. Master-planned, The Colonnade offers a complete business environment with essential services such as banking, shopping, restaurants, emergency health facilities, an athletic club and entertainment facilities.

This tradition and commitment to quality development ensure each addition to The Colonnade will

The National Bank of Commerce Building is one of 18 Trammell Crow Company projects in San Antonio.

HARTE-HANKS COMMUNICATIONS, INC.

Harte-Hanks Communications, Inc. is in the information and entertainment business with interests ranging from satellites to weekly shoppers.

For Harte-Hanks, that translates to many related media including daily and weekly newspapers, television stations, cable systems, direct mail, advertising operations, advertising shoppers, trade publications, city magazines, marketing research firms, and other marketing support and computer data base firms.

Bob Marbut, president and chief executive officer of the multi-dimensional business, explained the company's scope: "We have 115 different operating divisions that are part of 80 subsidiaries of the company. Those divisions are headquartered in 28 states and employ more than 10,000 people."

While the company's interests today are complex, its beginnings were much simpler.

Marbut recounted the company's early days:

"After Houston Harte moved from

The Abilene Reporter-News, shown here in the 1930s, was Bernard Hanks' contribution when the company was formed.

Missouri to California and other places, he moved to San Angelo in 1920 and bought the San Angelo Standard and later the Times. He was twenty-seven years old. Shortly thereafter, he met the owner and publisher of the Abilene Reporter-News,

Bernard Hanks. By the mid-'20s, they were pretty chummy and decided to buy other newspapers, all in Texas.

"They only bought newspapers in Texas because Mr. Harte said there wasn't anything worth buying on the other side of the Red River. He stuck to that.

"After the company was founded with two newspapers, it began to expand. They set out to buy either all or a minority interest in a number of newspapers, some of which they later sold. Later the company purchased the rest of the stock of the newspapers, as we did in Wichita Falls.

"By 1970 Harte-Hanks had accumulated the largest circulation collectively of any newspaper ownership in Texas. One of the major acquisitions was the San Antonio Express-News in 1962. It was the flagship of the company because it

History at a Glance   1962

Founded: *Mid-1920s in San Angelo and Abilene*
Moved to San Antonio: *1962*
Founders: *Houston H. Harte and Bernard Hanks*
Original name: *Harte-Hanks Newspapers*
Milestones: *1962 bought Express-News and KENS-TV; 1972 went public; 1973 sold Express-News, listed on New York Stock Exchange; 1983 became Fortune 500 company; 1984 went private; 1971 to 1984 made more than 75 acquisitions of different media; 1985 more than $550 million in sales with more than $100 million operating profit*
Headquarters: *40 N.E. Loop 410*
Principal owners: *Houston H. Harte, Edward H. Harte, A.B. Shelton, Bob Marbut, Larry D. Franklin*
Officers: *Houston H. Harte, chairman; Bob Marbut, president and chief executive officer; Larry D. Franklin, executive vice president and chief operating officer*
Employees: *10,000*
Divisions: *115 in 28 states*

This chapter was based on an interview with Bob Marbut.

Houston H. Harte

Bernard Hanks

involved two newspapers plus a television station.

"In the process of expansion, Harte and Hanks also got into radio for a while, but they divested of all their radio stations before 1970. In 1978 we re-entered the radio business for six years.

"The corporate office at that time was very small, just two or three people. They moved it from Abilene to San Antonio in the late '60s, and that's where it has been ever since. We sold the Express-News to Rupert Murdoch in 1973.

"Bernard Hanks was more on the financial, business and advertising side. He died in 1946.

"Houston Harte was a journalism graduate of UCLA. He was keenly interested in the editorial side and politics and was a legend in his own time in Texas. He had a very close relationship, for example, with Lyndon Johnson that started before Johnson went to the Senate.

"Somebody in his office one afternoon asked him how he thought the president felt about something and

Mr. Harte said, 'I don't know. Let's find out.' He picked up the phone and got LBJ on the line just like that.

"He went around to the newspapers in his earlier days and he would roll his sleeves up and work. He spent a lot of time in his own newsroom in San Angelo. He was a very strong-willed person whose mark was all over this company. No question about it. He was the only president the company had until I became president and chief executive officer in 1971. Mr. Harte was president for nearly 50 years.

"The influence of Mr. Harte and Mr. Hanks is very much a part of our culture today. One legacy is that each operation is a unique entity serving a unique market and, therefore, should have maximum operating autonomy. Secondly, each of our operations is an important institution in the community in which it operates. Therefore, it has a special responsibility — particularly if you're the only newspaper in town — to take a leadership role in that community. That translates to being responsibly active editorially in the case of our newspapers; it translates to being behind things that help the community to grow for all our divisions.

"A third piece of that legacy was the great importance of the operating division as a unique, separate company building block. We now have 115 of them. That's where the

Delivering the news is the KENS-TV Eyewitness News team, from left, Dan Cook, Chris Marrou and Albert Flores.

action is, and we try to get leverage at that point instead of trying to run things from San Antonio.

"They worked hard and created an environment of responsible local newspapers. There wasn't much corporate control or overhead in the early days. In fact, about the only things in the corporate office were an accounting department and an audit function, and they also bought newsprint centrally. All the rest was up to the local publishers.

"Houston Harte went around to the newspapers in his earlier days and he would roll his sleeves up and work."

"The uniqueness of each market and newspaper translates to a hands-off editorial policy. Each local newspaper should take its own position. We don't care what position they take; we just want them to be relevant to their marketplace, to speak a language the people there understand and to be perceived to be fair and credible.

"An example is when Houston H. Harte, the son, was publisher of the Express-News and his older brother, Ed Harte, was publisher in Corpus Christi. In the U.S. Senate race, Houston supported George Bush and Ed supported Lloyd Bentsen

Pressman in the 1950s worked with hot type at the Abilene Reporter-News.

editorially and financially. That made the point to everybody that it is up to the publishers to do their own thing.

"Another key player was Bruce

Today's Harte-Hanks leaders are Larry D. Franklin, left, and Bob Marbut.

Meador, who still lives in San Antonio. He joined the company in the mid-'40s as an auditor. When Mr. Hanks died, Bruce became managing trustee of the Hanks estate. He was the right hand of Houston Harte, and as Mr. Harte got older, Bruce's responsibilities grew. He was the traveling auditor among other things, so he was the one person from the corporate office who got into all the plants. As a result, he knew more about what was going on than anybody else in the company.

"Those were the days before many scheduled airline flights. So he would drive Mr. Harte around to visit the newspapers and make acquisitions. Bruce was the company's general manager by 1970. He was the one who was the real business conscience; he was the glue that held the company together.

"It was at that time the decision was made to go public. They had about 55 shareholders, publishers to whom they'd given a piece of the action, members of the Harte and Hanks families and Bruce Meador. It was desirable because some of these folks needed liquidity. So the decision was made to go public in mid-1970, and I came on board in 1970 to help take it public. We had the offering in early 1972 and were public for 12½ years.

"It's unusual to go the other way — from public to private — which we

did in 1984. But this was even more unusual because it was the same Harte and Hanks families represented by Ed Harte, Houston Harte and Stormy Shelton who were key shareholders, along with Larry Franklin and me, in going private again.

"There were several primary reasons. The most important was the recognition that what we wanted to do strategically could best be done in a private mode. For example, we were investing in cable television in a big way, and we had options to become a much larger and a very substantial cable operator almost overnight, but we needed financial flexibility.

"We had had 50 consecutive quarters of earnings growth while we were public. Only a handful of companies on the New York Stock Exchange have gone 12½ straight years with such consistent earnings growth and compounding at 17 percent.

"Despite this growth record, the stock market price did not reflect the real value of our company, or virtually any other communications company for that matter. Going private made it possible for all investors to realize a fairer value for their investment.

"Also, the disparity between the company's value as determined by the stock market and its real value would have eventually made Harte-Hanks vulnerable to unwanted takeover attempts."

San Antonio is the location of several Harte-Hanks units in addition to its corporate headquarters. This includes the group office for all Harte-Hanks Cable operations, San Antonio Monthly magazine and a division of Harte-Hanks Direct Marketing.

But the most visible Harte-Hanks operation in San Antonio is, of course, KENS-TV, which enjoys top market popularity and a new state-of-the-art facility at 5400 Fredericksburg Road.

"KENS-TV was not No. 1 in the market in the early days," Marbut said. "Some very special efforts

---

"For the last decade and a half, KENS has been the No. 1 station in this market in terms of market share, revenues and profits."

---

were made by two people in particular, Wayne Kearl, who was manager, and Bill Moll, who succeeded him. And now Linda Rios Brook is carrying on that tradition. She is surrounded by very talented people, and it is a very special station.

"Few people realize how special it is. For example, it consistently has been among the top five CBS affiliates out of more than 200 in the United States in terms of its acceptance. For the last decade and a half, KENS has been the No. 1 station in this market in terms of market share, revenues and profits.

"For two years now, our 10 o'clock news has been the No. 1 late news broadcast in the United States, all stations, all markets. We're very proud that it's in our headquarters town. That's also why we invested so much in the new KENS facility — to give it state-of-the-art capability and flexibility and expansion capability down the road. We probably had one of the worst facilities in the country — in the old garage of the Express-News building — and now

we certainly have one of the three or four best.

"The most important elements of KENS' success have been the management and people. For example, Bob Rogers, who has been news director for many years, deserves significant credit for building such a stable, No. 1 newscast.

"Some years ago, San Antonio had the TV news reputation, perhaps more than any other large city in the country, of having nothing but ambulance chasers. I think tastes in this market have changed. Enough people have said they wanted more information about what's going on, not just about who's getting killed in the bars or up and down the freeways. We ended up with a market willing to accept a more quality newscast.

"KENS is not a Chamber of Commerce kind of station, not totally a community cheerleader. KENS tries to be a responsible, objective broadcaster reflecting what this community really is. The fact that more people watch it day in and day out than any of the others demonstrates its audience perception and the station's credibility.

"In the new facility, we have a two-way satellite dish, which is unusual because we can originate broadcasts in San Antonio and uplink them throughout the country.

"For example, we use the uplink to provide a network for CBS for state news for five states, which still is an experimental process. We also provide local news inserts during the day to Cable News Network, and we are prepared to do other things such as weather in the future. This is the kind of programming you can do with a quality news operation and a quality facility.

"We also have KENS II, which is just like a separate television station using the talents, facilities and resources we have. It is unique in the country still. We have a library of nearly 1,500 films available to KENS II. We show Eyewitness News every two hours so people can get local news when they want it.

"Harte-Hanks always has and always will try to be responsive to what we see in the markets we serve. We define our business very specifically in terms of the needs we're trying to meet rather than the products

we're trying to produce. We're in the business of meeting people's needs for information and entertainment, which says that as the needs of the marketplace change so must we to stay in the mainstream.

"Part of our strategy was not to have all our eggs in one economic basket, namely Texas, and the other part of that strategy was not to have all of our eggs in one line of business, namely newspapers. So the combination of both geographic and line-of-business diversification gave us balance, like a gyroscope. When newspapers were having their troubles, television seemed to make up the difference and so on.

"We now have three core businesses: newspapers, television and shoppers. Those constitute the biggest piece of our revenue and profit bases. We have linked to those core businesses about 30 other businesses

The newsroom of the San Angelo Standard-Times, Houston Harte's first paper, buzzed with activity as reporters pounded out stories in 1952.

that are information or entertainment-related. Our strategy is to operate the core businesses effectively and to find other businesses that can, when linked, provide a unique kind of competitive advantage for us. We will stay close to the consumer.

"This strategy has resulted in making Harte-Hanks an integrated, but diversified nationwide communications company. We believe this positions us well for another 60 years of success." ⬛

TESORO PETROLEUM CORPORATION

Six million dollars in borrowed money, two decades of risk-taking, continued faith in an idea and years of hard work are the ingredients that mixed to form San Antonio-based Tesoro Petroleum Corporation.

Today the diversified petroleum company has a $3-billion-a-year level of gross revenues, approximately $1 billion in total assets and $435 million in shareholder equity.

The dynamic force behind Tesoro, Dr. Robert V. West, Jr., founder, chairman of the board and chief executive officer, explained his corporation's historic growth:

"My background was growing up with the petroleum industry in Tulsa, Oklahoma, which was then the center of oil in the country," West recalled. "The whole city of Tulsa woke up in the morning and went to sleep at night thinking oil and gas. So I had oil and gas in my veins when I enrolled at The University of Texas at Austin."

Armed with a master's degree in chemical engineering in 1943, West went to work for what today is Exxon Company U.S.A. in its Baytown refinery. But the energetic young man could not flourish in the confines of the regimented atmosphere and returned to UT-Austin to get a doctorate in chemical engineering and a minor in petroleum engineering.

Courted by major companies, West opted instead to work for the Slick-Urschel Oil Company in Midland, which had formed a "new, little independent oil company with two rather interesting gas condensate discoveries."

"I convinced Tom Slick he needed some bright, young engineer, which I thought I was, to work for him in West Texas. My professors thought I had prostituted my Ph.D. and should have gone back to some big company."

The subsequent relationship with the legendary oil family of San Antonio ultimately led to the establishment of Tesoro. By the late 1950s, West held high positions in Slick companies. When Slick died in 1962, West decided to buy out Slick's Tex-

---

History at a Glance   1964

Founded: *Dec. 16, 1964*
Founder: *Dr. Robert V. West, Jr.*
Original name: *Tesoro Petroleum Corporation*
Original employees: *125 including 30 in San Antonio*
Original investment: *$1,000 capital and $6.5 million borrowed*
Milestones: 1964 *purchased Texstar Petroleum Corporation stock;* **1968** *merged with Intex Oil Company and Sioux Oil Company;* **1969** *formed Trinidad-Tesoro Petroleum Company Limited and constructed new refinery in Kenai, Alaska;* **1974** *stock traded on New York Stock Exchange*
Lineage of presidents: *Dr. Robert V. West, Jr.; James C. Phelps; Dennis F. Juren*
Headquarters: *8700 Tesoro Drive*
Principal offices, subsidiaries and affiliates: *Tesoro Alaska Petroleum Company; Tesoro Bolivia Petroleum Company; Tesoro Crude Oil Company; Tesoro Drilling Company; Tesoro Gasoline Marketing Company; Tesoro Indonesia Petroleum Company; Land & Marine Rental Company; Tesoro Natural Gas Company; Tesoro Petroleum Distributing Company; Tesoro Pipeline Company; Tesoro Refining, Marketing and Supply Company; Tesoro Tank Lines Company; Tesoro Trading Company; Tesoro United Kingdom Company; Trinidad-Tesoro Petroleum Company Limited*
Owners: *13.7 million shares of common stock held by 9,000 stockholders; 5 million equivalent common shares of preferred stock held by 2,300 stockholders*
Employees: *2,970 including 1,720 in U.S.*
Units: *84 service stations in Alaska, 53 service stations elsewhere, 27 land and marine rental yards-stores*

This chapter was based on an interview with Dr. Robert V. West, Jr.

Dr. Robert V. West, Jr., left, visited an early Tesoro employee, Jeff Prater, at the Lopez Field in South Texas during the company's young days.

star Petroleum Company.

"It was not a large transaction by today's concepts — between $6 and $7 million — but my financial resources were almost zero," West said.

With endless perseverance and months of traveling from coast to coast, West finally secured enough financing to permit Tesoro Petroleum Corporation to exercise its option to buy Texstar stock in an eleventh-hour transaction.

For the name of the new company, West drew inspiration from Zapata Petroleum Corporation co-founded by Vice President George Bush and Hugh Liedtke, chairman of Pennzoil Co.

"I wanted a name like theirs that was symbolic of this region and had a ring to it. Tesoro means 'treasure' in Spanish and I came up with it by looking through a Spanish/English dictionary."

At the outset, Tesoro was poorly capitalized, a condition that became increasingly apparent during its first four years.

"When I started Tesoro, I couldn't read a balance sheet."

"Tesoro could not service its debt, pay its preferred dividends and still accumulate cash for reinvestment," West explained. "When I started Tesoro, I couldn't read a balance sheet. I'd buy paperbacks in airports and read about business law, accounting and finance on airplanes as I traveled around the country trying to raise money."

Tesoro was in debt to the Continental Illinois National Bank and Trust Company of Chicago, and the only viable means of repaying it was to make the company a public corporation.

"At the outset, my goal was to take the company public because that was the only way I could have access to significant outside capital sources."

But he was met with cold shoulders.

"I was perceived as a junior

Ground-breaking ceremonies were held in 1984 for the $90 million expansion of Tesoro's Kenai, Alaska, refinery. Dr. Robert V. West, Jr., left, was joined by Alaska Gov. Bill Sheffield, center, and Tesoro President Dennis F. Juren.

engineer from South Texas knocking on doors on Wall Street," he said. "Potential investors were dubious to the point they suggested they didn't think the company was ever going to make it."

At this point, West realized the best way to achieve his goal was to acquire control of a small publicly owned company and merge it with Tesoro.

"I spent nights at home in bed going through books trying to analyze what companies had in the way of assets and liabilities and whether their stock could be jarred loose."

West found two possibilities: Intex Oil Company in Bakersfield, California, listed on the American Stock Exchange, and Sioux Oil Company headquartered in Newcastle, Wyoming, traded over the counter.

E.F. Hutton & Company, Inc. went with West to the Chicago bank and helped convince its officers "their best bet of getting paid back was to loan me more so that I could acquire control of a public company. After repeated trips, they agreed."

The California company fought the takeover, but lost. Miraculously, the elderly heads of the Wyoming company asked to join the merger.

Simultaneously on February 1, 1969, Intex and Sioux merged with Tesoro. As a result of a public debenture offering a few months later, the Tesoro debt was wiped out, and West found himself with $19 million cash and a good cash flow.

"All of a sudden, we were rolling in money," he remembered.

Almost immediately after the merger in 1969, good fortune again shined on Tesoro, this time in the Caribbean tropics and the sub-arctic region of Alaska.

British Petroleum Company wanted to sell its oil and gas producing properties in Trinidad. Trinidad-Tesoro Petroleum Company Limited was formed with the government of Trinidad and Tobago.

Almost concurrently, Tesoro committed to build a new crude oil refinery in Alaska. The refinery required all of Tesoro's spare cash and the borrowing of more. The refinery is the leading gasoline refinery in Alaska and is capable of refining 80,000 barrels of crude oil a day. Tesoro today is the leading supplier of light petroleum products in Alaska.

"Both the Trinidad and Alaskan transactions required something a little different — financial creativity and corporate intestinal fortitude. In each case was a small company with limited financial resources going into new operating areas where it had no experience and making commitments that were significant in relation to its size. This has been the pattern of Tesoro. It takes creativity, guts and a lot of hard work."

To be successful, West believes, "You have to take risks, you've got to be entrepreneurial, and more importantly, you've got to be willing to work many, many long hours."

RALPH C. BENDER & ASSOCIATES, INC.

When Ralph C. Bender went into business for himself in 1966, he chose a company name that got right to the point: Ralph C. Bender — Urban Planning Consultant. He had no secretary and no staff, and his home was his office.

Nearly 20 years later, Bender oversees a staff of 60, specializing in architecture, land planning and landscape architecture, with clients nationwide. Now known as Ralph C. Bender & Associates, Inc., the company long ago left the founder's home. Its most recent move came in the fall of 1985 to a spacious office building in Woodway Park on San Antonio's Northwest Side.

The firm's expansion has paralleled and complemented the growth of San Antonio, which Bender says was regarded as a "sleepy little backwater Texas community" when he moved here in the mid-1950s.

But Bender's modus operandi is unchanged from his early days as San Antonio's assistant director of city planning: "We try and find out what the problem is, and then we address the problem.

"Many times architects and planners and landscape architects are so preoccupied with solutions that they don't ever bother to find out what the problem is," said Bender.

When Bender arrived in San Antonio in 1956, however, there were few challenges to tackle in land planning or design. The Alamo City seemed mired in the past, not caught up in the postwar boom of prosperity.

Bender, a native of Iowa, had seen the signs of the economic upswing in other cities. After serving in World War II, he had received his undergraduate degree in architectural engineering from Iowa State College

and a Master of Architecture degree from Cranbrook Academy of Art in Michigan, a school founded by modern architectural pioneer Eliel Saarinen.

After working for an Illinois architectural and engineering firm for a year and a half, Bender joined the Mobile, Alabama, architectural and planning firm of Arch R. Winter & Associates. He then spent four years preparing metropolitan area plans primarily in Louisiana.

When the urban planner decided to seek a position in a new locale, San Antonio was one of many cities where he made application. The city was not yet in the mainstream of urban America. It was so far from the current that, like most people, Bender knew San Antonio was located in Texas, but he wasn't exactly sure where.

Shortly after joining the City Planning Department, Bender was elevated to the directorship. While the planning department assisted in the design of numerous residential subdivisions as a service to developers, there otherwise was little to plan, Bender said.

An apartment developer from Houston, for example, visited Bender's office in the late 1950s to see how many apartments had been constructed in San Antonio. Bender knew that only a few had been developed, but directed the visitor to the city's building permit office for hard facts.

"When he came back, he was beside himself," Bender said. "There had been eight units built in the preceding five years. Not eight projects — eight units.

"The only things we built in San Antonio, and this was gospel truth, were single-family homes and gas stations. Regional shopping malls, high-rise office buildings and garden apartments were still just a dream for a city whose weather didn't even make the national news.

"I can remember getting irritated

Ralph C. Bender displays plans for his "dream come true" — the Westside Expressway.

Smolkin already had a place of honor in national home-building circles when he served as a marketing consultant on a project also assigned to Bender. As a result of their collaboration, Smolkin immediately began recommending the San Antonio planner for consulting jobs across the nation.

"Overnight I went from being a small local moonlighting consultant to a national consultant," Bender said. He and Smolkin still share projects, and Bender calls the New Orleans consultant "our patron saint."

Bender's firm has designed projects that span all economic housing markets from public housing to luxury housing. Locally the projects are as diverse as the federally assisted Lila Cockrell Apartments, a complex for senior citizens named after the city's former mayor, and the Thousand Oaks Racquet Club condominiums, a luxury development.

"Overnight I went from being a small local moonlighting consultant to a national consultant."

Bender is proud that much of his firm's work comes from repeat clients, many of whom he regards as close personal friends. By using his problem-solving philosophy, Bender's company has been instrumental in solving many problems confronting the housing industry and is regarded nationally as one of the foremost architects and planners addressing the needs of housing in the United States.

A former faculty member of Trinity University and an acknowledged public speaker on the subjects of housing and urban planning, Bender for many years has been a

sought-after speaker nationally. For that reason, his firm was better recognized outside of San Antonio than it was in the city.

Recently two significant San Antonio projects which carry the name of Ralph C. Bender & Associates have projected Bender and his firm to the forefront of this "Megatrend" city.

The Dominion, a luxury residential community of some 1,300 acres north of San Antonio, was designed and landscaped by the Bender organization. In addition, his firm performed the planning, architectural and landscape architectural work for The Dominion Country Club.

It has been said that The Dominion bridge, the information center, the tennis and swim club and the golf club — all designed by the Bender organization and associates — already are San Antonio treasures.

A second project destined to change the face of San Antonio is the creation of the Westside Expressway, a long needed — but abandoned as impossible to accomplish — transportation artery.

When Bender was retained by developer Charles Martin Wender to plan his 10,000-acre Westover Hills community, Bender found the project was the key to a door he had been trying to unlock for 20 years.

Bender convinced Wender and other landowners and developers to donate in excess of 90 percent of the right of way for the freeway, some 500 acres stretching over a 10.1-mile distance, and to fund one-half the cost of the access roads. The expressway plans went from idea to reality, with state construction funds being approved in less than 90 days.

Since his early years heading city planning, Bender has been a firm believer that private and public interests can join hands for the benefit of all. Always quick to give credit for success to his clients and colleagues, Bender said, "The many talents that created The Dominion and the many people who joined hands in the expressway effort are a constant source of satisfaction and amazement to me."

Bender identified two purely personal goals — "to enjoy learning the game of golf at The Dominion and to drive the first car down the Westside Expressway." [L]

by the fact that we were never on any national weather announcements. Mileage charts rarely listed how far it was to or from San Antonio. That's really how we were thought of," Bender said.

But Bender helped change the landscape of San Antonio, both in his municipal post and then with private developers whose housing projects grew as rapidly as the number of returning servicemen with Veterans Administration loans. Upon leaving city government, Bender worked as a national award-winning urban planner and designer, first with Ray Ellison, then with Quincy Lee — two major San Antonio builder-developers.

It was during the latter association that Bender began performing consulting work on the side with Lee's blessing. Through a fortuitous meeting with a New Orleans marketing consultant, Bill Smolkin, Bender became an overnight success on the national level, even when people in San Antonio were unfamiliar with his name.

LA MANSION HOTELS

A day or two after the birth of his eighth child in 1966, San Antonio attorney Patrick J. Kennedy gazed out a window of the Nix Medical Center and selected the site of his new career — the hotel business.

Built in 1852 as a boys' school, St. Mary's Law School provided the site for La Mansion del Rio in time for HemisFair '68.

The site was St. Mary's Law School from which he had graduated in 1952. The four-story building on the banks of the San Antonio River had been erected as a Catholic boys' school in 1852 by four brothers of the Society of Mary. It was about to be vacated as the law school moved to the suburban campus of St. Mary's University.

"I remember turning to my wife and saying, 'You know, San Antonio is preparing for HemisFair in 1968 and the city really needs some hotels. That would be a super location,'" Kennedy recalled.

At thirty-six, Kennedy had just completed major litigation in his private law practice and wondered what he would do next. Developing

La Mansion del Rio Hotel, one of only two major hotels built in downtown San Antonio in 50 years, became his next project.

The hotel, which opened in April 1968, not only launched a new career for Kennedy, it added a unique brand of first class hostelry to South Texas.

Nineteen years after its formation, Kennedy's River Hotel Company, which started with a 180-room hotel, now owns three hotels with a total of 1,000 rooms. In addition to La Mansion del Rio are La Mansion del Norte in San Antonio and La Mansion in Austin. Each is managed by the company's management affiliate, Texas Western Hotels, Inc. In addition, Texas Western Hotels, Inc. owns Computerized Hotel Systems, Inc., which develops computer software for the hotel industry.

From the beginning, La Mansion hotels have been singled out for their historical significance, unique atmosphere and service, and fine dining. La Mansion del Rio has been designated a Texas Historical Site and received an historical site award from the San Antonio Conservation Society. A river-view photograph of the hotel was selected for the official HemisFair '68 poster.

In 1980 it became the only San Antonio hotel — and one of only two in Texas — to be admitted to the prestigious Preferred Hotels Association. In 1984 La Mansion in Austin joined in the association's elite membership. La Mansion del Norte's San Angel Restaurant has received the coveted Holiday Magazine Dining Award annually since 1980.

Kennedy explained the progression of the company and where it is headed:

In turning a 116-year-old building into a first class hotel, Kennedy's goal was "to retain the charm of the architecture while bringing it into a condition that people in our current society are comfortable in."

"This is one of the philosophies that we have evolved in the company

History at a Glance 1966

Founded: *Nov. 1, 1966*
Founder: *Patrick J. Kennedy*
Original employees: *180*
Milestones: **1968** *opened La Mansion del Rio Hotel;* **1978** *opened La Mansion del Norte Hotel;* **1979** *completed 173-room addition, Las Canarias restaurant and Iberian Ballroom to La Mansion del Rio;* **1984** *opened La Mansion Hotel in Austin;* **1985** *completed total renovation of La Mansion del Rio*
Headquarters: *900 Isom Road*
Subsidiaries: *Texas Western Hotels, Inc.; Computerized Hotel Systems, Inc.; River Hotel Company*
Owner: *River Hotel Company owned by Patrick J. Kennedy*
Employees: *1,000 plus*

This chapter was based on an interview with Patrick J. Kennedy.

and still are refining. We are committed to a form of architecture — the Spanish hacienda — that is classic in form and has credibility in the authenticity of arches, columns and materials," Kennedy continued.

"We recognize that while the architectural style of the building may be 500 years old, the people inside are not. And they like comfortable things. A more traditional and Euro-

Patrick J. Kennedy

pean interior blends with the Spanish influence and is more compatible with our philosophy."

La Mansion del Rio opened to immediate occupancy, with an average of 92 percent of its 180 rooms filled for the first six months. After Hemis-Fair, however, it and other downtown hotels struggled until 1973 when La Mansion del Rio's occupancies exceeded the 80 percent mark and started a long-term, successful trend.

In 1979 an addition to the hotel brought the number of rooms to 354 and added the 5,000-square-foot Iberian Ballroom and Las Canarias restaurant. A total renovation in 1985 included expansion of the lobby, meeting rooms and restaurant.

Kennedy took his Old World hotel concept to San Antonio's fast-paced North Side in 1978. La Mansion del Norte with 300 rooms was the first major hotel built in a suburban location in San Antonio.

"All sorts of objections had been raised such as 'you don't have the

river out there' and 'you can't recreate that old, historic building,'" he recalled.

His biggest roadblock was difficulty persuading lenders to back the project. Finally, he won support from San Antonio Savings Association, which led a consortium of savings and loans to issue a permanent loan commitment.

The hotel proved an instant success, earning a profit its first full year of operation. Its grand opening was one of San Antonio's first fundraising galas, donating $10,000 to the San Antonio Symphony.

The company's first venture outside San Antonio was completed in 1984 with the opening of the luxurious 350-room La Mansion in Austin. It features fine restaurants and 18,000 square feet of function space including Austin's largest hotel ballroom.

"We have always tried to establish a link with the history of a community," Kennedy said. "In La Mansion del Rio, we named our meeting rooms after the San Antonio missions and our restaurant to honor the Canary Islanders who founded the city. In La Mansion del Norte, we named the ballroom the Madero Ballroom after Francisco I. Madero and invited the Madero family to the

---

"We have always tried to establish a link with the history of a community."

---

dedication. In La Mansion in Austin, we named function rooms for the empresarios who brought settlers to Texas including Stephen F. Austin."

Since 1971 La Mansion del Rio has provided refreshments and the starting point for Las Posadas, a Mexican Christmas tradition preserved by the San Antonio Conservation Society. Each December since 1980, the hotel has invited travel writers from across the United States, Canada and Mexico to witness this tradition

and observe the city's charming holiday celebration. The travel writers' weekend initiated by La Mansion and co-sponsored by the San Antonio Convention & Visitors Bureau has become an annual affair resulting in thousands of dollars of national publicity for San Antonio tourism.

Kennedy attributes the success of the hotels to "the uniqueness of our concept and our locations, the intense commitment of key personnel to refine our concept and their refusal to dilute it, and our willingness to let our 'product' evolve to meet the needs of the traveling public."

A strategic planning study with McKinsey & Co., a highly regarded international management consulting firm, concluded that River Hotel Company indeed has a unique concept and there definitely is a segment of the traveling public that likes what the hotels offer. Repeat business is far higher than the industry average.

"Through that study, we've developed a 10-year plan that calls for additional hotels. It's very likely there will be another in San Antonio," Kennedy predicted. ▐▌

La Mansion del Rio Hotel adds Old World charm to the San Antonio River.

RAND DEVELOPMENT CORPORATION

The force behind Rand Development Corporation, James A. Delaney, got into the development business by accident.

However unlikely, his start in real estate and construction was fortuitous. Eighteen years later, his highly successful company builds office parks, shopping centers and multifamily housing as evidenced by some of San Antonio's most unique and progressive developments.

Expert businessman and talespinner Delaney recalled how he began and where he is headed:

"I got into the development business accidentally. What I wanted to do was establish a restaurant downtown with a friend of mine, Jack Wysoki, who came in with me originally in this business. He was a butcher and we wanted to put a steakhouse in downtown San Antonio. When we looked for space, we found we could buy the Rand Building, the old Wolff & Marx Building, for approximately what it would cost us in rent. So we scraped up a down payment and bought this eight-story building. I went immediately from an almost-restaurant owner to an almost-developer.

"We put a 400-seat restaurant in the basement and called it the world's biggest steakhouse because it was eight stories high. We named it the Steak Cellar. We took the basement only because that would be the least desirable space in the building. We figured we'd rent the rest to other tenants. In about three years, we had that building 100 percent full."

If fate let Delaney fall into the restaurant business, it also pushed him out of it.

"One of our tenants was USAA. Eventually, they ended up with five floors of the Rand Building and then they wanted to lease the basement as well. So that forced me out of the restaurant business. I gladly gave it up.

"The real name of the old Wolff & Marx Building is the Rand Building. It's engraved in stone there. So we called our company Rand Development Corporation.

"In 1971 I bought El Tropicano Hotel in downtown San Antonio, and that was a success. In two years, we tripled the occupancy and doubled the revenue. Then I had a spectacular idea: I was going to fill that hotel and make it a household word in San Antonio in one gesture. So I arranged to have the Texas-Oklahoma football game televised on closed-circuit TV and sold the rooms at triple the rate.

"There were more Irish at the Alamo than there were Texans."

"I had the place packed. My restaurant was bulging and guest rooms had from 10 to 50 people in each. The TV sets were turned on at game time and the screen was blank. One of my engineers had repositioned the antenna. The game was being broadcast from Austin and San Antonio was blacked out. I couldn't get the game.

"These people went wild. They threw television sets in the pool and mattresses in the courtyard. I called the police. A policeman stood there and watched toilet paper being thrown down along with towels, table cloths and chairs. He said, 'I ain't going near these people, Mr. Delaney. You can stop it yourself.'

"About half time we got the film problem corrected and the game went on. But by then, these fans were insane and the place was a shambles. Anyway, my introduction to the hotel business was about as good as my introduction to the restaurant business."

Delaney found the hotel business too confining.

"I sold the Rand Building and the

History at a Glance 1967

Founded: *May 1967 at 100 E. Houston St.*
Founder: *James A. Delaney*
Original name: *Rand Development Corporation*
Original employees: *2*
Milestones: **1971** *acquired El Tropicano Hotel;* **1977** *first expansion outside San Antonio to Gresham, Wis.;* **1980** *expanded to Chicago;* **1983** *expanded to Dallas, Florida, California;* **1984** *expanded to New Mexico*
Headquarters: *599 Spencer Lane*
Employees: *104*
Motto: *Depressus Tamen Extollor*

This chapter was based on an interview with James A. Delaney.

hotel around the end of 1976. I took a year off to finish my obligations to various organizations like Centro 21, Incarnate Word College and so on.

"During that time, I reacquainted myself with M.H. Braden, who had a construction company. They needed some money and I had some, so we got together. Where I was just in development before, then I got involved in construction.

"H.B. Zachry underwrote my first performance bond. We had a contract to build the aircraft factory at Swearingen Aircraft Corporation. We built almost the entire Swearingen complex at San Antonio International Airport.

"Then about four or five years ago, we got involved in joint ventures with financial institutions across the country and now we probably have 22 projects under way. We have a pretty good concentration of our developments around Thousand Oaks — five multifamily complexes.

"My favorite kind of development is a massive thematic development like we're doing on the South Side in Mission Terrace, a 42-acre development by Mission San Jose. It enables us to maintain the harmony of architecture with the missions and to work with the government with the theme that is being maintained along Mission Parkway.

"The San Antonio Rose Palace is another favorite. It's a unique equestrian show and exhibition facility a Texas country mile from downtown. It has a ranch-style location on 72 acres. There is nothing else like it."

Of Irish extraction, Delaney also has developed a growing business connection between Ireland and San Antonio.

"Through my interest in the economics of Ireland, we have two companies there, an oil exploration company and a securities company. That has led us into investments in West Germany, Colombia, the Celtic Sea and the Gulf of Mexico.

"Through an organization I founded here about two years ago called the Irish American Unity Conference, I met Irish-American businessmen, lawyers, stockbrokers, attorneys and architects. Above our interest in Irish-American affairs, the Irish economy and political

scene, we have entered into business relationships.

"We've established a company called Texas Continental Securities, which is a repository for American investment funds in Ireland. We pool our capital resources and invest in the Irish economy and we promote exports into the American market. In one of our shopping centers, Waterford Square, we have the largest Irish goods store in the country, All Things Irish.

James A. Delaney is founder of Rand Development Corporation and often was mistaken for actor John Wayne.

"The last census revealed there are about 43 million Americans of Irish extraction. Texas has the third largest Irish-American population. As a matter of fact, of the 187 defenders of the Alamo, I think 12 were born in Ireland. There were more Irish at the Alamo than there were Texans."

Tall, rugged Delaney is accustomed to hearing that he resembles the late actor John Wayne.

"When 'The Alamo' premiered in San Antonio, I happened to get a ticket to the movie and a reception at the St. Anthony Hotel.

"At the reception, I met John Wayne. He remarked that we must have been the two tallest people in the room. He asked, 'How tall are you?'

"I said, 'I'm six-foot-six.'

"And he said, 'Well, you've got me by an inch and a half.'

"We soon discovered our Irish connections and he mentioned that he is

Scotch-Irish from the northern part of Ireland. He said his real name was Morrison. When I was in Ireland later, I went to the county where my grandmother was born and I sort of tracked him down. I found a relative of my grandmother whose name was Morrison. I never went beyond that, but I found out that my family was also from the northern part of Ireland. I've got to pursue that someday. I'm going to find out that John Wayne and I are distant cousins.

"As to the future of Rand, I see us getting more into international securities, finance, information processing, technology transfer and that sort of thing. We will get involved in the electronic network around the world with the sophistications developing in earth satellite data transmission and laser technology.

"We like to think we're keeping up with the leading edge of technology. I see us becoming more international." ⬛

DILLARD'S

A simple philosophy catapulted Dillard's from a single store in Nashville, Arkansas, to one of the fastest growing retailers in the country: Give the customer his money's worth.

A reputation for honesty, value and a broad selection of merchandise has made Dillard's the fourth largest department store group in the nation. The chain, based in Little Rock, Arkansas, boasts more than 100 stores and an annual volume of $1.5 billion.

San Antonio is home to four Dillard's stores, a divisional office which runs the Texas/New Mexico Division with 23 stores, and a distribution center which supplies merchandise to Dillard's stores in the Rio Grande Valley, Corpus Christi, Austin and College Station as well as San Antonio.

Other Dillard's stores are in Arizona, Arkansas, Louisiana, Missouri, Kansas, Nevada, New Mexico, Oklahoma and Tennessee.

Fred T. Johnson, vice president in charge of sales promotion for the Texas/New Mexico Division, traced the

A parade goes by the first Dillard's store in Nashville, Arkansas, in 1940.

History at a Glance   1968

Founded: *1938 in Nashville, Ark.*
Opened in San Antonio: *1968*
Founder: *William Thomas Dillard*
Original investment: *$8,000*
Original employees: *3*
Milestones: **1983** *named No. 1 store chain in the nation by manufacturing marketing executives;* **1984** *sales in chain exceeded $1 billion, and stock traded on the American Stock Exchange jumped from 27th place to second place among retailers;* **1985** *cited by Forbes Magazine as first in growth and earnings per share and fourth in profitability among general retailers, and William Dillard honored as Menswear Retailer of the Year*
Headquarters: *Little Rock, Ark.*
Officers Texas/New Mexico Division: *Charles E. "Chuck" Franzke, chairman; Jim Wilson, president; Dick Roberds, vice president, merchandising; Wynelle Chapman, vice president, merchandising; Mitchell Parrish, vice president, director of stores; Fred T. Johnson, vice president, sales promotion; Gat Lemoine, vice president, personnel and operations*
Employees in San Antonio: *1,000*
Units: *More than 100 stores including four in San Antonio*

This chapter was based on an interview with Fred T. Johnson.

personal success story behind Dillard's, the chain's incredible growth and its impact on San Antonio:

"Our founder, William Thomas Dillard, became interested in retailing in his father's general merchandise store in Mineral Springs, Arkansas. After graduating from the University of Arkansas, Mr. Dillard earned a degree in retailing from Columbia University. While in college in New York City, he sold shoes for I. Magnin. He then worked for Sears in Tulsa before returning to Mineral Springs.

"With $8,000 borrowed from his mother, he opened a store in his wife's hometown, Nashville, Arkansas. Ten years later, he opened a store in Texarkana, Arkansas, launching a remarkable expansion program."

Dillard's growth since then has been divided between opening new stores and buying existing ones.

Modern Dillard's are anchor stores in malls across the country.

Stores which have come under the Dillard's banner in the past 25 years include Mayer & Schmidt in Tyler; Leonard's in the Dallas/Fort Worth area; Pfeifer's and Blass, both in Arkansas; Diamond's in Arizona and Nevada; John A. Brown and Brown-Dunkin, both in Oklahoma; and Stix, Baer & Fuller in Missouri.

"A Dillard's store is full of merchandise and full of customers."

In 1964 Dillard opened a store in Austin. It was his first store in a shopping center, the first in Texas and the first built under the Dillard's name. The store's success prompted Dillard to look 80 miles south to San Antonio.

Dillard's opened in Central Park Mall in 1968. Six months later, a store was opened on Southwest Military Drive. Stores opened in Windsor Park Mall in 1976 and Ingram Park Mall in 1979.

"Mr. Dillard makes a statement every time we open a store that 'no business can exist without integrity.' That sums him up. He's an unbelievably honest man who doesn't believe in lying to himself, to his employees or to his customers," Johnson continued.

At seventy, Dillard still runs the company as chairman of the board. He visits each store two or three times a year.

"When he comes to San Antonio, he is on a first-name basis with the longtime employees. He's very observant of how the store looks. He believes if the store doesn't look like it's full, customers will think we don't have enough money to fill it up.

"In an interview in St. Louis after he bought a store there, Mr. Dillard was asked if he was going to change the name to Dillard's. He replied, 'Not until it looks like a Dillard's store.' He then was asked, 'What does a Dillard's store look like?' He said, 'It's full of merchandise and full of customers.'"

"Mr. Dillard has been quoted as saying his stores are operated on three basic principles: 'First, we present to the customer the best merchandise available in famous name, nationally advertised products. Second, all Dillard's stores offer outstanding values at a pleasing price because of our cost-control techniques and volume buying. Third, we believe in the principle of truth in advertising.'"

Dillard's customers are in the middle- to upper-middle income brackets as well as people of lower and upper means. In recent years, the store has upgraded its merchandise mix.

Dillard's believes in leaving a nest egg to the community.

For example, Dillard's is a major sponsor of the Miss Texas U.S.A. Pageant. The pageant which began in El Paso in 1975 was moved to San Antonio in 1983. Dillard's furnishes the winner a $6,000 wardrobe and sponsors a substantial portion of the statewide telecast which showcases San Antonio as well as the contestants.

Dillard's remains a family business. The family owns 51 percent of the stock in the corporation and all five of the founder's children are in Dillard's management. William Dillard II is president and chief operating officer; Alex Dillard and Mike Dillard are executive vice presidents; Drue Dillard Corbusier is vice president of merchandising for the Fort Worth Division; and Denise Dillard is divisional merchandise manager of the Little Rock Division.

Dillard's ambitious growth plan includes expansion in San Antonio.

"Our next store will be in a mall to be built at the intersection of Nacogdoches and Loop 1604. We probably will open there in the fall of 1987. Next on the drawing board will be an anchor store in a mall at Interstate 10 and Loop 1604.

"Mr. Dillard believes the name of the game is growth." ⬛

BRAKE CHECK

Brake Check is the largest brake speciality company in the country and plans to double its size within the next five years.

With 27 service centers in San Antonio, Houston, Austin and Corpus Christi, the 17-year-old locally based firm services more than 150,000 cars per year.

Brake Check has earned a reputation as a trend setter in the auto repair industry because of its imaginative willingness to do things differently.

The innovator behind Brake Check is owner John A. Peveto, Jr. The self-made businessman is highly visible as the spokesman on Brake Check television commercials. The son of a Baptist preacher, Peveto was a Marine, aspiring actor, fry cook and tire salesman before managing his first brake repair shop in 1968. His story is the story of Brake Check:

"My first job was being janitor of my father's church in Dallas when I was nine years old. I got my first paper route at eleven. Later I worked at a gas station and bought my own car with the money I saved. I did all my own work on that car; I've always been interested in cars.

"At eighteen I went to Howard Payne College, but left to join the Marine Corps. I literally grew up in the Marines. After my tour of duty, I was discharged in California, where I stayed for a while and sold tires at Sears. A friend encouraged me to try for an acting career, but it didn't

take long to find out that was not for me. Eventually, I returned to Texas.

"I've always considered myself to be permanently enrolled in the school of life. I learn from books and from everyone I meet. I believe we are the same people today that we were 10 years ago or that we will be 10 years from now except for what we learn from the books we read and the people we meet.

"When I was thirty-two, I had a wife and two sons and I was looking desperately for an opportunity. I was offered a chance to go to San Antonio to try to turn around a failing brake repair franchise. Little did I realize that the store on Interstate 10 behind Wonderland Mall would be the start of what is now the largest company in the United States specializing in brake repair.

"When I took over the store, it hardly had enough business to keep the doors open. I knew that I had to do something different.

"I would go across the street to the Rodeway Inn, introduce myself to people checking in and ask them if their cars needed any work done. I introduced myself to the merchants in the nearby mall and asked for their business.

"I even stood out in front of my store and waved and hollered at passing cars on the freeway just to

John A. Peveto, Jr.

get their attention.

"I'll never forget one of the first jobs I sold because of my waving at traffic. Three women carpooling to work passed by every day. After about a week, they stopped and asked, 'Why do you wave and holler at traffic every day?'

"I told them candidly, 'Because I'm going broke if I don't get some more business soon.'

"It was lucky that they stopped;

"Sometimes you have to do something really different to attract attention."

---

the car needed new brake linings and the drums turned. I learned from that experience that sometimes you have to do something really different to attract attention.

"Basically, I didn't want Brake Check to be like other companies that repaired brakes. While working for a restaurant years before, I learned the value of offering customers something they could not get anywhere else.

"So at Brake Check, I started accepting cars up until 6 p.m., and we didn't go home until we finished repairing every car. The customer didn't have to do without his car

---

History at a Glance   1968

Founded: *September 1968*
Founders: *Fred W. Bell and John A. Peveto, Jr.*
Original Name: *Brake-O*
Original employees: *3*
Original location: *6746 N.W. Expressway*
Headquarters: *10107 McAllister Freeway*
Subsidiaries: *Better Brake Parts, Inc.*
Current employees: *350 plus*
Service centers: *27 stores in San Antonio, Houston, Austin and Corpus Christi*

This chapter was based on an interview with John A. Peveto, Jr.

John A. Peveto, Jr., is highly visible in television commercials for Brake Check.

overnight, and we didn't have business hanging over from the previous day. Our customers appreciate it. And we never charge overtime.

"Also, Brake Check mechanics don't work on commission. They get paid an hourly wage plus overtime. There's no incentive for our mechanics to recommend a part or service a customer doesn't need. Our mechanics also work for an opportunity to grow with the company. We don't hire managers; we promote from within. The key qualifications for being a Brake Check manager are not the attributes of a good salesman; they're knowing how to fix the brakes on a car and doing it right. All our managers started as trainees.

"We don't have 'Employees Only' and 'Keep Out' signs at Brake Check. We welcome our customers to watch as we work on their cars.

"Another thing that's different at Brake Check is our transferable guarantee. While a standard guarantee is good only as long as you own the car, a Brake Check guarantee automatically transfers to the new owner if the car is sold.

"We've always advertised dif-ferently, too. It's misleading to advertise a specific price for a brake job because every car is different. Buying a package price brake job can easily result in a customer buying parts and services he doesn't need. And some price advertising for brake jobs is plain old 'bait and switch.'

"All Brake Check stores are company owned. We have much greater control over day-to-day operations to ensure high quality service. We've had the opportunity to go the franchise route many times. But I don't want to be big just for the sake of being big. I want Brake Check to grow only as long as we can develop people who accept opportunity with the proper responsibility.

"The service business is a people business. Each employee has individual needs and characteristics. A company that treats its employees as if they were robots cannot last long. If you treat your employees like machines, they will treat your customers in the same uncaring manner. That's why we have a policy of selling our customers only what their cars need. We want to be part of the solution, not part of the problem.

"I'm often asked why I'm in so many Brake Check commercials. It's because I want people to know that I personally stand behind every job Brake Check does. We're human, and we make mistakes. But when we do, we're fast to admit it and correct it. I want our customers to know that if they aren't satisfied, I want to

---

"We may be big. And we'll grow bigger. But we will never lose the personal touch."

---

know about it. And I will do something about it.

"We may be big. And we'll grow bigger. But we will never lose the personal touch. Caring about people — our employees and our customers — is what got us here. And it's what will get us where we eventually want to be."

CRAIN DISTRIBUTING COMPANY, INC.

"The beer business is the only business I've ever known. I have been involved in this industry for more than 30 years and I really believe that Anheuser-Busch produces the finest products that are available on the market."

Thus William J. Crain, Crain Distributing Company, Inc. president, described his life's work.

As an Anheuser-Busch distributor, Crain's company sells Budweiser, Bud Light, Michelob, Michelob Light, Natural Light, Busch and LA, a low-alcohol product. The company services Bexar, Frio, Medina, Wilson and Atascosa counties.

"In 1984 we sold approximately 4 million cases, which represents more than $35 million worth of business," Crain explained. "We employ 158 people and operate a fleet of more than 100 vehicles. Our growth rate over the past three or four years has averaged between 15 and 20 percent annually.

"Today we occupy a six-acre complex with two brand new buildings. The main building houses our offices and the environmentally controlled beer storage vaults. The other building provides indoor parking for our fleet and a full-service fleet maintenance center. Together these buildings cover almost 150,000 square feet."

Crain recalled his earlier years: "But it hasn't always been like this. I had been a beer distributor once before as a young man. But I obviously wasn't a very good businessman back in those days because I went broke. I then went to work as a salaried salesman for a major brewer, but I felt that this was not the way to get ahead. I kept my eyes open for the right opportunity and when the Anheuser-Busch distributorship in San Antonio came on the the market, I made my move."

In October 1969, Crain purchased his business and moved to San Antonio.

"At that time, we occupied an old beat-up building and had about 20 employees. That first year, our eight or nine routes sold about 270,000 cases," he remembered. "So we have

"I kept my eyes open for the right opportunity and when the Anheuser-Busch distributorship in San Antonio came on the market, I made my move."

grown tremendously over the years. But this growth has been very gradual and difficult to come by because this business has always been intensely competitive.

"In those days, our main competitors were Pearl, Lone Star, Jax and Falstaff. Budweiser was the No. 1 brand nationally, but it had never really caught on here. I felt that the opportunity for growth of Budweiser and the other Anheuser-Busch brands was tremendous. The timing was just right and things started to slowly fall into place. We greatly improved service to our customers, added more routes, expanded the sales force and became more professional in our efforts.

"But this gradual growth has taken place over a 16-year span. It has taken a lot of patience, hard

---

History at a Glance   1969

Founded: *1969 at 403 Dawson*
Founder: *William J. Crain*
Original name: *Crain Distributing Company, Inc.*
Original employees: *25*
Original investment: *$50,000*
Milestones: **1975** *began service to Frio, Medina, Wilson and Atascosa counties;* **1978** *reached 1 million cases in sales;* **1980** *built 75,000-square-foot building at 611 N. Cherry St., purchased corporate stock of original investors and accepted sons as partners;* **1983** *sales reached 3 million cases;* **1984** *added fleet maintenance and vehicle storage facility*
Employees: *158*
Service area: *3,600 retail outlets*
Motto: *Making friends is our business.*

This chapter was based on an interview with William J. Crain.

William J. Crain, center, and his sons, Glynn Crain, left, and Andrew Crain, make their distributing company truly a family enterprise.

"Both of my sons are involved very closely in the business," Crain said. "My oldest son, Glynn, is 29. He worked part time for the company until he was 16 and became full time after graduating from St. Mary's University in 1977 with a bachelor's degree in marketing. He has served as a warehouseman, route helper, driver/salesman, draft system installer, warehouse foreman and sales supervisor. Today he is vice president of the company with responsibilities for financial planning, forecasting, sales reporting and computer development.

"My other son, Andrew, is 25 years old and attended Southwest Texas State University. He has followed in his brother's footsteps by serving in the warehouse and on route trucks as both a helper and driver/salesman. He is currently a sales supervisor and we expect him eventually to move into the sales manager position.

"My sons now have become my partners and each of them owns 25 percent of the company. So now it is truly a family business. I feel that our situation is ideal.

"The fact that our industry is so competitive is merely icing on the cake. Happiness to me is competition, and I wouldn't have it any other way." **LI**

work and a tremendous capital investment over the years. There is no way that I could have purchased a business like this one today with what little money I had back then. Our facilities alone are probably worth in excess of $6 million.

"It required a fortune to develop this market, but it has been done over a long period of time. This slow, steady and controlled growth over a number of years is what has made it all possible."

Crain believes the selling methods of today's beer business have evolved over the last 20 to 30 years.

"No longer does a big man walk into a bar and set up the house," he said. "Today we employ sophisticated marketing techniques to advertise and sell our products. Methods unknown to this industry until relatively recently now have become commonplace such as market segmentation, target marketing, cost per thousand and demographics.

"Today we would be lost without the instant access to vital marketing information which the computer now provides. These new methods and techniques, we must always remember, are merely tools which assist our sales force in their day-to-day dealings with our customers."

Today Crain Distributing Company is a family enterprise.

Millions of dollars worth of Anheuser-Busch beers pass through the company's environmentally controlled storage facilities annually.

ORAH WALL

What started as a small concrete wall business has flourished in only 15 years into an international company with multifaceted operations ranging from construction to medicine.

Efraim Abramoff

Orah Abramoff

"The company started in 1971 with a system of poured-in-place concrete into aluminum forms for warehouse walls," said Orah Abramoff, company co-founder.

Since the system was new to San Antonio, the Abramoffs had to educate local builders about the method.

"Efraim had to work very hard even to demonstrate," Orah Abramoff recalled. "A friend of ours had an apartment complex, and Efraim said, 'Let me pour a wall for you, so when I speak to people about what Orah Wall can do or about this system, they will understand me.' "

In the beginning, the company had only one employee, a part-time secretary. The first full-time employee was Robert Garcia, who worked with the Abramoffs as a laborer and is still with the company.

From this small beginning, the company has become international in its scope.

"We feel like the world has become very small because the same needs are here that are in Europe, Israel, South Africa, South America and Japan," Orah Abramoff said. "People are looking for better, more effective ways in any field from construction to high technology and agriculture."

Efraim Abramoff's background is in construction, having worked in his native Israel for one of the largest companies in the Middle East.

Orah Abramoff described her husband this way:

"He is open-minded and learned many aspects of the company as it was growing. He came to the States to study to become an architect. That was his life's dream. He also has a good sense of business and real estate. He loves land. He says land is something you can touch; it is real.

"Efraim is an achiever because he has the courage to overcome obstacles. We passed through very bad times like everybody else in business. Because we came from another country, everything was new and success was not easy. Efraim believes, always, in not giving up. I think it is in his nature, and I, too, have learned to respect and to use this quality. You can change your life and you can change the world with positive attitudes."

The turning point for the company was in 1980 with the purchase of the Horizon Hill property on Interstate 10 West.

"It was a big change," Orah Abramoff remembered. "Efraim had the foresight to see that this would be the next major growth area in San

History at a Glance   1971

Founded: *1971 at Fresno Street and Interstate 10*
Founders: *Efraim Abramoff and Orah Abramoff*
Original name: *Orah Wall Construction Company*
Original employees: *3*
Original investments: *$6,000, 1 pickup truck, handsaw, desk and 2 chairs*
Milestones: *1975 purchased Missouri-Pacific Depot; 1976 incorporated; 1978 Aerogate Office Center; 1979 Energy Plaza; 1980 Horizon Hill land transaction; 1982 corporate operations consolidated at Horizon Point; 1983 Ariel House opened; 1984 established Orah Wall Research & Technologies Corporation and international trade office in Den Hague, Netherlands, and Tel Aviv, Israel*
Subsidiaries: *Ophira, Inc.; Orah Wall Investments, Inc.; Shield Investment Corporation; Energy Plaza Ltd.; Abramoff-Kuras Associates; Abramoff Associates; Abramoff-Shweiki*
Assets: *Company's vision for the future — ability to look forward and meet tomorrow's challenges*

This chapter was based on an interview with Efraim Abramoff and Orah Abramoff.

Abramoff 'Thinks Big'

Efraim Abramoff plans to build a new landmark for San Antonio and the State of Texas. "This new project is one of my highest ambitions," he stated with great conviction.

The unique development is the European Economic Community Center (World Trade Center) — a 1.5-million-square-foot facility. This 46-story, blue reflective glass building features a horizontal structure supported by four paralleled towers.

"I love San Antonio," Abramoff said. "San Antonio has done a lot for me and I want to return some of that to the city.

"You have to think big," he continued. "I think this project will enhance San Antonio and bring people here. It mainly will be a trade center dedicated to meeting all the needs of international corporations in one totally planned environment. The brokers and businessmen from Europe and Japan are eager to do business here in the middle of the

Efraim Abramoff believes his unique European Economic Community Center will be a new landmark for Texas.

Americas."

The huge development will take about three years and close to $200 million to build. The dynamic design is unique and will encompass both working and living environments for its tenants.

Abramoff believes one of the keys to success is learning to live with people.

"You can be good at finances, but if you do not know how to deal with people, sooner or later you will lose your effectiveness.

"Most people see only what they need today. I am an open-minded thinker. I see many years ahead of me and see what can be accomplished. The progress that I have made thus far continues to make me look forward, striving for tomorrow's visions today."

Ashford Oaks Executive Office Tower is one of many Orah Wall projects in San Antonio.

Antonio. We started building apartments on this land. I was also interested in condominiums, so I got a real estate license and could devote more time to the company."

Another project, the Ariel House, a private club, is one of Orah Abramoff's favorites. She directs the club and chairs its Key to the Arts Program.

It was meant to be more than a club. One of the major objectives in opening Ariel House was to offer the finest in dining and a place which enhances the arts for San Antonio. "You cannot have a city without culture and art," she said.

One subsidiary of Orah Wall is Orah Wall Research & Technologies Corporation. It is directly involved with Degem, a computerized learning system developed in Israel. The system can train any group from elementary schoolchildren to factory workers in the specific skills of such diverse areas as high tech-

nology, electronics and farming. Orah Wall plans to locate a Degem training school in San Antonio in one of the company's buildings.

Another division of Research & Technologies is Medical Enterprises, which is involved in the development of imaging centers. These diagnostic centers, which provide medical test results in one day while cutting labor and paper work costs, are innovative technologies for tomorrow's medicine. The company currently is building two imaging centers in San Antonio and has expansion plans for the entire Southwest.

"It is not very easy participating in so many different things," Orah Abramoff said, "but we continue to diversify the company. We find the best people we can to make up Orah Wall's team for meeting the challenges of the future. We believe the more you work, the more time you have to spend in learning."

EMBREY INVESTMENTS, INC.

Walter Embrey, Jr., started his real estate development company in 1974 during the worst recession the construction industry has suffered in the last 30 years.

Unique project concepts combined with caution, determination and sound management launched his company while established firms were going broke.

Today Embrey Investments, Inc. is primarily a real estate development company with $130 million annual volume. The firm constructs and manages its own commercial development properties including office complexes, retail centers, industrial buildings, condominiums and apartments.

With headquarters in San Antonio, the company builds in Texas, Florida, Arizona and Tennessee.

Still under forty years old, Embrey has had a meteoric rise to success in construction and development. He explained how he did it:

"I always had some interest in construction. As a child, I played hooky from school so I could spend a day on a construction site. I probably wouldn't have gotten caught except that I brought home scraps of wood to build things with.

"I started young. I'm from San Antonio and went to Thomas Jefferson High School. I married my high school sweetheart, Diana Richter, while I was attending The University of Texas, and I needed to get started on a career. So before my senior year at Texas, I got into the construction and development business part time.

"I worked part time for Walter Carrington, the second largest home builder in Austin. After I graduated in 1968, the company hired me full time. I thought with a degree in finance that I would start in some unique finance job. Instead, I was given the keys to a truck.

"That was the best thing that ever happened to me because I had an opportunity to learn how to construct housing. I started building houses and duplexes as a superintendent, working long hours and weekends and learning everything I could.

"From the construction side, I moved into design and marketing. This company used creative California architects and started a lot of exciting concepts in design and land use. We did hundreds of single family homes which gave me an opportunity to understand design and building concepts.

"Next I became a partner and executive vice president of Jagger and Associates in Austin. By the time I left in 1974, the company was one of the largest multifamily builders in the United States. As executive vice president of Jagger, I became involved with finance, administration and overall running of the operation.

"I always had some interest in construction."

"I couldn't have picked better individuals to work for. Both Carrington and Jagger had great talent in design, finance and administration. It's amazing that they gave me the responsibility they did when I was so young.

"In 1974 when I started my own company, my first project was to develop one of the largest undeveloped tracts of land on Loop 410 North. It was an area called Northcross at Loop 410 and Austin Highway.

"The building recession was tough; it almost killed me trying to make it through that era. Many companies were going broke and financing was hard to get. But we started one of San Antonio's first office warehouse centers, Northcross Business Center. That kicked off the project and we were able to develop the area.

"We've developed more than 50

History at a Glance   1974

Founded: *1974 at 7224 Blanco Road*
Founder: *Walter Embrey, Jr.*
Original investment: *$50,000*
Milestones: **1975** *completed first major project, Northcross Business Center;* **1976** *completed first project outside San Antonio, Spyglass Apartments in Austin;* **1983** *completed first project outside Texas, Chesapeake Apartments in Tampa, Fla.*
Headquarters: *750 E. Mulberry Ave.*
Subsidiaries: *Embrey Construction Co.; Trinity Management Co.*
Owner: *Walter Embrey, Jr.*
Officers: *Walter Embrey, Jr., president; Roger Bowler, senior vice president, finance; Ken Nichols, senior vice president, development; John Echols, senior vice president, development; Arun Verma, president of Embrey Construction Co.*
Employees: *100*
Offices: *Texas, Florida, Arizona and Tennessee*

This chapter was based on an interview with Walter Embrey, Jr.

major projects since 1974, representing an investment of more than $400 million. Over the last five years, we have been increasing our commercial development activity to balance out with our multifamily operation.

"Much of our success can be attributed to good management skills and good people. Most of our key people have partnership interest in the projects, so we have a system of ownership which creates tremendous incentive to perform.

"We take risks, but only very calculated risks. Some people think we're fairly conservative. But we've never had an unsuccessful project. We do a lot of market research. We calculate what the risks are and what the rewards are and decide whether a project is worth doing.

"We're also very detail-oriented. We try to be very precise about the product we're going to build. We

have no uniformity of product. Some of our competitors build the same thing over and over, but we tailor our projects to the site and to the market. We also have developed some great relationships with strong financial institutions and are very cautious about arranging the best financing packages.

"One of my favorite multifamily projects was Las Cimas with more than 250 units off Fredericksburg Road near the Medical Center. We found a beautiful tract of land with 794 oak trees surrounding the old Frost family estate, a beautiful 7,000-square-foot summer home built around 1910.

"We were able to keep more than half of those oak trees. The house was very expensive and not well-suited to our site plan. But we refurbished it and made it the club and leasing facility for the project. The

living space at Las Cimas was leased in three to four months at what then were the highest rates in the city.

"In commercial projects, I have most enjoyed the Trinity Plaza project in San Antonio. Several years ago, we were looking for a unique area to build office buildings other than on Loop 410 or Interstate 10. We put this land at Mulberry and McAllister Freeway under contract and had a hard time financing it.

"We take risks, but only very calculated risks."

Many major financial institutions around the country thought it was too much of a pioneering effort.

"We decided to go ahead with the project. We felt good about it; the inner city area was next to Brackenridge Park, Trinity University and many neat restaurants plus it had easy access to downtown and the airport.

"We built the smallest building first, Trinity Plaza, also known as Trinity National Bank Building, to test the market. It turned out so well we started our second building across the street. While it was under construction, American Security Life Insurance Company joined the project as a venture partner and became the anchor tenant with five of the nine floors. The third building is a 12-story building to be completed by 1987. We also are developing a mixed-use complex with retail, hotel and offices on St. Mary's Street west of McAllister Freeway.

"We do what we call bread and butter in the major growth areas, but we also like to find unique opportunities. We've grown very steadily over the last 11 years. Our goal is to maintain our work force in the San Antonio area and our Texas operation while generating new activity in other locations. We will add new partners and locations selectively over the next few years.

"There's a lot left to do." ⌑

Walter Embrey, Jr., stands before one of his most visible San Antonio projects, Trinity Plaza, at Mulberry and McAllister Freeway.

G.I.C. INSURANCE COMPANY

G.I.C. Insurance Company services the insurance needs of employees of some of the largest and most prestigious entities in the area including the City of San Antonio and Bexar County, and its annual premiums total approximately $60 million even though the company is less than a decade old.

Founder and owner Michael W. Keogh has set high goals for his young legal line reserve life and health stock insurance company, whose main thrust is in group life and group major medical hospitalization insurance.

"We are in the throes of advancing the company," Keogh explained. "We hope for a growth pattern of approximately 20 percent a year. Fortunately, for the last four years we've had that growth pattern and we hope to maintain it in the future.

"Since 80 percent of G.I.C.'s business is in group life and hospitalization and 20 percent is in life insurance, we're the opposite of the major companies, who have been in business for 100 plus years and are heavily into individual life insurance," he continued. "What we

do is a sideline to them.

"In Texas very few of the domiciled companies are involved in group life and group health products. We specialize in the medical field and, therefore, we can give more personalized service. Our policyholders are not computer numbers."

Keogh believes his company has only begun to touch the potential in the medical insurance business.

"Texas, of course, is in a boom area, the Sun Belt," he explained. "We've got a lot of companies with employer/employee-related fringe benefits to pursue in this state. At this point, we're licensed only in Texas."

Keogh's history in the insurance business began in 1954 when he came to San Antonio and worked as

a salesman for Blue Cross and Blue Shield of Texas, Inc. Nine years later, he opened the first regional office in Texas for American United Life Insurance Company headquartered in Indianapolis, Indiana.

"In 1969 I started a consulting firm called Group Consultants, Inc.," Keogh explained. "I hung my shingle and went to employers and said, 'Let me handle all of your insurance, your employer/employee benefits package for group life or hospitalization or disability income or cancer or whatever policies you want.'

"In 1977 I serviced quite a block of business and was consulting with employers for new insurance products. I was placing that business with other life insurance companies, and one day I said, 'They're making money, so why should I place all that business with them? Why not just start my own?' So I started looking for a company to buy in Texas and found one in Frier.

"I went to Frier and bought Richmond Life Insurance Company on October 6, 1977, and moved it to San Antonio that same day. I immediately transferred the majority of the business I was servicing to my own company, G.I.C. Insurance Company.

"When I purchased the company, there were 18 people working with me in the consulting firm. I came back one day and said, 'Now we're a life insurance company.'

"The first year, we had phenomenal growth; we turned about $5 million worth of premium. Seven years later, we have $60 million worth of premium."

G.I.C.'s logo is a familiar one: a reverse 'G' and 'C' with a reclining 'I.'

"I had that logo with my first firm, Group Consultants, Inc.," Keogh said. "After eight years in business,

History at a Glance   1977

Founded: *May 16, 1972, in Frier*
Opened in San Antonio: *Oct. 6, 1977*
Founder and owner: *Michael W. Keogh*
Original name: *G.I.C. Insurance Company*
Original employees: *18*
Original investment: *$300,000*
Milestones: 1972 *incorporated;* **1977** *Michael W. Keogh became sole owner, moved to G.I.C. Building;* **1982** *expanded outside San Antonio*
Headquarters: *9100 Interstate 10 West*
Employees: *130*
Locations: *San Antonio, Houston, Dallas-Fort Worth*
Assets: *$25.1 million*

This chapter was based on an interview with Michael W. Keogh.

people knew me by that logo and I wanted to maintain that image.

"Technically, the initials G.I.C. don't really stand for anything. However, having been asked that question for the last eight years, we have come up with an answer. Now we say the 'G' stands for group insurance; the 'I' for individual insurance; and the 'C' for credit insurance."

Keogh has proved wrong many insurance industry people who warned him that administration and sales, his forte, don't mix.

"The majority of the people in the industry would say not to let salesmen run companies because they don't pay attention to details," he said. "The man who taught me the business suggested if you're going to run a company, you must get your administration end set up first and your sales will come second. If you don't have the administration to take care of the sale, you'll lose the sale. Fortunately, I always had the sales end of it down pat and have learned the inside since 1977."

G.I.C. is a general agency company.

"I hung my shingle and said to employers, 'Let me handle all of your insurance.' "

"Basically, we don't accept business from agents and/or brokers," Keogh explained. "We have 15 general agents, who act as regional arms of the home office. They have agents and brokers to bring them business and then they submit it to us. We give the quote back to them and they take it to their agents and brokers who sell it.

"Because we're predominantly in medical insurance, our business has changed due to the continuing rampant inflation growth in the medical business. Recent medical trend factors and hospital and doctor cost factors are around 14 to 15 percent.

G.I.C.
Insurance
Company

Michael W. Keogh turned a small insurance company into a multimillion dollar business.

"When I started 10 years ago, we would see claims in the $2,000 to $5,000 area. They were considered large claims that we audited. Today we don't audit claims under $10,000. The largest claim G.I.C. has had was in 1983: a $281,000 hospitalization claim.

"The new cost containment facilities are all very active now," Keogh said. "The new trend is to chop some of the extraordinary costs of going into a hospital by increasing outpatient care. The theme now is to go to doctors, clinics or outpatient departments and have pre-hospital testing done there before reporting to the hospital for surgery in the morning. A lot of people are convinced that second opinions are necessary. One doctor may want to treat with drugs rather than through more expensive surgical procedures.

"Competitively speaking, what is offered now is the service that goes along with the sale of the policy and the processing and payment of the claims."

Statistics indicate 71 percent of the U.S. population is covered by hospitalization insurance through employer/employee groups, and 13 percent is covered through Medi-Care. Almost all companies with 10 to 15 people or more have a group

---

"It's nice to deliver one of those checks to a widow or take care of a child. It's a good business."

---

hospitalization plan for the employees.

"Insurance is a must," Keogh believes. "Twenty years ago, that was not the case. Because it is a corporate or company write-off, the majority of companies are paying 100 percent of the individual employee's policy cost and then the employee pays only for his family's coverage.

G.I.C. offers a member participant association plan.

"For instance, we have a master contract on an association plan with the Greater San Antonio Chamber of Commerce," Keogh said. "The chamber wanted that because many of its members have fewer than 10 employees, which is not a true group in Texas."

Keogh recalled his company's turning point:

"People said to me, 'It will take five years to build a company and get over the problems. You won't make any profit for five years.' I said, 'That's not true. We can handle that.' Around 1981 I started realizing that they may have been right. After that fifth year, 1982, we finally realized the company was big and strong and that we were a factor to be reckoned with.

"We owe our success to the people here at this company. I still maintain that there has to be communication and loyalty. If you don't have those two things, there's going to be a divorce if it's a family unit or a breakup if it's a business. These

Some 125 employees work for G.I.C. including these on the staff of 40 in the claims department.

folks here have stayed with us, learned and had the hard knocks. We've got some fine people. We have 125 people in our building and we're bulging at the seams. We have to look for more space.

"To write an account like the City of San Antonio for 7,600 employees is a very presitigious piece of business. When Mayor Cisneros signs our contract for the city each year, it's a good feeling to know that

in our own community of San Antonio, we are a real force. Almost any day at any time, you can see a policeman walking into G.I.C. with his claims. We tell clients to sit down, have a cup of coffee and give us the claim. We process it and they leave with a check."

Other groups with insurance through G.I.C. include Bexar County, Southwest Texas Methodist Hospital and the National Guard of the State of Texas.

Keogh wishes he had gone into business for himself 20 years earlier.

"This is such a satisfying business," he said. "It's nice to deliver one of those checks to a widow or take care of a child. It's a good business, it's a clean business, it's very competitive and it's very self-satisfying. I wish I had done it years ago." ⌶

G.I.C. has a full-service issuing department for new policies.

NASH PHILLIPS/COPUS

Nash Phillips/Copus has been ranked the No. 1 home builder in the state by Texas Business Magazine and is No. 2 in the San Antonio market.

This rapidly growing firm based in Austin operates in five Texas metropolitan areas in addition to San Antonio — Austin, Houston, Dallas/Fort Worth, Temple/Killeen and Bryan/College Station. NPC also is active in Colorado, Arizona, Virginia and Florida.

"In San Antonio, our company's first operation was in home building. We've expanded that to commercial development, residential land development and brokerage services," Louis Kirchofer, Jr., president of the San Antonio division of Nash Phillips/Copus, explained. "Our goal is to be a complete real estate service company. In 1984 we built about 850 homes here."

Kirchofer explained what prompted NPC to enter San Antonio:

"We had watched the San Antonio market for about five years. Coming here was in response to two things: We thought there was great opportunity in San Antonio and that coincided with the company's desire to expand.

"Historically, we had been primarily an Austin builder. During the 1950s, however, we were also in the oil patch in West Texas — Lubbock, Midland/Odessa and Amarillo.

"Our founders, Nash Phillips and Clyde Copus, are Austinites. But Mr. Phillips grew up in San Antonio. His dad was a surgeon at Fort Sam Houston and the family lived in the Alamo Heights area when it wasn't quite the same place it is today. He still talks about the horse he kept in the fields by Alamo Heights.

"They started this company out of their hip pockets, with less than $10,000. Their first operation was headquartered in a basement off Congress Avenue in the old Austin Alamo Hotel.

"After World War II, Mr. Phillips opened his own real estate brokerage
in Austin. He had been in operation for six to nine months when Mr. Copus joined the firm as a salesman. When Mr. Phillips saw his high performance standards, he realized he needed to offer Mr. Copus a partnership.

Louis Kirchofer, Jr.

"After the war, the country experienced a housing shortage. Mr. Phillips and Mr. Copus did so well in the general real estate business they ran out of houses to sell. There wasn't enough housing inventory and that's really how they got in the home-building business. The builders were not providing adequate inventory to sell. The same thing led them into the land development business. There became a severe shortage of lots and they didn't believe anybody was being aggressive enough in the development business.

"Mr. Phillips and Mr. Copus have an unusual arrangement. It's very rare that two individuals can keep a partnership going over a 40-year span. They're completely different personalities and they really complement each other.

"Their diverse perspectives have been a kind of insurance for each of them. Mr. Phillips is a real generalist; he's very knowledgeable

History at a Glance 1979

Founded: *1945 in Austin*
Opened in San Antonio: *January 1979*
Founders: *Nash Phillips and Clyde Copus*
Original employees: *3*
Original investment: *$10,000*
Milestones: *First in Austin to introduce energy-saving homes; first major home builder in Austin to build condominiums;* **1984** *acquired Security Financial Corporation and Capital City Savings in Austin, received Builder of the Year award*
Headquarters: *Austin*
San Antonio location: *13441 Blanco Road*
Services: *Commercial and residential development; single and multifamily home construction and sales; commercial construction and brokerage; property management; residential brokerage; corporate relocation; financial services; construction and manufacturing*
Employees: *1,500 plus*
Total sales volume: *$400 million*

This chapter was based on an interview with Louis Kirchofer, Jr.

about real estate in general and keeps an overall perspective. His primary interest is land development and overall project planning. Mr. Copus is a driving person, a real motivator of people. He is very involved on a day-to-day basis, all the way down to the placement of windows and the particular design of a fireplace. He has an extreme influence on our architectural department. You'll frequently see both men out on construction sites.

"San Antonio has a lot of NPC's attention. We believe there is real opportunity here. When we entered the San Antonio market, we initially built expensive custom homes. But one thing that's unique about our company is that we build in all price ranges. With prices from $40,000 to $600,000, we try to hit all segments of the market. A real entrepreneural spirit exists in our company and we're never afraid to try something new.

"Each division president operates autonomously and is encouraged to go in new directions. We do extensive market studies. We don't like to have failures.

"We obtain lots from other developers and also develop our own communities. NPC developed Northwest Crossing and has been the primary builder in the Great Northwest. The entire Stone Ridge development was a major endeavor. We built out the balance of Whispering Oaks and the Castle Wood Forest subdivisions. We really are attracted to being in a subdivision with other builders.

Nash Phillips, left, and Clyde Copus are the duo behind NPC.

"In the San Antonio market, we've found the demand for quality to be much higher than it is in other cities. I would rank San Antonio highest in

"They started this company out of their hip pockets."

Texas in terms of quality of overall builders. There are more experienced buyers here because of the number of military buyers. They've bought multiple homes and they demand quality. About 40 percent of our sales are military.

"The best housing value in the na-

tion is in San Antonio. I would have said four or five years ago that it was in Austin. But Austin is in a boom cycle and there has been tremendous land speculation that has impacted the price of houses. The medium price of a home here in 1984 was about $83,000, while in Austin it was $109,000. There probably was not that much difference in the size or the features of that medium home.

"We envision tremendous opportunities in the future. We're probably the most aggressive home building firm in the nation right now. Four years ago, we would have ranked No. 7 or No. 8 in Texas and now we're No. 1. We've been received well in the other markets that we've entered. And the way Mr. Phillips and Mr. Copus have structured management, I see a glowing future for the company." 🖵

Two-story home in The Hills of Northwest Crossing exemplifies construction skills which have made Nash Phillips/Copus the city's No. 2 home builder.

GARDEN RIDGE POTTERY & WORLD IMPORTS

Size is a secret to the success of Garden Ridge Pottery & World Imports. The mammoth mass merchandiser, which built its reputation on pottery and baskets, features 5½ acres of household merchandise at discounted prices.

And its two massive, bright orange buildings, warehouses and expansive parking area on Interstate 35 North use only 20 of the 31 acres the rapidly growing business owns.

Six years after it opened, Garden Ridge sells a seemingly endless array of domestic and direct-imported goods such as silk and dried flowers, floral supplies, baskets, candles, figurines, glassware, brass, toys, miniatures, furniture, souvenirs, dinnerware and housewares.

Founder and owner Eric W. White explained how he began the popular operation, its phenomenal growth and plans for expansion:

"I started in 1979 with a 22,500-square-foot building with pottery, baskets and some accessories. At that time, the availability of quality goods at discounted prices was scarce for San Antonio consumers. Immediately, I saw the store was too small. So we added on the same year. And we've just kept adding on.

"This type of business needed to be on the outskirts of town. We cater heavily to tourists who travel Interstate 35. I drove up and down the freeway looking for a location. There was a Garden Ridge exit on both sides of the interstate. It looked like this area had potential for growth. Of course, the Austin-San Antonio corridor has been talked about a lot since then, but at the time it just looked good to me," he said.

The turning point in the success of Garden Ridge was its expansion to 100,000 square feet.

"At that point, I had enough merchandise and was able to advertise more. We really had struggled the first two years. But I didn't worry; I knew in my mind that the store would make it.

"When I started, I tried to tell people about the growth I envisioned and they laughed at me. But I knew this operation had to be big to justify being this far out of town. Then when

"In my opinion, a store can't get too big."

I added on, I again went against everybody's advice. But I like to get advice from as many people as I can, think it through and then make my own decisions," he said.

Direct importing keeps prices low by eliminating the middleman. White makes three or four month-long buying trips a year to the Philippines, Hong Kong, Taiwan, China and other destinations in the Far East.

History at a Glance   1979

Founded: *March 1979 at 17975 Interstate 35 North*
Founder: *Eric W. White*
Original investment: *$600,000*
Original employees: *12*
Milestones: 1979 *expanded to 52,500 square feet;* **1980** *expanded to 92,500 square feet;* **1981** *expanded to 124,000 square feet;* **1983** *added south building with 112,500 square feet;* **1985** *opened store in Oklahoma City*
Owner: *Eric W. White*
Employees: *175*
Motto: *There's nobody like us.*

This chapter was based on an interview with Eric W. White.

He buys directly from factories and cottage industry operations and usually buys $2 million in merchandise each trip.

"Buying overseas is all bargaining. It's very important that you know approximately what the price is of the product you're buying because the vendors are very sharp. We buy in such large quantities we've got to know prices," he explained.

Orders for Garden Ridge's Christmas season must be placed at least eight months in advance.

"We have a longer Christmas season than most stores. At the customers' request, we put out Christmas merchandise in August and the season continues to the first of January. We have to be so far ahead of the trends," White said.

The average Garden Ridge customer browses three to four hours.

"A lot of people plan a day around Garden Ridge. They bring their out-of-town relatives and spend the whole day. Many have said they enjoyed it as much as strolling down the River Walk or seeing any other tourist attraction. We also get a lot of customers on bus tours."

As to how White keeps up with his 236,500 square feet of merchandise, he observed, "That seems to bother everybody but me."

White attributes his store's success to growth.

"We always try for a 50 percent increase per year, and we've met this since we've been here. In five years, we went from a $1 million operation to a $10 million operation. Hard

Owner Eric W. White sells pottery and direct-imported goods in his 236,500-square-foot buildings.

"In five years, we went from a $1 million operation to a $10 million operation."

---

work is important, but I've gathered a lot of good people around me to help.

"In the near future, we plan to double our space and widen our stock. There are a lot of things we would like to add before we've got everything.

"In my opinion, a store can't get too big." **LJ**

The shining white roofs of Garden Ridge Pottery & World Imports cover acres of shopping space.

SAN ANTONIO MARRIOTT RIVERWALK

In 1927 J. Willard Marriott opened a root beer stand with nine seats and a slat roof in Washington, D.C. His first expansion was adding chili dogs to the menu.

With foresight, hard work and sound management, he turned his first venture into the Marriott Corporation, a multicorporation composed of first class hotels, suite hotels and economy hotels as well as fast-food operations, cruise lines, theme parks and in-flight food service. Annual sales volume for the corporation is $3.5 billion.

A major business magazine recently rated Marriott as one of the top managed companies in the United States. In another journal, its sales force was designated the best sales team in the hotel industry.

The San Antonio Marriott Riverwalk is one of the 141 hotels which have contributed to the success and good reputation of the Marriott Corporation. The local hotel, which opened in December 1979, overlooks the San Antonio River and the Henry B. Gonzalez Convention Center.

The 30-story hotel features the only indoor/outdoor swimming pool in downtown San Antonio, 502 deluxe guest rooms, a 10,000-square-foot ballroom and 14,000 square feet of meeting and banquet space. Visitors enjoy Cactus Flower restaurant in the hotel. Popular clubs are the convenient lobby bar and Gambits with its two-decked lounge and riverside patio.

A 35-story companion Marriott hotel will add 1,000 rooms to downtown hostelry in 1988 when the Tiendas del Rio Mall project is completed.

The first venture for J. Willard Marriott, left, was a root beer stand in Washington, D.C.

Christopher Hosmer, director of marketing for Marriott Riverwalk, traced the background of the company and explained the plans for the second Marriott downtown:

"J. Willard Marriott, a Mormon from Salt Lake City, Utah, went to Washington, D.C., in the 1920s and married his wife, Alice. Near the 14th Street Bridge, he started his business with a nine-seat root beer stand and soon moved up to selling chili dogs, too.

"His stand was close to National Airport. One day an airline had problems with a plane on the ground and came to him for sack lunches for waiting passengers. That's how in-flight service started," Hosmer said.

Before his death in August 1985, Mr. Marriott frequently visited his hotels and checked the kitchens and inspected the rooms. Though he remained active in the business, he had turned over some of the operations to his son, J. Willard Marriott, Jr.," Hosmer said.

Much of the company's success can be attributed to the elder Marriott's philosophy that if the

History at a Glance   1979

Founded: *Marriott Corporation, 1927 in Washington, D.C.*
Opened in San Antonio: *1979*
Founder: *J. Willard Marriott*
Original name: *Marriott — Hot Shoppes Inc.*
Original employees: *2*
Milestones: **1957** *entered lodging field with Twin Bridges Marriott in Washington, D.C.;* **1967** *added Big Boy restaurants;* **1968** *added Roy Rogers restaurants and Sun Line Cruise Ships;* **1982** *acquired Host International and Gino's Inc.;* **1979** *Mariner Corporation built Marriott Riverwalk;* **1984** *Marriott Riverwalk sold to Montgomery Realty*
Headquarters: *Washington, D.C.*
Owner: *Marriott Corporation*
Employees: *120,000 worldwide*
Units: *141 hotels, 1,000 restaurants, 70 U.S. and international flight kitchens and more than 260 food-service management accounts*
Motto: *When Marriott does it, we do it right.*

This chapter was based on an interview with Christopher Hosmer.

company takes care of the employee, it will reflect in the way he or she takes care of the guest. That, in turn, will ensure repeat guests.

"Marriott believes in the guarantee of fair treatment. If an employee isn't satisfied with decisions by his superiors, the employee can go up the chain of command, all the way to the top if necessary.

"We're totally non-union. For such a large company to be non-union, we have to give our employees better benefits than any other hotel company," Hosmer said.

The Marriott Riverwalk sits on an area beside the San Antonio River where barges once were stored. The river was extended past that area to reach the convention center prior to HemisFair '68.

"The Marriott added another destination to the River Walk. People like it because there's a park area in between. The new hotel will make this end of the river a main attraction of the River Walk," Hosmer said.

The second downtown Marriott will be a major part of the Tiendas del Rio Mall project begun in 1985. The project will add another leg to the San Antonio River, making it flow underneath Commerce Street and into the mall.

Thirty-story Marriott River-walk overlooks the San Antonio River and the Convention Center.

"One day an airline had problems with a plane on the ground and came to him for sack lunches for waiting passengers. That's how in-flight service started."

In addition to the Marriott, the project will include a shopping mall, high-rise office building and shops and eateries along the River Walk.

Plans for the new Marriott include a ballroom with more than 25,000 square feet, three times the size of the ballroom in Marriott Riverwalk. The hotel also will have a 15,000-square-foot junior ballroom and an indoor/outdoor pool. A sky walk likely will connect the two hotels.

"With the expansion of the convention center to 362,000 square feet of meeting and exhibit space, we're seeing a demand daily for a megahotel. The Marriott will be it," Hosmer said.

The combined number of rooms in the two Marriotts will be 1,500, more than twice the rooms of the next largest hotel in San Antonio, which has 633. The two Marriotts will complement rather than compete with each other. They will have separate sales forces, but will be able to combine facilities to accommodate large groups.

"We can go after much larger conventions with the total hotel space we will have in 1988," he said.

Some 60 to 65 percent of the Marriott Riverwalk's current business is from groups.

"But we're also fortunate to have very strong weekend business from Austin, Dallas and Houston. These are families bringing the kids here to absorb the tourist sights."

Among the famous guests hosted by the Marriott Riverwalk are President Reagan, Vice President Bush and Mikhail Baryshnikov as well as stars of TV soap opera "General Hospital," "Sesame Street," Ice Capades and the Muppets. National Basketball Association teams stay overnight when in town to play the San Antonio Spurs.

"Our forte is really our service. People know that when they come to this Marriott or the Marriott in Maui, the service they will receive will be the same good, consistent, caring service whether it's from the housekeepers, the front desk or the catering service. Our service is the best in the business — always." 🔲

FISHER BROTHERS LUMBER COMPANY

The Fisher family came to San Antonio purely by chance.

"My wife, Diane, and I were in the Caribbean in January of 1979 on vacation from our home in South Africa. We were trying to go to Miami and Los Angeles to sort out some immigration papers. We got to Miami just in time to see our plane take off," recalled Ian L. Fisher, half of the twin brother team which founded and owns Fisher Brothers Lumber Company."

"So Diane and I were standing by the ticket counter kind of forlorn, and a really big old cowboy came up with a face and hat bigger than I've ever seen. He leaned over to the lady behind the counter and said, 'Ya'll goin' to San Antone?' "

Fisher continued, "I was listening with half an ear and I asked Diane, 'What did he say?' She hadn't understood a word either. I asked the ticket lady what he said. She said he wanted to know if they had a flight to San Antonio.

"Then Diane remembered we had a couple of very good friends who moved here. So we also got tickets to San Antonio and visited our friends for one day. We liked the look. So when our green cards finally came

through, we moved here. I'd like to say I did all these interesting surveys about the Sun Belt and why it's such a wonderful place. But we simply came across the city by pure chance. Very, very fortunate. We met such super people on that brief visit that we felt sure we would settle well in San Antonio. Most of those people are still our very close friends."

Since the early '60s, the Fishers' native South Africa has had tremendous political pressures and problems.

"They have a situation there with the blacks and whites that is going to get more troublesome," Fisher explained. "The long-term future for our kids just wasn't what we would like it to be. We were also worried about our business future. If you build up a business there and end up leaving the country, you really have worked for nothing. You've left it all behind because they have exchange control regulations which don't allow you to take much money out of the country. You just run and start again some place else.

"Diane had always been very committed to leaving South Africa. She had lived out of South Africa as a teen-ager for a few years and had always thought after we were married that we should begin our lives in a new country.

"So in 1977, my twin brother, David, and I decided that one of us would be out by 1980 and start again. My background was in lumber and his was in accounting. We thought it better for me to leave first because my kids were older and it would be easier to get them into schools. That's why we left first.

"It was a family decision. The major turning in my thinking was in 1976 when they had a lot of riots in South Africa and people burned cars and threw stones in the streets. We sold our company in 1984, and my

The Fisher brothers are most proud of their building center, which opened in 1983.

brother will join me in this business after fulfilling a work contract in South Africa."

By the time they sold out, the Fishers owned the largest private lumber company in South Africa. Fisher recalled how they got started:

History at a Glance   1980

Founded: *1975 in Johannesburg, South Africa*
Moved to San Antonio: *1980*
Founders and owners: *Ian L. Fisher and David R. Fisher*
Original employees: *6*
Original location: *8,000 square feet in South Africa; 2 acres in San Antonio*
Milestones: **1981** *land doubled;* **1983** *Fisher Building Center opened;* **1984** *Fisher Millwork opened and land expanded to 20 acres*
Headquarters: *Interstate 10 West at Camp Bullis Road*
Employees: *141*
Stores: *3*
Motto: *Nice people to do business with*

This chapter was based on an interview with Ian L. Fisher.

"When I left the Air Force in 1967, I started working for a lumber company that was part of a chain which had 40 or 50 branches through South Africa. I started out in the yard loading rail cars and was kind of a short-pants sweeper-type. I worked for them until 1973 and worked my way through the company. I wanted to do more. And like most people, I felt like I was running the business, so why shouldn't I do it for myself? My father had been in that same company all his life and was almost ready to retire.

"I left them in April of 1975 and started in business with my brother. I took a second mortgage on my house of $10,000 for start-up capital. I went to suppliers who gave us 30 days and 60 days and some even 90 days to pay. It was very difficult because we started in a yard that was one side of a duplex house no larger than 10,000 square feet. We had a little hardware store there where we sold really small things and hand tools. We gradually rented more and more pieces of land around us, but we still had to store most of our lumber on the sidewalk outside for lack of space. We hired a very loyal black night watchman and bought him a German shepherd dog to guard our lumber at night. It was ridiculous."

Even with such a small beginning, the company grew rapidly.

"We were very fortunate," Fisher remembered. "We worked extremely long hours. We started with two or three people. Eventually, we had probably 450 people working for us in the seven yards we finished up with."

To repeat that success in San Antonio, Fisher first had to find an appropriate spot for his new business.

"To find a location here, I started downtown on one of the rail lines," he explained. "I walked out of town on the rail and wrote down pieces of land and addresses as I went. I always liked this area on Interstate 10 where we finally located. This piece of land wasn't for sale at the time. It was owned by Howard and Betty Watson, a really dear couple, who have lived out near Camp Bullis for years. Mr. Watson was not at all keen to sell the land because he did not want any unsightly enterprise next to his ranch. I was determined

Twin brothers David Fisher, left, and Ian Fisher combined their skills to form Fisher Brothers Lumber Company.

that this location was the piece that I wanted to buy because it was flat, on a rail track and visible.

"I spent many an afternoon drinking coffee and eating an assortment of delicious cakes baked by Mrs. Watson, who is a super cook. I also introduced them to my wife, Diane, and my two daughters, Lauren and Daniella. Finally, one afternoon after about four or five weeks, Mr. Watson said, 'Well, you must want to buy that land real bad.'

"I told him to put any price on it and that would be fair. I didn't know the price until almost the day we closed, but I had the utmost trust that the Watsons were very fair people. We've got a workable nine acres now.

"When I first came to San Antonio, I walked on job sites at 5 or 6 o'clock in the afternoon when workers were going home. I'd pick up the pieces of lumber with the grade stamps and call the Lumberman's Association of Texas and ask, 'What does this grade stamp mean?' or 'What does this species look like?' It really was a whole new learning experience because the sizes, species and qualities were very much different from those in South Africa. Everything is much bigger in the U.S.A., and frankly, the quality is much better as well.

"It took me perhaps five months until it all came together. Our first office was a 600-square-foot wood framed building on 10 foot-high piers, which was built in the evenings and on weekends by my close friends Marty Wender and Raul Vieyra and me. We moved into our 'Taj Mahal' in May 1980 and used that little blue office building very happily for two years until we were all sitting almost shoulder to shoulder in the office.

"Our growth pattern was very good from day one. Needless to say, the extremely long working hours put tremendous pressure on Diane, but she stood foursquare behind me always. However tough our new start-up was, I think it was probably more difficult even for Diane, who had the children to contend with as well.

"I'd say the biggest business milestones we have accomplished so far have been the openings of the building center and millwork shop. My personal milestone is that we've managed to build up a super group of people. We started out here with six people and now we have close to 150. We always try to hire the best quality people and are very proud of all the people we have working with us. Everybody is an extension of what you are." $\square$

HYATT REGENCY SAN ANTONIO

The roots of San Antonio's largest hotel, the Hyatt Regency San Antonio, are steeped in history.

Ancestors of part-owner Belton Kleberg Johnson founded the legendary King Ranch and helped preserve the Alamo.

The Paseo del Alamo, the hotel's terraced waterway, has become the pedestrian Main Street of San Antonio linking the city's oldest and most popular tourist attractions, the Alamo and the San Antonio River. And the hotel was developed through a landmark blending of forces from both public and private sectors.

The unique 16-story Hyatt features 633 guest rooms and 25,000 square feet of meeting space including the city's largest hotel ballroom.

Guest rooms face the Alamo, a historic section of San Antonio or an atrium garden lush with tropical plants and a palm grove. Water flows through the hotel's river level lined with one-of-a-kind shops. For dining and entertainment, the Hyatt boasts the Crescendo, La Puerta and Chaps restaurants as well as the River Terrace lounge and Jim Cullum's Landing, a landmark San Antonio jazz club.

Johnson, head of Belton Kleberg Johnson Interests, and Ben A. Yeakley, sales manager of the hotel, explained how the creation of Hyatt Regency San Antonio made and preserved history:

"My maternal great-grandfather, Capt. Richard King, founded the King Ranch in Kingsville, which still remains in the family. I was raised on the ranch and worked there summers as a boy and full time as a young man. Later I was a shareholder and director," Johnson said.

"But my family and I have had a long association with San Antonio. I attended San Antonio Academy and Texas Military Institute, I have had offices in San Antonio for 20 years, and I have lived here for the last 10.

"The King Ranch family used to stay at the Menger Hotel next door to the Alamo. It was the gathering spot of ranchers and cattlemen for years. Capt. King died there in 1885.

"My other maternal great-grandfather, Robert Justus Kleberg I, guarded Gen. Santa Anna after his capture at the Battle of San Jacinto.

"Another family connection we're quite proud of is the close friendship of my mother, Sarah Spohn Kleberg Johnson, with Clara Driscoll, who saved the old convento of the Alamo from being razed. My mother helped her in that crusade.

Belton Kleberg
Johnson, right,
and ranch
manager Pete
Emmert oversee
operations of
the family's
Chaparrosa
Ranch at La
Pryor.

History at a Glance 1981

Founded: *December 18, 1981, at 123 Losoya St.*
Owners: *Belton Kleberg Johnson, Mexican American Unity Council, Hardin Investment Associates and Samuel G. Friedman*
Management: *Hyatt Hotels Corporation, Chicago, Ill.*
General manager: *Norman A. Howard*
Employees: *550*

Ben A. Yeakley was director of sales at the Hyatt Regency San Antonio from September 1, 1979, until his death April 23, 1985, at the age of 47.

Yeakley was active in the hotel business in Texas for nearly 20 years and brought a tremendous amount of enthusiasm and creativity to every project he undertook. Through his dedication and leadership, he made Hyatt Regency San Antonio one of the most successful hotels in the State of Texas. Due to his tireless efforts, the hotel had more advance group bookings prior to its opening in 1981 than any other Hyatt hotel in the history of the company.

"Ben was a 'people' person who touched people's lives in a very deep and meaningful manner. We dedicate this section of The Businesses That Built San Antonio *to the memory of Ben Yeakley, as he will forever be an inspiration to the people who work in this hotel," said Norman A. Howard, general manager.*

This chapter was based on an interview with Belton Kleberg Johnson and Ben A. Yeakley.

"Long before the idea of building a hotel in the area, my wife, Patsy, and I wanted to do something in San Antonio in memory of our parents. When the prospect appeared for the Paseo del Alamo, we knew that was the perfect tribute."

The connection between the River Walk and the Alamo was for many years the dream of San Antonians. That dream finally became a reality when Johnson joined with Hardin Investment Associates, a development firm in Atlanta, and the City of San Antonio to build the hotel and the Paseo del Alamo. The architects were Thompson, Ventulett & Stainback of Atlanta with local assistance from Ford, Powell & Carson, Inc.

"Almost 150 years ago, the Mexican Army laid siege to the Alamo on that site."

"In a little cafe on the river, we asked O'Neil Ford, one of the nation's great architects, what his thoughts were about a linkage. On the back of a small cocktail napkin, he drew the pictures that formulated the ideas for the Paseo," Johnson recalled.

"There's no better location for something like this," Yeakley said. "Almost 150 years ago, the Mexican Army laid siege to the Alamo on that site. The ground the hotel sits on is special because it represents the defense of democracy and the free enterprise system."

During excavation for the Hyatt and Paseo del Alamo, archeologists unearthed artifacts such as musket balls, bullets, buttons and pottery, many of which are displayed at The University of Texas at San Antonio.

The most significant discovery, however, was the finding of an outer wall of the Alamo. The design concept of the terraced waterway was modified to include a window to display a small portion of the wall.

The Hyatt is a prime example of cooperation between the public and

The Hyatt Regency San Antonio provides easy access to the San Antonio River through its lower lobby.

private sectors — the U.S. government through an Urban Development Action Grant, the City of San Antonio and private developers.

"This was the first large-scale development of its kind on the river," Yeakley said. "But the Paseo del Alamo wasn't a new idea; maps of early San Antonio show an acequia going from the Alamo straight down to the river.

"The hotel has introduced two things to America — a beautiful waterway system flowing through a hotel, and fajitas. Most hotels throughout the country are serving fajitas, and we were the first hotel to start it," Yeakley said.

The Hyatt's success inspired the redevelopment and restoration of historic buildings in the area.

Renovations include the Crockett Hotel; the Landmark Building, now the Emily Morgan Hotel; the Maverick Building; and the Giles Building.

When the Paseo del Alamo was dedicated in December 1981, a bronze plaque placed beside the fountains recorded the event for posterity. Its inscription capsulizes the importance of the historic project:

"The past, the present and the future are all embodied in this project to rejoin the historically inseparable Alamo and the San Antonio River. Community spirit, individual dedication and generosity, and intergovernmental cooperation, have all combined to make the Paseo del Alamo a reality." ◪

TETCO, INC.

Tetco, Inc. is one of San Antonio's newest corporations, but its history is centered around a local legend: the rise of Sigmor Corporation and the Tom E. Turner family who masterminded it.

Tetco was formed after Sigmor Corporation, the largest independent service station organization in the United States at the time, was sold to Diamond Shamrock in 1983. Today its scope includes such varied interests as trucking, auto parts manufacturing, warehousing, hotels, a 400-acre wholesale plant nursery, radio stations, banks, savings and loans, a professional baseball team and real estate developments.

The success story began with a small family enterprise more than 50 years ago, and today's new business is still family owned and family run, a fact the Turners are particularly fond of pointing out.

In San Antonio, Tetco is well-known for its participation in Sonterra, a prestigious planned community; the San Antonio Dodgers, Radio Station KBUC-AM & FM; Safeguard Security Group; Safeguard Security Services; Mission Petroleum Carriers; Bexar Savings; Thousand Oaks National Bank; and Capital Bank Northwest.

Tom E. Turner, Jr., part owner in today's ever-expanding enterprise, tells the family's story:

"My dad was a young seventy when we sold Sigmor, and he had no intention of going home, sitting down and watching TV," Turner explained. "So we decided to go back into business. We named the company Tetco, initials for Tom E. Turner Company, and now it is a 100 percent family owned corporation.

"Most of our real estate holdings are in San Antonio," he explained. "Sonterra is a 715-acre development between Highway 281 and Blanco Road north of Loop 1604 in which Tetco is the managing partner, owning 51 percent of the project. The balance is owned by other San Antonio businessmen. It will have around 1,000 families living there, a 36-hole golf course and all the other amenities that make an outstanding country club.

"Tetco has built three large local shopping centers: Adobe Creek, Carillon Hills and Leon Creek. The company is also developing a residential subdivision and office buildings. With Bexar Savings, Tetco built a 15-story office building on

Tom E. Turner, Sr.

Loop 410 to house its corporate headquarters and Bexar Savings."

The interest in real estate evolved from the challenge the family found in locating new service stations.

"Before we sold Sigmor, we were becoming interested in buying property, building a shopping center on the bulk of it and then putting the service station on the corner," Turner explained.

But the story of the Turner empire goes back to the late 1930s when Tom E. Turner, Sr., left Fort Worth for San Antonio.

"He went to work for Sig Moore, who had a group of service stations called Midway Oil Company,"

Fred A. Turner

Turner explained. "He started as a helper and then became the night manager and later a manager. Then he became a supervisor who handled a group of service stations for Mr. Moore.

"In the early '40s, Mr. Moore decided to sell out and loaned my dad money to go into business for himself.

"Originally, he leased a service station on East Commerce near the old Friedrich Air Conditioning plant. That was our first location. When we got our second service station, my dad ran it and my mother ran the first one. She was a pioneer for women working in a service station.

"We learned early the togetherness of a family business."

"Then my dad bought an old truck. He would haul our own gasoline because we saved money buying it directly from the refinery. When he got off work, usually at 6 or 7 o'clock in the evening, he would pick up gasoline and deliver it to the three stations. He would usually go home around 9 or 10 o'clock and he was at work at 6 o'clock the next morning seven days a week.

"My dad encouraged my brother and me to go to work at an early age, so we learned early the togetherness

of a family business. My dad is president and chairman of the board, and I'm executive vice president. The two of us and my brother, Fred, as senior vice president, are the owners. I have three sons, and my brother has three sons and two daughters. My dad always said he was building the company for his family, and it was a foregone conclusion that we would continue on.

Tom E. Turner, Jr.

"The growth of the company in the early stages was financed strictly from available cash flow. My dad was brought up very conservatively, and he didn't believe in borrowing. He never bought anything until he could afford it.

"Hard work is a big part of our success, but there are a lot of people who work hard all day and do not become successful. Success is also

coming up with ideas, using them properly and having the common sense to know when something is or is not the thing to do.

"If I had to select one major reason for the business' success, it would be our ability to pick the right people. They stayed with us and grew with us. I think that's really why we've continued to be successful.

"In the early days, we grew within the family. Of course, you ran out of family pretty soon, so you had to start hiring people. We were able to get people who were very loyal to us."

Tetco continues to hire the best management personnel available to help run the company's varied operations.

"We have a management staff that meets with us periodically to go over each company and make recommendations," Turner explained. "We have reached the size now where we have a management team in each company, and they handle all the day-to-day problems."

Of the varied businesses the Turners own, trucking remains their largest in total revenues, operating more than 500 trucks in 48 states.

"It would be fair to say trucking is the favorite business because it is something we've been doing since my dad opened the third service station," Turner said. "The rest of them are fun, but we just haven't been doing them as long." **LJ**

Sonterra's prestigious club offers the finest facilities.

DIAMOND SHAMROCK REFINING AND MARKETING COMPANY

Diamond Shamrock Refining and Marketing Company was born in January 1983 when its parent company, Diamond Shamrock Corp., acquired the refining and retail marketing assets of the well-known San Antonio-based Sigmor Corporation.

But its roots lie in the past.

Seventy-five years ago in Pennsylvania, a soda ash company, Diamond Alkali, was started by a group of glass manufacturers who poured $1.5 million into a venture to service the needs of their glass business. And in 1929, an Irishman founded Shamrock Oil and Gas Co. in the Texas Panhandle, which lost millions of dollars during its first few struggling years.

Those two divergent businesses half a continent apart — Diamond Alkali and Shamrock — combined forces in 1967 to form Diamond Shamrock Corp., with 1984 revenues of $4.5 billion.

The new company with sales of $324 million in its founding year continued to do what it did best: find new reserves of oil and gas and manufacture quality chemicals. The chemical operation benefited from additional cash flow and assured itself of the petrochemical raw materials it required.

Today San Antonio-based Diamond Shamrock Refining and Marketing Company has two refineries, both in Texas; thousands of miles of

Roger Hemminghaus, president, fills his car with gasoline at a local Diamond Shamrock retail unit.

pipelines; 15 terminals across the Southwestern United States; and more than 2,000 Diamond Shamrock-branded stations including about 500 company-owned and operated units.

Roger Hemminghaus presides over the local company. He explained his company's history and its operations:

"Diamond Shamrock Refining and Marketing Company refines crude oil at two refineries," he said. "One is the McKee Refinery in the Panhandle; it includes one of the largest gas processing facilities in the country and is the finest refiner in its class. The other is in Three Rivers between San Antonio and Corpus Christi. The combined capacity of

---

History at a Glance   1983

Founded: *Jan. 14, 1983*

Founding companies: *Diamond Shamrock Corp., Dallas, acquired the refining and marketing assets of Sigmor Corporation, San Antonio*

Milestones: 1910 *Diamond Alkali was founded in Pittsburgh, Pa.;* **1929** *Shamrock Oil and Gas Co. was founded and headquartered in Amarillo;* **1943** *Tom Turner bought his first service station in San Antonio and called it "Sigmor;"* **1952** *Sigmor Corporation incorporated;* **1960** *Sigmor became a jobber for Shamrock;* **1967** *Diamond Alkali and Shamrock Oil and Gas Co. merged;* **1978** *corporate headquarters relocated in Dallas*

Lineage of presidents: *Riley Epps, Roger Hemminghaus*

Headquarters: *3643 E. Commerce St.*

Owners: *Publicly held corporation listed on New York Stock Exchange with about 75,000 stockholders of record*

Employees: *3,933 Refining and Marketing Company employees in the world; 1,100 in San Antonio*

Revenues: *$4.5 billion for Diamond Shamrock Corp., $2.3 billion for the Refining and Marketing Company*

This chapter was based on an interview with Roger Hemminghaus.

those plants is about 120,000 barrels per day of crude oil."

Hemminghaus continued, "We have 2,000 miles of crude oil gathering lines. After refining we take the product from those refineries and move it by 2,000 miles of pipeline, barge and exchanges to nearly 30 terminals (15 owned and operated by Diamond Shamrock) in the Southwest.

"Those terminals supply a retail marketing organization of more than 500 Diamond Shamrock-owned stations."

In addition, these terminals supply products to a jobber network of independent businesses which buy products and market them through more than 1,500 Diamond Shamrock-branded stations.

Because of the addition of retail stores to the service stations, a popular convenience for customers,

"To survive in a mature business with the major companies, you have to be a little different."

"we say we are not only in the motor gasoline selling business, but the convenience business," Hemminghaus said.

Now 75 years old, Diamond Shamrock Corp. began in Pittsburgh, Pennsylvania, when the century was young.

"Some businessmen got together to make soda ash, a major component for the glass industry," Hemminghaus explained. "That started in 1910 and the company was called Diamond Alkali. That company developed as a major chemical company during the 1920s. Parallel to that development was Shamrock Oil and Gas Co., which incorporated in 1929 and developed as an independent oil and gas company. It built a

small refinery in about 1933. That small plant developed into our McKee Refinery that today processes more than 80,000 barrels of crude oil each day.

"The first company gasoline service station was built in Sunray in Moore County also about 1933.

"In the late '60s, Diamond Alkali and Shamrock Oil and Gas were merged and became Diamond Shamrock Corp. At the time of the merger, the company was about 80 percent a chemicals company and 20 percent an oil and gas company. Today it has just about flip-flopped. We are 80 percent an oil and gas company and about 20 percent a chemicals company."

When Diamond Shamrock acquired Sigmor in 1983, the San Antonio-based company was one of the largest independent service station companies in the United States.

"Tom E. Turner, Sr., started Sigmor in 1943 when a service station operator he had been working for, Sig Moore, decided to sell out," Hemminghaus explained. "As the story goes, he loaned Mr. Turner $350, which he used to get his own

single station. The company just kept growing until 1983. When Diamond Shamrock acquired Sigmor, Diamond Shamrock combined its refining and marketing operations with Sigmor's, which is the genesis of our company here.

"We respond quickly to the competitive situation on the street."

"Ours is a very competitive business. The gasoline business is not growing in this country; it's a rather mature business. To survive in a mature business with the major companies, you have to be a little different. You've got to do things a bit more efficiently and effectively, provide a bit more convenience for the customer and keep a smile on the face of the attendant behind the counter.

"We have carved out a niche as a regional company that is growing. We see a significant amount of expansion for this company in the marketing area in the Southwest, in Texas and in the surrounding states.

"Our headquarters will remain in San Antonio, a delightful place to live. We are the largest marketer of motor gasoline in San Antonio and the surrounding area. The city is between our two refineries and in the heart of our market, a great place to be headquartered. When we consolidated our headquarters in San Antonio, we moved 70 families here from Amarillo and Dallas.

"Including our office staff and employees in our retail stores, we have in excess of 1,100 employees in the San Antonio area. We are a significant factor in the economy here.

"Following the merger, we've made significant changes in our retail operation, not the least of which are the color and graphics changes at all of our company-operated Diamond Shamrock stores. We have rebuilt or significantly remodeled about 50 stores and added around 20 new stores. We have a modern, crisp look on the street now. We have 70 stores in the greater San Antonio area."

Diamond Shamrock is recognized for competitive prices.

"Being competitive doesn't mean that we set the lowest or highest price," Hemminghaus said. "When people leave a Diamond Shamrock retail store, we want them to feel they bought quality products at competitive prices and that they will come back the next time they need motor fuel or convenience items. We can do that because as a company we are flexible, we communicate, we are tightly manned, we operate as efficiently as anybody in the business and we make decisions very quickly. So we respond quickly to the competitive situation on the street.

"From a revenue standpoint, Diamond Shamrock Refining and Marketing Company would fall within the top 200 U.S. corporations if it were a stand-alone company. It's big business. Moving that much crude oil and products is a big operation. In 1984 our revenues for the refining and marketing company were in the neighborhood of $2.3 billion.

"You've got to be very nimble and a bit lucky to make money in the current environment. We are one of the survivors in the business and plan to grow not only in San Antonio, but in other parts of Texas and the surrounding states." ⬛

The familiar green cloverleaf Shamrock brand marked Sigmor's stations for about 20 years before the Diamond Shamrock sign was adopted in the early '80s.

Convenience Name of Game

Diamond Shamrock was the first gasoline company in the San Antonio area in the early 1970s to include convenience store items to its service station-related products, and a few years later it was among the first here to offer self-service.

"We have been ahead of the pack in the store business as far as traditional gasoline companies are concerned," said Joe Walden, vice president of retail marketing for Diamond Shamrock Refining and Marketing Company.

Convenience is the name of the game today for Diamond Shamrock, whose easily accessible stores provide everything from motor oil and filters to candy, ice, bread and milk.

After gasoline, however, the top sellers are tobacco products, beverages and fast foods.

Boasting its own credit, the Diamond Shamrock card now can be used to purchase any merchandise in the store as well as gasoline.

And today Diamond Shamrock's convenience also includes access to cash. With the addition of San Antonio Savings and Loan Association's automatic teller machines in 1985, customers also can stop at local Diamond Shamrock stations to make deposits or withdrawals or check the balance of their SASA accounts.

"The customer now can come in and deposit his paycheck, pull out cash, fill up the car and buy bread and milk and a snack for the road," Walden said.

A less expensive gasoline — due in part to a decrease in the number of people needed to run a station — is a side benefit customers of the self-service stations enjoy.

We've seen big changes in automobiles so that they just don't require the amount of service they

Joe Walden, vice president, poses inside a Diamond Shamrock station/convenience store.

did some 10 to 20 years ago," Walden said. "Every service station used to have two or three bays. Many dealers made a lot of their money washing cars, changing oil and greasing cars. That has changed."

A Diamond Shamrock subsidiary, Industrial Lubricants Company, is a motor oil canning and automotive accessory business, which serves as a major wholesaler and distributor of motor oil to Diamond Shamrock stations and others who retail these products. Big Diamond Tobacco and Candy Company, a

subsidiary located in San Antonio, also supplies the station-stores with candy and cigarettes.

Diamond Shamrock sees itself as a company that provides quality products and a range of conveniences in attractive stores. Customers believe they can purchase motor fuel and other products at a competitive price.

"We're unique in that we have our own supply capabilities both from the gasoline side and from the store merchandise side," Walden said.

"Quality and convenience at competitive prices — that's what we want to be known for."

Diamond Shamrock owns and operates about 500 gasoline retail units in Texas and Louisiana.

Diamond Shamrock's convenience stores offer fountain drinks and snacks among a variety of products.

ADVANCED TOBACCO PRODUCTS, INC.

The combination of J. Philip Ray's scientific capabilities and the entrepreneurial talents of Gerald R. Mazur materialized in the form of Advanced Tobacco Products, Inc., the smokeless cigarette company.

"Our smokeless cigarettes provide tobacco pleasure and satisfaction like conventional cigarettes," explained Mazur, chairman and chief executive officer of the new San Antonio firm. "But they do so without being lighted. In other words, the cigarettes provide nicotine satisfaction without the byproducts of combustion — tars and carbon monoxide. In my view, this is the first real technological advance in the tobacco industry since the advent of snuff."

The Ray-Mazur relationship goes back to the late 1960s when the two formed Datapoint Corporation. Mazur was chairman and chief executive officer; Ray was president. Both left in the early 1970s.

Mazur recalled, "I heard in 1978 that Phil was working on a smokeless cigarette. My first reaction was, 'Is he out of his mind?' Later a lot of other people asked the same question about both of us.

"I'm often asked, 'Why did Phil think of this? What caused him to try to develop such a product?' He was a three-pack-a-day smoker with an insatiable scientific curiosity. Phil wanted to know why he smoked. More importantly, he was aware that his smoking was offending others.

"So the question he was asking himself was, 'How can I continue to smoke without forcing other people to smoke whether they want to or not by just inhaling what I exhale and generate?'"

Mazur continued, "To make a long story short, Phil developed the product. He started reading and identified all the really outstanding authorities in the world. There were only six or eight and he went to see them all."

Ray formed a research and development partnership and Mazur helped him sell it before joining the company full time in 1982. Three factors tempted Mazur to join this unique enterprise.

"One motivation — and I'd be a hypocrite and a liar to say anything else — is I like to start companies. I saw something that looked tremendously promising here. The other thing is I like to make money, and I plan to. The third thing is that I thought the cigarette smokers of the world would be happier if they could take in just the nicotine, the habituating thing, without being forced to inhale the products of combustion, the tars and carbon monoxide."

> "FAVOR® is a way of enjoying tobacco pleasure in those environments in which smoking is either prohibited or socially unacceptable."

The world market for tobacco prior to the price increase in May 1985 was $160 billion per year. The U.S. and Canadian markets combined at that time were $30 billion in round figures and the European market including the United Kingdom was $50 billion. Japan is about $15 billion. Because of these figures, Mazur calls the potential for smokeless cigarettes "mind-boggling."

Additionally, the time is ripe for Advanced Tobacco's product. "In San Francisco, it's practically illegal to smoke any place but on the street," Mazur explained. "Los Angeles just passed similar legislation. This is happening in many different cities. It's illegal now in California to smoke in any state office. The timeliness of the product couldn't be better."

The smokeless cigarettes have a patent with 34 claims and the name FAVOR is registered.

History at a Glance 1983

Founded: *1983*
Founders: *Gerald R. Mazur and J. Philip Ray*
Milestones: **1984** *public offering;* **1985** *moved to new facilities and introduced product*
Headquarters: *121 Interpark Blvd.*
Officers: *Gerald R. Mazur, chairman and chief executive officer; J. Philip Ray, president and chief of technology; James D. Simonsen, executive vice president and chief operating officer*
Assets: *$7.4 million*

This chapter was based on an interview with Gerald R. Mazur.

Philip Ray, left, and Gerald Mazur are the duo behind smokeless cigarettes, the first major technological breakthrough in the tobacco industry since snuff.

Smokeless cigarettes work like this: "Phil discovered nicotine is volatile; that was a very exciting thing to learn. He learned that the amount of nicotine necessary to satisfy the cigarette smoker is about 2 percent — one-fiftieth of the amount of caffeine a coffee drinker requires for satisfaction. So you have minute quantity and volatility. You can induce volatility by pressure change.

"We put a minute quantity of solution, containing nicotine and flavorants, in a synthetic fiber material that looks like a cigarette filter-rod and is contained in a tube that is made to look like a conventional cigarette. When you take a drag, there's enough pressure change to release an amount of nicotine that's sufficient to be perceived as providing the same satisfaction that you get from a drag off a burning cigarette. It's that simple."

The amount of nicotine in one FAVOR approximates that in one conventional cigarette, yet it pro-vides the tobacco satisfaction of about five because of its efficiency.

"With a burning cigarette, a tremendous amount literally goes up in smoke between puffs. Then a third or a half is thrown away," Mazur explained. "You'll put FAVOR in your pocket, take it out, take a few drags, put it back in your pocket and

---

"I think this is the best thing I've ever done."

---

take it out when you want another drag."

Advanced Tobacco Products makes no health or cessation claims. "FAVOR is a way of enjoying tobacco pleasure and satisfaction in those environments in which smoking is either prohibited or socially unacceptable."

The targeted FAVOR customer is the adult cigarette smoker.

"He or she is going to keep regular cigarettes in a pocket or purse and also carry a pack of FAVOR," Mazur believes. "In an open environment, the smoker will probably light up a conventional combustible cigarette. But in restricted environments — in a theater or on an airplane or the non-smoking section of a restaurant or the increasing number of places where one can't light up — he or she is going to reach for a FAVOR."

FAVOR is manufactured in a facility at 121 Interpark Blvd. The current space will accommodate eight production lines which have a production capacity of more than 20 million packs per year.

"I think this is the best thing I've ever done," Mazur said. "I've been involved with many companies. Characteristically, my interest span is short, but I get more excited everyday about FAVOR. It's a great interest-span extender." ⌷

INTERCONTINENTAL BANKSHARES CORPORATION

InterContinental Bankshares Corporation started as an American channel for the banking needs of its founder, Dr. Burton E. Grossman, who was among the largest, most successful bank owners in Mexico.

Now with two banks — InterContinental National Bank-Lackland and InterContinental National Bank-Starcrest — the young holding company plans to expand by acquiring existing banks.

The corporation's banks handle all types of commercial banking such as financing of businesses and industries while also helping individuals with their banking needs.

Grossman, the force behind the banking corporation, told how he and his business came to be in San Antonio:

"Originally, we came to San Antonio to acquire the Lackland National Bank to handle business for our banking group in Mexico," Grossman explained. "We had a 74-branch banking group in Mexico, which was the 13th largest in the country in assets. We did a lot of business in the United States and needed to consolidate our banking rather than using banks in different parts of the country.

"We requested permission of the Mexican government to acquire a bank in the States as a part of our banking group in Mexico City, Continental Banking Corporation, or as a part of our holding company, the Continental Group Corporation in Tampico. The government said it preferred us to buy Mexican banks," he continued. "As a result, I personally purchased the Lackland National Bank in San Antonio in 1982."

Grossman's timing was fortuitous.

"A few months after I purchased the Lackland bank, the Mexican government expropriated all private banks in Mexico. The government tried to make it appear as though we were a bunch of foreigners. Not one of us was a foreigner; we were all Mexican.

"So we decided we ought to expand our banking business in San Antonio since we had lost the banks in Mexico. That's the reason we obtained a permit to open the Starcrest bank. It opened in December 1983."

Grossman also owns control of the Continental Group Corporation, which controls 33 corporations including 12 Coca-Cola syrup manufacturing and bottling operations in Mexico. The soft drink operations use 57 distribution centers serving 75 cities in Mexico.

Born and raised in Corpus Christi, Grossman was educated at The University of Texas. He moved to Mexico following his U.S. Army service in World War II.

"Banks should be more than just lenders of funds."

"I wound up the last several years of World War II as a commandant of two Army units in Dallas," he said. "At the end of the war when Japan surrendered, some Mexican businessmen happened to be in Dallas and offered me an opportunity to go to Mexico.

"I had specialized in advertising and public relations at The University of Texas Business School. At that time, there were no advertising and public relations specialists or business administration graduates in Mexico. I thought it was a very good opportunity. I worked for that group for 15 years before going into business for myself.

"I've lived in Mexico for 40 years and I am a Mexican citizen," Grossman explained. "To be in the banking business and in the soft

---

History at a Glance   1984

Founded: *1984*
Founder: *Dr. Burton E. Grossman*
Original employees: *3*
Holding company officers: *Dr. Burton E. Grossman, chairman and chief executive officer; Russell Brown, president and chief operating officer; Bruce Grossman, executive vice president*
Bank officers: *Russell Brown, president and chief executive officer, InterContinental National Bank-Starcrest; James W. Capps, president and chief executive officer, InterContinental National Bank-Lackland*
Employees: *50*
Units: *2 banks*
Motto: *Personal, friendly service*

This chapter was based on an interview with Dr. Burton E. Grossman.

drink business in Mexico, you have to have Mexican citizenship."

He also owned the Cattleman's Bank, the last Tampico-based bank formed by the local citizenry, until the expropriation 2½ months after the purchase. Other holdings expropriated were an insurance company that was a division of his banking interests, and a corporation that provided financing for equipment, machinery and buildings on a leasing basis.

Grossman continues as a member of several business and industrial boards in Mexico. He also is chairman of the board of trustees of The University of the Americas and the Institute for Higher Learning of the State of Tamaulipas, Mexico.

He looked toward Texas for a bank because of its proximity to Mexico.

"We looked at banks in Houston and Dallas but felt the Lackland National Bank was the size and type we needed," Grossman said. "We've been very pleased."

He owned Lackland Bank until the holding company was formed. He then transferred his holdings to the InterContinental Bankshares Corporation of which he is the principal stockholder.

Grossman's philosophy holds that "banks should be more than just lenders of funds."

"We always try to help a customer by analyzing what his needs are and trying to advise him on the kind of financing that would serve him best and at the same time would be good business for our banks," he said.

"We practice professional banking and adhere to banking ethics and integrity. We believe financing should be equitable. If we believe financing is not good for the customer and not good for us, then we don't engage in it. We have always asked that we be judged on what we do and not by what we say. There are a lot of talkers in this world and we prefer to be judged by our actions rather than on talk."

Grossman looks forward to expanding his operations "so that we can be even more important to the financing of the economy in San Antonio."

"We are anxious to have more banks, but we would prefer to buy banks that are already in existence rather than to obtain a charter for a new bank," he explained. "When we came here three years ago, there were only 40 banks in San Antonio; now there are around 70. Banking is quite competitive not only for funds but for good bank executives.

"We compete on a basis of personal service," Grossman said. "Our policy in Mexico was to give personal, friendly service and that's what we're trying to do up here. We think there always is going to be a place for banks our size where customers will feel that they're being treated individually rather than just as a number."

InterContinental National Bank-Starcrest is one of two local banks that make up Inter-Continental Bankshares Corporation.

BIBLIOGRAPHY

A Century of Service to West Texas 1884 to 1984, San Angelo Times.

"A Store Where the Salespeople Sell," Fortune, January 1950, pp. 80-83.

Bennett, John M. *Those Who Made It.* San Antonio, 1978.

Brandt, Floyd S. and Larry Secrest. "Transcribed Interviews with Mr. Sam Lucchese." Oral History Business Project, Graduate School of Business, The University of Texas at Austin, 1971. (Unpublished.)

Burkhalter, Lois, "The Enjoyable Joske's Story," The San Antonio Light, April 15, 1973.

Connor, Seymour V. *Texas, A History.* Lubbock: Texas Tech University, AHM Corp., 1971.

Dunn, Edward Clare. *USAA: Life Story of a Business Cooperative.* New York: McGraw-Hill, Inc., 1970.

Evert, Alice. *A Man A Dream A Company.* San Antonio: American Security Life Insurance Company, 1980.

Everett, Donald E. *San Antonio Legacy.* San Antonio: Trinity University Press, 1979.

Fehrenbach, T.R. *The San Antonio Story.* Tulsa: Continental Heritage, Inc., 1978.

Fehrenbach, T.R. *Seven Keys to Texas.* El Paso: Texas Western Press, The University of Texas at El Paso, 1983.

"Frost Bros. A San Antonio Tradition," Ultra, April 1985, pp. F2-F10.

Hornor, Sidney H. "A Short History of the Security Building and Loan Association Which Became The First Federal Savings and Loan Association of San Antonio." San Antonio: First Federal Savings and Loan Association, 1960. (Unpublished.)

Mason, Herbert M. with Frank W. Brown. *A Century on Main Plaza: A*

History of the Frost National Bank. San Antonio: The Frost National Bank, 1968.

McLemore, David. *A Place in Time.* San Antonio: Express-News Corporation, 1980.

Odom, Marianne and Gaylon Finklea Young. "Early Days of the San Antonio Conservation Society." Oral History Project for the San Antonio Conservation Society, 1984. (Unpublished.)

Park, David G., Jr. *Good Connections.* St. Louis: Southwestern Bell Telephone Company, 1984.

Pool, William C. *A Historical Atlas of Texas.* Austin: Encino Press, 1975.

Ramsdell, Charles. *San Antonio, A Historical and Pictorial Guide.* Austin: University of Texas Press, 1959.

Richardson, Rupert N., ed. *Texas, The Lone Star State.* New Jersey: Prentice-Hall, 1981.

Schmitz, Joseph William. *The Society of Mary in Texas.* San Antonio: The Naylor Company, 1951.

Schuchard, Ernst. *The 100th Anniversary Pioneer Flour Mills, San Antonio, Texas 1851-1951.* San Antonio: The Naylor Company, 1951.

Simpson, Arthur J., ed. *The Century in Southwest Texas.* San Antonio: Southwest Publications, 1937.

Smith, Charles. *San Antonio Chamber of Commerce: A History of Its Organization for Community Development and Service 1910-1960.* San Antonio: 1965.

Wise, T.A. *Peat, Marwick, Mitchell & Co.* Peat, Marwick, Mitchell & Co., 1982.

Woolford, Sam, ed. *San Antonio, A History for Tomorrow.* The San Antonio Light. San Antonio: The Naylor Company, 1963.

LIVING LEGACIES

Living Legacies is a San Antonio-based public history service which specializes in historical publications and oral histories for businesses, organizations and families.

Founded in 1983, the company makes voice recordings and video tapes, compiles archives and publishes historical works.

Life cycle events such as anniversaries, memorials, weddings and birthdays lend themselves to the services offered by Living Legacies.

For the corporate community,

Living Legacies produces brochures, reports and books; oral histories of business leaders; archives; and retirement gifts.

Founders are Marianne Odom and Gaylon Finklea Young, who have a combined 30 years of journalistic experience in research and publications.

Journalist and educator Marianne Odom has taught journalism and English at San Antonio College and Tyler Junior College. As award-winning fashion editor of the San Antonio Express-News, she covered markets in Paris, Lon-

don, New York, Los Angeles and Dallas. She holds a master's degree in journalism from East Texas State University and a bachelor's degree from North Texas State University.

Gaylon Finklea Young is a nationally acclaimed writer and editor, who has made a name for herself in San Antonio through her work in such publications as SA magazine, San Antonio: The Magazine, The San Antonio Light, San Antonio Express-News and the Jewish Journal. Nationally, her writing has appeared in Newsweek, and she has won national awards for coverage of social issues and the war in Lebanon. Her journalistic career began with a bachelor's degree in journalism from The University of Texas at Austin.

Their oral history experience includes interviews with such well-known personalities as Dan Rather, Debbie Reynolds, Mary Martin, Aaron Spelling, Lady Bird Johnson, Dr. Denton Cooley, Sandy Duncan, Jimmy Dean, Ray Price and Kathryn Crosby.

Authors Marianne Odom and Gaylon Finklea Young are co-owners of Living Legacies.

CREDITS

The Businesses That Built San Antonio was produced in San Antonio with the following assistance:

"San Antonio: Then and Now" was researched and written by Robert H. Carlson.

Special photographer was Harry Young of Harry Young Photography.

Printing was by American Printers.

San Antonio has come a long way in the three-quarters of a century since wagons and touring cars competed for parking space near Alamo Plaza.

PHOTOGRAPHS

Sources for photographs and art appearing in this book are noted here in alphabetical order and by page number. Numbers in parentheses indicate position of photographs on a page; photographs are numbered clockwise beginning at 12 o'clock. Photos and art not listed here were provided by the companies in whose chapters they appear.

Abilene Reporter-News: Abilene, Texas: Page 144; 146 (2)

Andie & Barbara, San Antonio, Texas: woman's clothing courtesy of: Page 5 (2)

Photo by Weissgarber, San Antonio, Texas: Page 136; 173 (1)

Leslie W. Bland Custom Photography: Page 107 (2)

Joe Chavanell, San Antonio, Texas: Page 77 (2)

Daughters of the Republic of Texas, Alamo, San Antonio, Texas: Page 7 (1); 11 (2,3); 12 (2);
Also:
   Grandjean Collection: Page 41 (3)

John Dyer Photography, San Antonio, Texas: Page 187

Thom Evans, San Antonio, Texas: Pages 80-81

Flash Photography, Lebanon, Tennessee: Page 45 (4)

Goldbeck Company, Gary W. Yantis Collection: Page 77 (1)

Bruce Grossman, San Antonio, Texas: Page 189

Library of Congress, Washington, D.C.: Page 15 (1)

Bob Maxham, San Antonio, Texas: Page 146 (1)

Audie L. Murphy Memorial Veterans Administration Hospital, San Antonio, Texas: Page 6 (1)

National Park Service: Page 13

Harvey Patteson & Son: Page 100 (1); 101

C.R. Randow, San Antonio, Texas: Page 111 (1,2); 112 (1,2); 112-113; 113 (1,2)

Al Rendon Photography, San Antonio, Texas: Page 63 (2); 93; 94 (1,2); 95 (1,2,3)

San Angelo Standard-Times, San Angelo, Texas: Page 147

San Antonio Express-News, San Antonio, Texas: Page 21 (2) and 192 by Scott Sines; 26 (1) by Charles Barksdale

The San Antonio Light, San Antonio, Texas: Page 10 (2) by Martin D. Rodden

Emily Morgan Hotel, San Antonio, Texas: Page 32 (2)

San Antonio Museum Association, San Antonio, Texas: Page 16 (2)

Bud Shannon/Photography, Inc., San Antonio, Texas: Pages 142-143; 143 (1)

Craig Stafford, San Antonio, Texas: Page 153 (2)

Harvey Smith Photo, San Antonio, Texas: Page 99 (2); 100 (2); 102 (1,2); 103 (1); 129

Dana Spring: Page 145 (2)

Studio Six: Pages 108-109

John Tedrowe Photography, San Antonio, Texas: Page 167; 168; 169 (1,2)

Texas State Library, Archives Division, Austin, Texas: Page 6 (2); 25 (2)

The University of Texas Institute of Texan Cultures at San Antonio, Files of: Page 42 (4);
Also:
   Robert Ashcroft, San Antonio, Texas: Page 5 (3)
   Robert M. Ayres Estate, San Antonio, Texas: Page 10 (1) ; 191
   Ann Russell, San Antonio, Texas: Page 30 (2)
   The San Antonio Light Collection: Page 14; 17 (2); 22 (1,2); 24; 25 (3); 27; 41 (2); 55 (1)
   Mr. and Mrs. Rudolph R. San Miguel: Page 15 (2)
   Marshall Steves, San Antonio, Texas: Page 44 (4)
   Mamie Bizy Swatek, San Antonio, Texas: Page 16 (1)
   Capt. T.K. Treadwell, Bryan, Texas: Page 21 (1)
   Mrs. Homer Verstuyft, San Antonio, Texas: Page 17 (1)

Xavier Vazquez, Collection of: Page 130; 131 (1,2,3,4); 132 (1,2); 133 (1,2); 134 (1,2); 135 (2)

Harry Young (Photography), San Antonio, Texas: Page 4; 5 (1,2); 6 (3); 7 (2,3,4); 8-9; 10 (3); 11 (1); 12 (1); 18 (1); 19; 20; 23; 25 (1); 26 (2); 28-29; 28 (2); 29 (1); 30 (1); 31 (1,2); 32 (1); 41 (1); 45 (1,2,3); 82; 85 (1,2); 104-105; 105 (1); 155; 161 (1,2); 165; 176; 177; 190

Zavell's, Inc., San Antonio, Texas: Page 65 (1)

Zintgraff Photographers, San Antonio, Texas: Page 65 (2); 84; 87; 91; 100 (3); 107 (3); 137; 153 (1); 181 (1)

Charlie Urton, Commercial Photographer: Page 106 (2)

ACKNOWLEDGEMENTS

A book of this magnitude requiring slavish attention to detail could not have been accomplished without the assistance of many dedicated individuals.

Obviously, the credit for the heart of this book goes to the 72 spokespersons who told the human and historic tales herein. Their names are listed in each chapter.

For providing guidance, their own unique skills and unfaltering support, we extend extra special thanks to Gen. William V. McBride (USAF Ret), Samuel P. Bell, Mayor Henry G. Cisneros, Jack A. Maguire, Keith A. Woods, Monica Hasbrook, Harry Young, Robert H. Carlson, Derek P. Dutcher, Darwin Sealy, Jan Almon, Sean McNulty, Richard H. Noll, Nelson Norman, Dr. Gregory M. Jackson, Woodie Goodspeed and Stephen A. Nathanson.

For inspiration and advice, we thank Esther MacMillan, Mildred Stern, Charles Stern, John Goodspeed, F. Ronald Callaway, Pam Plocher and Larry Odom.

Thanks also go to our energetic sales force: Melissa H. Hinton, Ellen Elbaz and Paula Kaufman.

Professionals in public relations and advertising who assisted include Kay Sharp, Carl Mertens, Jim Dublin, Linda A. Valdez, Mary Ann Bengtson, Wanda Mann, Jack Pitluk, Bob Sinclair, Julius Germano, Edward Fong and Cindy Mills.

Thanks also go to Carrie Harrell, Jean Van Gee, Ben Horny, Lisa Grahmann, Loyce McCarter, June Meyer, Rollette Schreckenghost, Lois Burnett, Ken Baker, JB Hazlett, Jack Newman, Jill L. Campbell, Loydean Thomas, Eddie Morris, Gary Morris, Irene Banks, Dr. Donald Everett, Dr. Thomas L. Charlton, Dr. Thad Sitton, Richard W. Francke, Deborah Cano, Mike de la Garza, Maria Elena Torralvo, Shirl Thomas, D.B. Harrell, Diane Taylor and the San Antonio Sesquicentennial Committee.

Our appreciation also goes to Josephine Myler, Nancy A. Roth-Roffy, Bill Cothren, Cathy Garison, Mel Lemler, Virginia Gonzales, Allen Walsh, Walter Patterson, Gail Berish, Sally Sealy, Charlotte Dill, DG Rich-McNiel, Janie Hagelstein, Amy Abdalla, Elvin Schofield, Martha Dikeman, Joe Deres, Don Rogers, Michael Gillette, Walter Bell, Freeman Fisher, Donna Schweitzer, Ken Higgins, Donna Muslin, Woody McPike, Toby Coltellaro, Steve Foster, Robert D. Nelson, Maria Casas, Carol Payne and Virginia Dayton.

Also, Roger L. Williams, John C. Walmsley, Beth Pyndus, Jon R. Sandidge, Shirley L. Mayer, Doris Conley, Lee Page, Anne LaFave, C.S. "Sam" Netterville, Karlene Krueger, Cathy Obriotti Green, Emma Leigh Carter, Barbara Henk, Jeanette Westbrook, Dina Dorich, Diana Hawley, Gay Goddard, Vernon Schrader, Debra Wainscott, Robin Barnes, Mary Ann Jacko, Jim Tilton, Charalyn Bishop, Wanda Bartholomew, Suzy Thomas and Gene M. Patton.

Also, Bobbie Lyda, Nancy Johnson, Madeline Harlan, Ann Downing, William M. Sims, Evelyn Lewis, Dan Talbot, Paul Dailey, Sylvia Gutierrez, Barbara Pope, John La Framboise, Linda Bailey, Charles Franzke, Dana Simpson, Barry Gardner, Karen Narciso, Kyle Saunders, Dayna Boren, Sheryl Wood, Norman A. Howard, Dayton Simms, Connie Boose, Kathy Stancek, James D. Simonsen, Sally Forester, Jamie Maverick Killian, Cathy Speegle and Iris Schoultz.

Heartfelt gratitude goes to Dorthy Finklea, Floyd H. Finklea, Laura Odom and Patsy Callaway.

The Greater San Antonio Chamber of Commerce also acknowledges L. Lowry Mays, 1985 chairman of the board; Samuel P. Bell, 1986 chairman of the board; and Gen. William V. McBride (USAF Ret), president.

Also, the 1985 board of directors composed of Barbara Banker; Sam E. Barshop; Glenn Biggs; Narciso Cano; Charles E. Cheever, Jr.; Stephen Dufilho; George Fischer; Ed Gistaro; Martin Goland; Cipriano Guerra; Dr. John P. Howe III; Leonard Huber; James E. Ingram; H.D. "Curly" Johnson; Mark M. Johnson; Fred Lepick; Dr. Earl M. Lewis; Mike Manuppelli; Bob Marbut; Stephen McNeeley; Theodore J. Michel; Palmer Moe; Clifford E. Morton; Glenda Musser-Kratzer; Emilio Nicolas; Dan Parman; James Reed; Robert Rork; Conrad Rotenberry; Bill Roth; John K. Spruce; Bill Thomas; Dr. James W. Wagener; and Charles "Marty" Wender.

Also, the chamber staff including Anne Adley, Kristin Athas, Therese Bass, Diana Benavides, Sandra Brown, Sylvia Camarillo, Frances Collins, Janice Smith, Kathy Duncan, Donna Enney, Paul Fairchild, Randy Felker, Beth Thurber, Madeleine Henggeler, Randy Hutchison, Helen Knapp, Michele Krier, Patti Larsen, Hilda Lopez, Charles Mangold, Nick Milanovich and Helen O'Hara.

Also, Tony Milligan, Elsie Pagliei, Pauline Pezina, Mary Ellen Pfeifer, Andrea Pinc, Toni Renfrow, Steve Schultz, Susan Shepherd, Oscar Smith, Allen Sonnenburg, Elaine Spalding, Diana Tamez, Rita Thompson, Jose Trujillo, Rose Valdez, Alice Velez, Angie Villarreal, Keith A. Woods and Bill Wroten.

— *Marianne Odom and Gaylon Finklea Young*

Nowhere but San Antonio can rush-hour traffic have its share of lighter moments.